A Kaleidoscope Book

Also by Kim E. Woods

Audio:

all about abundance: guided meditations to increase the flow of abundance in your life

all about magic *beginnings*: guided meditations to tap into your magical side

all about calm: visualizations and guided meditations for you, your teens and children

Books:

all about magic *beginnings*

all about calm

Heart Around Ankles

Alex & Chloe Meet the Men in the Head ®

Surprise!

So Big!

all about abundance

Kim E. Woods

Written by Kim E. Woods
Cover design by Moira Abram-Hale of m. abram creative

CreateSpace Independent Publishing Platform, North Charleston, SC
Categories: Body, Mind & Spirit / General
ISBN-13- 978-1977532978
ISBN- 1977532977

First Edition

To Greg –

The Magician.

Table of Contents

Abundance in Motion

TENETS FOUNDATION LAYERS

TOOLKIT WEAVING

"Abundance is not something we acquire. It is something we tune into."
— Wayne Dyer

Why Abundance?

As a business consultant and now a revealer, you can imagine how many requests I've had from clients to help them increase revenues, improve bottom lines, boost prosperity, enhance resources and basically, build wealth.

Everyone wants abundance yet don't understand the first thing about it.

"I want to make more money."

"I need an increase in salary."

"I'm going to work at this job and save money, so I can take a vacation or so I can retire."

Even if people are more aligned with the mysteries of life, the approach is still the same.

"If I spend more money, my money will multiply."

"I just have to open myself to receive and the money will come to me."

"I'm going to wish for more money and send the wish out into the universe."

Money. Money. Money.

Everyone asks for money.

And everyone who does – is missing the point – entirely.

When you talk about abundance and ask for money, it's like asking for a drop of water when the entire ocean is available.

Imagine standing in front of God and she says, "Ask me anything you want child," and you say, "How do the lights work?" She'll answer you, of course, because you asked the question, but think of the questions you could have asked instead.

What's the meaning of life? How does the Sun rise and set every day? How was the Earth created? How many other galaxies are there? Is there life on other planets?

Nope. You didn't ask those questions. Instead, you asked "How do the lights work?" and got an explanation on electrical wiring.

It's the same thing when speaking of abundance and asking about money.

It's way too small.

In fact, it's infinitesimal.

Don't limit yourself. You're worth way more than that.

In fact, you're worth everything. You're worth so much more than money.

So, when you ask for abundance, ask for everything.

Don't leave anything out, because when you ask for abundance, you're asking for everything from yourself.

Also, the money?

The money is the easy part. The money flows once you've aligned your heart, mind and will to step into the divine flow of life.

What is Abundance?

According to the Merriam-Webster dictionary, abundance is defined as;

> ➤ *an ample quantity or relative degree of plentifulness;*
> ➤ *affluence, wealth;*
> ➤ *a large quantity of valuable material possessions or resources.*

And this definition is awful. No wonder no one knows what abundance means.

Even the dictionary's definition is too small.

So, what is abundance?

Abundance is magic.

Abundance is making your life flow in perfect alignment, rhythm and order.

Abundance is about recognizing the truth in your life and seeing its meaning and purpose. It's about getting what you want and appreciating it for its worth. It's about living in calm, passion and joy. It's knowing exactly who you are and what you want in life. It's about being in the divine flow of life.

That's the real meaning of abundance and the basic tenets are all about you.

The basic tenets to introduce abundance into your life are:

1. Know the True You
2. Step into the Infinite Flow
3. Welcome an Abundant Life

The first tenet:

1. Know the True You

Getting to the root of who you are is the essence of abundance. It's about realizing you are worth everything – absolutely everything in the world.

How can you get to your core truth? How can you know yourself intimately, realistically and openly?

Firstly, you want space. You want space to make connection to your inner knowing. You want to give yourself permission to take time for YOU to enjoy the silence and in that silence, make abiding connection with yourself. You also want to connect to the infinite flow of life and recognize your magic and power.

Secondly, you want to clear your mind, open your heart and set your will. Getting your mind, heart and power into alignment makes you unstoppable.

Thirdly, you want to let go of any fear or belief that's in your way to allow joy into your life.

Finally, you want to allow yourself to be you – authentically and unapologetically.

You are the magic and abundance you've been looking for all of this time.

Oh, and don't worry – the money will follow.

It always does.

2. Step into the Infinite Flow

There's a rhythm to the infinite flow of the Universe and respect for this flow allows for more abundance in your life.

Think of the Sun and the Moon, the tides and your breath – there's an expansion and a contraction. The Sun rises and sets, the Moon waxes and wanes, the tides are high and low. For every inhale, there's an exhale.

It's beautiful, really, this dance of life.

It's the infinite flow of life and it's literally the figure 8 – the sign of infinity.

Anyone who knows of abundance and blessings appreciates the number 8. Eight signifies plenty, wealth and prosperity in numerology. In Feng Shui, it means harmony. In the Tarot, it means balance.

There's an elegance with the eight. There's a flow. There's a give and a take, a yin and a yang, an action and a breath.

Abundance is supported by this flow – it's the infinite and natural flow of the world.

This infinite flow relies on balance, so there needs to be harmony and relative equality in flow in order to allow for movement. It's the natural cycle of expansion and contraction.

Now, fear arises when you contemplate contraction and that's okay. It'll be discussed in the following sections. For now, just recognize that it's part of the elegant and sophisticated dance of the universe.

There are names for these cycles. There are methods and correspondences. It's about the doing and being in life.

Expansion	Contraction
Yang	Yin
Doing	Being
Movement	Stillness
Masculine	Feminine
Sun	Moon
Manifesting	Receiving
Praying	Meditating
Asking	Accepting
Giving	Letting go
Releasing	Surrendering

As you're doing, there should be time for rest. As you're talking, there should be space for listening. As you're giving, there should be opportunity for receiving.

The infinity flow is the natural cadence of life.

As you line up your mind with your heart and your will, you'll naturally begin to align with the universal flow.

In this alignment, abundance reigns. Then, the next step is welcoming abundance into your life.

3. Welcome an Abundant Life

Welcoming an abundant life means saying 'Yes'.

It means saying yes to you, saying yes to the infinite flow and saying yes to all of the magic and abundance available in the world.

This isn't a one-time yes and you're done.

It's not an 'Okay, I'll work now' and then forget all about it kind of thing.

It's a repeated yes.

Think about it.

Do the flowers and trees stop saying yes after one springtime?

Do the fruits and vegetables stop saying yes after one harvest?

Do the Sun and Moon stop saying yes after one day, one week or one year?

The answer is 'No, they don't stop'.

Neither can you.

You must say 'Yes'.

Repeatedly.

Say 'Yes'.

Yes. Yes. Yes.

Foundation of Abundance

"You create your own universe as you go along." – Winston Churchill

As most other things, abundance is layered. There's a layering that involves the basic tenets, natural law, practical methods and magical tools.

The basic tenets are the footing. They're the support that all of the other components utilize for reinforcement.

Three of them have been covered in the introduction – knowing you, aligning with the flow and saying yes - repeatedly.

The action of *doing* these is required in relation to the *being* nature of these next two.

The *being* tenets involve – the Law of Attraction as it relates to all of the Hermetic Principles and the power of the inner life.

Simply put, the **Law of Attraction** is *"like attracts like"*.

The Law of Attraction is one of the universal principles, so it's a Law of Nature.

It's based on the Hermetic Principle of "As above, so below. As within, so without," from the Emerald Tablet circa 3000 BC.

In *The Secret* by Rhonda Byrne, the Law of Attraction is based on the creative process. This process is boiled down to three steps:

1. Ask
2. Believe
3. Receive

By delving further, there are sub-steps:

1. Ask

    a. Clearing your mind

    b. Clarifying your intention

2. Believe
   a. Acting, speaking, thinking as though you've already received it
   b. Law of Attraction works to give you what you want
3. Receive
   a. Feeling the way you would once you've received it
   b. Lifting your vibration or frequency to receive your desire

The power of positive thinking can change your life. Good, right?

Yet, *The Secret* hit the bestseller list in 2006, so why hasn't everyone attracted everything they want?

Let's look further into the power of positive thinking with this creative process.

The power of thinking goes back to the 1800's with the New Thought philosophy based on works by Phineas Quimby of Maine. In New Thought philosophy, the **Law of Attraction** is the belief that by focusing on positive or negative thoughts a person brings positive or negative experiences into their life.

The belief is based on the idea that people and their thoughts are both made from "pure energy", and that through the process of "like energy attracting like energy" a person can improve their own health, wealth and personal relationships.

So, there's a magnetic power or attraction due to everything being energy. So, it's more than positive thinking.

The Secret deepens this theory to include the gratitude and intentional processes. It speaks to lifting your vibration with gratitude and fueling intentions through visualization. This adds punch to the Law of Attraction.

But, again, why hasn't everyone who's read *The Secret* and followed its teachings, created life to its fullest and highest potential?

Because, there's more.

When looking at the Emerald Tablet, there's more information. There are other Hermetic Principles to take into account.

The Secret covers the following:

Principle of Mentalism

"All is mind. The Universe is mental." – The Kybalion

Hence, the power of positive thinking. Check.

Principle of Vibration

"Nothing rests, everything moves, everything vibrates." – The Kybalion

Raise your vibration, raise your attraction manifestation. Check.

There are five other principles. The Principle of Correspondence is partially covered by the Law of Attraction.

Principle of Correspondence

"As above, so below; as below, so above." – The Kybalion

Your inner life reflects your outer world. So, as "like attracts like". Partial check.

Your inner life is reflecting your outer world.

Principle of Polarity

"Everything is dual; everything has poles; everything has a pair of opposites; like and unlike are the same; opposites are identical in nature, but different in degree; extremes meet; all truths are but half-truths; all paradoxes may be reconciled." - The Kybalion

There is mental alchemy when using the art of polarization to transmute a state from one end of the pole to the other. For example, changing evil to good, hate to love or dislike to like.

So, opposites are two sides of the same coin. Have you developed the ability to transmute a positive into a negative and vice versa?

Without this ability, polarity exists on Earth. The world has duality.

- Up, down.

- North, south.

- East, west.

- Left, right.

You need to become completely absent of judgment. Nothing is good. Nothing is bad. Everything is both good and bad.

It doesn't mean to ignore the 'bad', 'dark' or 'evil' aspects of life. These exist. It means to embrace them completely and know they are relative to their counterparts.

In addition to what's covered in *The Secret*, there are three more principles.

These three are in tandem with one another.

Principle of Rhythm

"Everything flows; out and in; everything has its tides; all things rise and fall; the pendulum-swing manifests in everything; the measure of the swing to the right is the measure of the swing to the left; rhythm compensates." - The Kybalion

Everything has a manifested motion along the Principle of Polarity as there is always action and reaction, expansion and contraction.

Principle of Cause and Effect

"Every Cause has an Effect; every Effect has its Cause; everything happens according to Law; Chance is but a name for Law not recognized; there are many planes of causation, but nothing escapes Law." - The Kybalion

Nothing happens by chance. There are higher planes that dominate the lower ones, but all is in accordance to Law.

Principle of Gender

"Gender is in everything; everything has its Masculine and Feminine Principles; Gender manifests on all planes." - The Kybalion

Every state of matter has both the masculine and the feminine.

So, there's a being and doing, a giving and receiving, an expanding and contracting element to life.

The power of gratitude and intention speaks to this rhythm and are amplified with the force of creation and destruction, joy and fear and authenticity and forgiveness.

Using the Law of Attraction

Using the Law of Attraction is more complicated than stating positive statements. That's a good step, but it's not even close to being complete. The Law of Attraction works when you're open to receive and actively giving to the universe. It works when your mind and heart are in alignment with your true self.

There are layers to abundance and you'll be pulling back these layers throughout this book.

You'll be getting to the core of yourself.

You'll be tuning into the infinite flow of life.

You'll be welcoming the abundance of the universe into your world.

Story: Below the Water Line

"Why aren't I getting the results I want?"

"I work really hard and don't seem to make any progress."

"I use the Law of Attraction and it's not working!"

I hear these comments from my business clients over and over again throughout the years. My clients do get results. They get results from using the tools of strategic, leadership and financial methods. They work smarter, make more money and improve their bottom line. They're happy for a while.

Oftentimes, the happiness doesn't last. The improvement isn't as much as they desire. It's because they haven't actually achieved happiness. They've just smoothed things out for themselves.

"It's because you haven't gotten to the root of your issues," I say. "You need to go within yourself to find what you seek."

Those who are brave enough, listen when I tell them to look below the surface, to go inside and to get to the root of the problem.

They hear me when I explain, "If you don't delve below the surface, you won't have a chance of getting what you really want."

Those who aren't brave enough like riding on the surface as it's familiar and known. It's safe and secure. There's no possibility of discovering hidden things or feeling uncomfortable emotions.

However, there's also no possibility of revealing wholeness, of letting go of things no longer in service or of discovering the true self.

That's too a high price.

You see, life is like a glacier. It's lived mostly below the water line. Recognizing most things are happening beneath the surface allows you to see, learn and uncover more aspects of you. It allows you to accept yourself as you are, discover things you want to change and realize your passions and inspirations.

The benefits of swimming into the depths far outweigh any discomfort.

Once I widen my practice to include the personal side of life, I can assist so many on the inter-workings between the inner life and outer world. I even comprise a methodology for doing so to ease individuals through the process.

Your inner life involves your physical, emotional, mental and spiritual connections. These each directly affect the aspects of your life on the surface or outer world.

Your living conditions, career or job, friends and family connections and ability and willingness to explore beyond your usual borders reflect the parameters of your outer world.

Abundance requires aligning your mind, heart and will as well as getting into the natural flow of the universe. Delving into your inner life goes hand in hand with this alignment.

The outer world flow comes easily once you dive into the inner life to release and manifest.

Refer to the image below to depict the areas of the inner life to explore when welcoming abundance into your life.

Kaleidoscope Wheel of Life™

There are aspects of your inner life to fully explore and strengthen to help you improve your outer world:

- o *Create wellness* – bolster your physical, emotional, mental and spiritual health
- o *Spark mind* – open your mind, improve your intuition and increase your awareness
- o *Satisfy heart* – discover your heart's desires, tap into your passion and enliven your creativity
- o *Fill soul* – connect to your inner knowing and follow its direction

There are steps interwoven throughout this book to assist in diving into your inner life. To highlight:

- o Make space.
- o Go with the flow of the mind.
- o Be inspired.
- o Find power in alignment.
- o Overcome fear.
- o Discover the true you.
- o Make it real.
- o Keep going.
- o Have fun!

These steps become evident as you continue your exploration of abundance throughout this book.

"Air sings of intelligence and bravery, fire speaks of action and growth, water teaches flexibility and power, and earth expresses firmness and balance." – Yung Pueblo

The layers of abundance involve the foundational tenets as described in the previous two sections:

Doing	Being
Knowing You	Law of Attraction
Infinite Flow of Life	Inner Life Power
Saying Yes - repeatedly	

The foundation is key, however, there are elements to layer into the process to make gaining abundance attainable and fun.

When I say elements, I mean it literally.

I'm talking about the natural elements of ether, air, fire, water and earth. These are the paint box of the natural world and as such affect you in ways you may not be aware.

Additionally, they align with your bodies – spiritual, mental, emotional and physical and your bodies tap into your energy centers or chakras as follows:

Element	Body	Chakras
Ether	All	Crown
Air	Mental	Third eye, throat
Fire	Spiritual	Heart, Solar plexus
Water	Emotional	Sacral
Earth	Physical	Root

Note: There's an overlap with the chakras per body, however, these are the clearest delineations.

As you're clearing your mind, opening your heart and powering your will to align with the infinite flow of life, the elements assist in many ways.

Natural Elements

The natural elements involve ether, air, fire, water and earth.

Beginning with ether makes sense as it's the most accessible and closest to the spirit world.

<u>Ether/All</u>

Spirit is the center of all that is and is also known as 'akasha'. It is said that ether makes up the heavens.

Ether is the element that connects all that is.

Magical power: To be

Every time you meditate, you have the opportunity to connect to ether.

It's affiliated with your crown chakra.

Air/Mental

The air element involves movement, freshness and is invisible to the naked eye. It relates to communication and intelligence and aligns with the mental body. It's active, so it's considered to be yang energy.

The air element is the imagination, visualization and wishes. It's vital for giving life to all living things and acts as the glue that binds everything together.

Magical power: To know

Call on air when your thoughts are stuck, momentum is stopped or new life needs to be breathed into a project or area of your life.

Air is associated with your third eye and throat chakras.

Fire/Spirit

Fire is hot, active and alive. It's a source of energy as it creates warmth, however, it must be contained as it's also a destructive force. It has masculine qualities, so is considered to be in the yang category. It's strong, forceful and intense. It requires sources of energy in order to burn and needs air to feed on itself.

Magical power: To will

Call on fire when you desire creation, connection to spirit, protection or cleansing.

Fire relates to your heart and solar plexus chakras.

Water/Emotional

Water is necessary to sustain life and it's an element of spiritual regeneration. It's a yin or feminine energy. Water is healing, loving and refreshing. It's also cleansing.

It relates to the emotional body, intuition and the natural mysteries.

It's a receptive force and can help with dreams, sleep and peace.

Magical Power: To dare

Call on water to tap into your intuitive side. Also call on it for strength.

Water is affiliated with your solar plexus and sacral chakras.

Earth/Physical

Earth is terra firma, representing stability and security and physical form. It's receptive, yin or feminine energy. It's the element of wisdom, strength, growth and prosperity.

It's the physical plane and nothing exists without it.

Magical power: To be real

Call on earth when you want to make things real.

Earth is your root chakra.

Tools

The tools are the practical and magical aspects of the universe woven together.

The union of these brings abundance into your world.

The magical tools of intuition, energy and connection to the divine and the practical ones of focus, determination, vitality and action combine beautifully to align with the abundant flow of life.

Magical

Tools for connection, divination, vibration and inner guidance provide loft to the tide of divine flow. There's magic in this world and tapping into it can increase your abundance and blessings in life.

Practical

Practical instruments leverage the natural abilities of your mind, heart and will. Your mind allows you to clarify and set intentions, your heart accepts support and renewal and your will helps you achieve goals and lean into action.

Moving through the layers of abundance gives you harmony and balance by being in the flow. It creates space, clears your mind, opens your heart and ignites your passion. It brings you to your true self.

Using the practical and magical tools make the process easier and more fun.

The next section delves into some of the magical tools as you may be unfamiliar at this point.

"You pray in your distress and in your need; would that you might also pray in the fullness of your joy and in your days of abundance." – Khalil Gibran

The abundance toolkit involves your intuition, your energy centers or chakras, and magical tools of divination and vibration.

Knowing a little bit about each or at least their definitions helps you use the methods in this book to attract abundance into your life.

If you require more information about any of these topics, refer to my *all about magic – beginnings* book.

This section covers a brief description of the following:

- o Intuition
- o Energy
- o Chakras
- o Magical tools:
  - Numerology
  - Pendulums
  - Oracle cards
  - Colors
  - Crystals and stones
  - Astrology
  - Fairies
  - Lunar cycles
  - Animal spirits
  - Angels
  - Goddesses

Intuition

What is Intuition?

> *the ability to understand something immediately, without the need for conscious reasoning.*

> *a thing that one knows or considers likely from instinctive feeling rather than conscious reasoning.*

How do you tap into your intuition?

The short answer is:

You lean into it, you use it, you say **YES**.

Say YES to your intuition and use it. Practice makes it stronger.

Heart Activation

Engaging your heart helps you use your intuition. Working your heart muscle for tapping into your intuition is the quickest way to activate your magical gifts.

Simply enter a meditative state.

Once there, breathe deeply and fully. Focus your attention on your heart chakra and start breathing into it. As you inhale, expand your heart center and feel it opening. Feel it filling with love. As you exhale, feel your heart extend its love into the space in front of you and behind you. Continue to breathe, opening and extending your love. Ask your heart what it wants you to know. Does it have any messages for you? Feel its love for you.

Take a few moments. Thank your heart for its health in keeping you alive, for its passions, messages and all of its love.

When you're ready, take a nice full breath and bring your awareness back into the room. Exit your meditative state and close your energy.

Energy

There's energy all around you.

In fact, you're made of energy.

Successfully navigating your world involves successfully navigating the energy around and within you.

Once again, <u>everything</u> is made up of energy. Recognizing this and becoming aware of energy involves tapping into your senses and working energy within and without.

So, working with energy becomes important as everything is made up of it.

Chakras

Chakras are energy centers located within your body.

These involve the root, sacral, solar plexus, heart, throat, third eye and crown chakras. Each chakra has a particular meaning as described in the following color and chakra table.

Chakra	Location	Color	Intention	Potential Issues
Root	Base of spine	Red	Foundation - grounded	Survival, physical and financial
Sacral	Lower abdomen	Orange	Desire Accept others and new experiences	Emotional, abundance, well-being, pleasure, sex
Solar Plexus	Upper abdomen	Yellow	Willpower Confidence and control	Self-worth, confidence, esteem
Heart	Center of chest	Green	Ability to love and be loved	Love, joy, inner peace
Throat	Throat	Blue	Communicate and speak our truth	Self-expression, communication
Third Eye	Forehead between the eyes	Indigo	Focus on big picture, intuition	Imagination, wisdom, make big decisions
Crown	Top of head	Purple	Connected to spirit	Inner and outer beauty, spirituality - bliss

Divination Tools

Numerology

Every number has a unique meaning. Positive whole numbers begin with 0 and go to infinity. The individual whole numbers from 0 – 9 represent the arch of life.

Numerology is the study of the corresponding numbers to letters, words, names and ideas. It's also the belief of the divine meaning of numbers relating to coinciding events.

Pendulums

Pendulums are a great divination tool to begin using magic.

A pendulum is a small weight suspended on a piece of string, thread or chain. It may be a ring at the end of thread, a stone at the end of string or a small crystal at the end of a chain.

Oracle cards

Oracle cards represent the energies of the symbols of the cards. So, the animals, plants or angels pictured on each card represent the energies of its symbol. Connecting to the cards is actually connecting to the energies of their symbols.

Tarot cards have been used to gain wisdom, to predict the future, to activate intuition and to work as a roadmap for life. Tarot cards involve a deck of 78 cards with 22 cards in the Major Arcana and 56 in the Minor Arcana. The 22 Major Arcana cards correspond to the 22 branches of the Tree of Life. The additional 56 Minor Arcana cards follow four channels of life; the body, heart, mind and spirit.

Vibrational Tools

Colors

Colors have meanings and they also resonate at a certain frequency, so are involved with vibration and can be used for healing.

Crystals and stones

Crystals and stones have vibrational healing properties and are used by complementary healing practitioners by placing on the body for chakra or energetic healing.

The vibrational properties of crystals may also be used in your environment, in a flower essence blend, carrying in your purse or bag or by wearing as jewelry.

Cycles and Seasons

Astrology

According to the Merriam-Webster dictionary, astrology means:

> ➢ *the divination of the supposed influences of the stars and planets on human affairs and terrestrial events by their positions and aspects.*

The Hermetic Principle of Correspondence '*As above, so below*' explains astrology more expansively than the dictionary definition. The stars reflect our consciousness and vice versa. There is the placement of the stars as of the minute you are born and then there is the movement of the planets over the years.

In other words, our inner life is reflected in our outer world and astrology depicts this by the positioning of the planets, signs and houses.

Lunar and Seasonal Cycles

The Moon passes through phases every month and enters a new zodiac sign every few days. This is important as the earth and its inhabitants are directly tied to the Moon.

The Moon travels around the Earth as the Earth rotates around the Sun. The monthly phases occur and move through the celestial signs with the Earth on a yearly basis.

As the Moon moves through the signs with the Earth, each month the Moon interacts with the Sun. During a Full Moon, the Moon and the Sun are opposite each other and during the New Moon, the Moon and the Sun are blended together.

The Full Moons involve the Sun and Moon being in opposite zodiac signs and the New Moon involves the Sun and Moon being in the same sign.

Every season brings its own energies and you can relate them to the directions, elements, lunar cycles and time of day.

Fairies

Fairies help with healing, manifestation and in relationship. They help with gardening and lifting spirits. They bring joy, laughter and fun.

They help with creativity and tapping into spiritual connection.

They help heal Mother Earth and all of her beings. They help connect to the natural realm.

Inner Guides

Magical or Higher Self

Your magical self is also known as your *higher self* or divine self. Your higher self is the highest aspect of you that can be reached while in the physical body. It's the part of you that holds your highest potential of evolution here on Earth.

Animal Spirits

Animal spirits are known as power or totem animals and animal guides. Animals love to give you messages. They show up when you call them, but they also show up when they have a message for you.

Angels

Angels provide love, guidance and support without question. You can call on them at any time without any special innovation or prayer. They're always at the ready to help. Just think, 'angels' and they'll come immediately to assist.

They bring joy, grace, love and happiness into your life.

Goddess

The earliest evidence of a Goddess temple dates back to the Paleolithic times about 25,000 BC. Humans are paying homage to the Goddess before the Gods come onto the scene.

Most of these female deities represent the Sun, Moon, heavens and stars. Their worshippers pay homage as their lives depend exclusively on living off of the Earth's bounty.

Practical Tools

The practical tools are ones needing no definition:

- Focus and discipline
- Willingness to dive into your wholeness
- Commitment to yourself
- Opening your mind, heart to growth and will to action

Open your mind and heart to use your intuition and energy and advance your basic knowledge and acceptance of the chakra system and natural elements to being using your magical tools.

Open your will to action by making a commitment to yourself to delve into these activities deeply and willingly.

Once again, if you want more information on any of the magical tools, refer to my book *all about magic – beginnings.*

Weaving Abundance

"Strong emotions such as passion and bliss are indications that you're connected to Spirit, or 'inspired,' if you will. When you're inspired, you activate dormant forces, and the abundance you seek in any form comes streaming into your life."
- Wayne Dyer

The recipe for abundance seems cumbersome at first glance, however, there's a dance taking place. If you look closely enough without pre-condition, you can see it.

There's an interweaving or linking that happens between the basic foundational tenets, the elements and the tools.

First, the basic tenets of knowing your true self, aligning with the infinite flow and welcoming abundance into your life are the foundational keys.

As always, you connect to you. You do this by knowing yourself deeply and intimately. You become aware of the infinite flow of the universe. Then you say 'Yes' – repeatedly - to the magic, wonder and abundance of the world.

Next, you begin the initial steps of utilizing the universal law of attraction in an expanded way as you realize the effects your inner life have on your outer world.

Then, you layer the art of doing and being by navigating the natural elements connecting you to universal source energy. This, in turn, drives the power of this infinite flow to your very core and grounds this force into the Earth to make it real.

You step through ETHER as you make connection, lean into AIR to clear your mind, unleash FIRE to open your heart and activate your will and dive into WATER to overcome fear and lean into joy. Lastly, you ground into EARTH to make everything real.

Through the elements, you clear your mind and connect to your heart, your body and your soul.

Up until now, your mind has been doing the yeoman's work, so it's time to give it a rest.

Your heart has something to say and wants to be heard. Your soul yearns and wants to connect. Start from the top with ETHER as it's always the first step in any connective process.

Turn the page to allow yourself to make space and connect to All That Is.

Abundance in Action

ETHER   AIR   FIRE

WATER   EARTH

Ether: Connection

"You try to pull away the experiences until you get to the core of humanity, and you find that light that exists in everybody. It's that light that I'm searching for in all of my work - is that connective thing, that ether that enters all of us - you know what I mean? That's a part of God." – Forest Whitaker

Using ether for abundance creates space in your life and allows connection to spirit and all that is. Creating space spirals inward and outward simultaneously.

For your inner life, it involves calming down your thoughts and connecting to your spiritual side.

For your outer world, it involves solving problems to free yourself to be available to live a larger life.

There are four components entwined with the inner life and outer world aspects:

~ Make space ~ Find calm ~ Summon spirit ~ Maintain connection ~

These sections in ether involve:

- o *Making space* - by solving your problems.

- o *Finding calm* - by clearing your thoughts through breath and meditation.

- o *Summoning spirit* - by fostering association with your higher self and awareness centers.

- o *Maintaining connection* - by dancing with the infinite abundance of the universe.

Exploring the realms of ETHER is the first step in welcoming abundance and blessings into your life.

"The longest journey begins with a single step." – Lao-Tzu

Story: Blank Pages

I walk into the room to greet a prospective client, extending my hand to firmly shake his and sit down, nodding to the roomful of executives.

I take a seat, take out my portfolio and my sacred pen, and unfasten my portfolio to reveal a blank pad of paper. As I turn my pen to its ready position and open my mouth to ask my first question, I hear a **quick intake of breath** run throughout the room.

The prospective clients are **aghast**. They're expecting a presentation. They're expecting handouts, templates and proposals on my plan to walk them through their potential strategic project. They're expecting razzle and dazzle.

I can hear them thinking that surely, I have a plan. Surely, I'm going to walk them through my process. Surely, I'm going to **amaze and astound them** with my brilliance. Surely, I'll give them much information so they can review, analyze, assess and make a decision on whether to go with my firm. Surely, this is going to happen.

No, actually it's not. It's not going to happen like that at all. My plan is different. My plan involves listening, listening and more listening.

I smile. Of course, I expect this. It happens every time. I'm going to ask questions and I'm going to listen. I'm going to listen to what's being said and what's not being said. I'm going to observe. I'm going to observe what's really going on beneath the words and silences.

Of course, I have a plan. I know exactly how to perform a strategic project for any size client, in any industry, of any size. Yes, of course, I do.

But, they're not ready. They're not ready to start a big strategic project. No one is. No one's ready because strategy is NOT top down. It's NOT step 1 through 10. It's not that straightforward - YET.

"I do strategy sideways," I tell my perspective client. "I need to ask you questions and listen to your answers. I need to create space for you BEFORE you begin your strategic project."

Intrigued and a little perturbed, the clients let me begin. Once they start hearing my questions, they relax and realize I'm not leading them astray. I have the skills and abilities to help them and they begin to see this for themselves. After 60 – 90 minutes, I know what the client's issues are and I tell them. I tell them exactly what they need, how to achieve those needs and ask if they want my help.

They say yes. They say yes - every single time. They say yes, because they now see that they do need space and a little relief before they take on a big strategic project. They need to take a breath, tackle some critical issues and

THEN step back to visualize greatness, think big and make a plan to get from here to there.

You do too.

Resolve Issues

How does this relate to you and creating abundance? Your big strategic project is creating abundance and guess what? You need a little space and bit of relief before you begin.

Just as you can't stuff any beautiful brand new clothing you may have purchased into a completely overstuffed closet, you can't fill an already jam-packed life with abundance. You need to clear some space in that closet and then put those beautiful new clothes into it. It's the same thing with abundance. You just can't pack more and more and more. You need space. You need breath. You need ease to be able to create abundance.

So, your first step in this longest journey is to make space. You're going to create abundance by going 'sideways' for this first step.

Depending upon the season, you may have space made for you just by the start of the summer, a vacation or holiday season. If you have school-age children or are involved in schools yourself, you have space made for you automatically. Yay you. Now, you have a choice. You can either skip this step or you can be uber-vigilant and continue forth and create even more space for yourself. It's completely up to you.

For everyone else, there's also a tiny bit of space created in the summer or while on vacation. It happens automatically. The days are longer, the schedules a little easier due to holidays and vacations, so a bit of breath is created. You can take advantage of this space.

However, you may want to make *actual* space. You may want to make space for you that will last beyond the summer or vacation. You want abundance to be huge, not little, and you don't want to cram it into the little bit of space that seemingly longer days create. You want your abundance to be bigger than just one season or one moment.

Okay, here you go. Fair warning. I'm going to ask you to do a few things that you do NOT want to do. It's inevitable when you think about it. You would be living in abundance now if you've been making space in your life on a regular basis. Obviously, something is holding you back.

You'll need a notebook to answer the following three questions:

1. <u>What's keeping you up at night?</u>

    Whatever is keeping you up at night is typically your biggest problem. It's the gnarly, thorny, nasty problem that may not have an easy solution. If it's a recent problem, then give yourself an hour with paper and pen and outline a solution. It could be a complex issue that just needs some focus and critical thinking, so give it the attention it deserves. Pushing it off is only going to make it worse, so draw up a plan and start whittling away at it.

    However, if it's a chronic problem that's keeping you up at night, the problem needs a different approach. Whether it's your job, finances, relationship, or family, you're a smart person and this problem is bigger than you right now. So, here's the thing, you need to give yourself permission to ask for help. That's right – you need help and you need to ALLOW yourself to ask for it.

    Think about someone who can help you find a solution and ask for help. If it's a family member or friend, great – call him up. If it's a professional, also great – call her up. If you need multiple people to help, great – call them all up. You've given yourself permission to get help with this problem, so get some help and start on your solution.

Seriously, start getting the help you need to solve the problem. You won't be able to create space otherwise.

2. <u>What continues to be on your list (either mental or physical) that you keep pushing further down the line?</u>

You know what I'm talking about, that pesky little thing that just keeps getting pushed along day after day. Today is the day you're going to do it. Today. Right now. Do it.

Pick up the phone, craft and send the email, write the letter, find the bill, pay the bill, set up the files, clean out the drawer – whatever it is, just do it.

No excuses. Get it done.

3. <u>What's right in front of you that bothers you whenever you see it?</u>

What do you keep walking by that compels you to say for yourself, 'Just ignore it, it doesn't matter, just ignore it'? Okay, notice it today and make a plan to clean it up, organize it, give it away, tear it down, move it or whatever.

Make a plan in the next week to get it done.

The first step to creating abundance is not a fun one. By working on your biggest problem, by putting a stop to procrastinating, by tackling that niggling issue, you're getting rid of noise. By getting rid of this noise, you're making space to allow room for abundance. So, think of it that way. You're doing these pain in the A@$ things so you can make room for abundance.

Making Space

With your newfound space, you can do the following:

- o Breathe
- o Go to yoga
- o Spend time in nature
- o Be creative
- o Visualize
- o Meditate
- o Have a massage
- o Get energy work

Look at your calendar to determine ways to incorporate 3 of the things on the above list into your days.

Schedule them.

Do them regularly.

Weave space throughout your life in order to create available moments for abundance to come into it.

Find Calm

"Calmness is the cradle of power." – *Josiah Gilbert Holland*

Americans are an anxious bunch. There are societies, associations and institutes that study and create solutions for the various levels of anxiety and stress.

There's the American Institute of Stress, The Stress Management Society, The Anxiety and Depression Association of America (ADAA), American Psychological Association and Social Anxiety Association to name a few.

With so many institutions to study stress and anxiety, there's certainly a need for strategies to create more calm in your life.

According to the Merriam-Webster dictionary, calm is defined as:

➤ *a state of tranquility.*

Tranquility? That sounds amazing and a few ways to achieve this state are breathing, visualization and meditation.

Breathing

Breathing is calming, centering and grounding. When you're feeling disconnected, remember to take a few deep breaths.

Take frequent breath snacks throughout the day – in the shower, at a traffic light or while making dinner.

Number of Breaths

You have the choice in the number of breaths.

One Breath

Take one full and complete breath.

Inhale deeply and exhale fully.

Three Breaths

Take three full breaths.

- Inhale. Exhale.
- Inhale. Exhale.
- Inhale. Exhale.

10 Breaths

Take 10 full and complete breaths to change your mood and to create a sense of connection.

Types of Breathing

You also have the choice of different types of breathing.

Try these different ways to see which one works best:

- o Full breathing
- o Equal breathing
- o Deep breathing
- o Alternate nostril breathing
- o Yogic breathing

Full Breathing

Full or complete breathing is just that. Completely fill your lungs as you inhale and completely empty your lungs as you exhale. Take breaths slowly and deeply.

Equal Breathing

While breathing through your nose, count to four while you inhale and then count to four when you exhale. You can count to four or six or eight, whatever is comfortable for you.

Deep Breathing

Place one hand on your chest and the other on your stomach. Breathe in and feel your lungs expand and as you continue breathing, push your breath deeper into your stomach and feel it extend with each inhale. Keeping your hand on your stomach, continue breathing into your belly. This is deep breathing.

Alternative Nostril Breathing

Place your right thumb on your right nostril and inhale through your left nostril. Then, place your left ring finger over your left nostril and exhale through your right one. Immediately, inhale through your right nostril, place your right thumb over your right nostril and exhale through your left one.

Alternate your inhale and exhale from side to side.

Yogic Breathing

Place your hands on your belly and begin breathing into it. Then place your hands on your lungs and breath into them. Feel your lungs expand and contract with each inhale and exhale.

Now, you're ready to begin yogic breathing. Inhale by filling the belly, then ribs and then lungs. Exhale by emptying the lungs, then ribs and then belly. You're filling our body from the bottom up and emptying it from the top down.

Choose the type of breathing and the number of breaths that appeals to you.

Remember to take frequent breath snacks throughout the day.

Visualization

Visualization is a type of meditation involving mental imagery. It typically takes less time than meditation as you're focused on seeing with your mind's eye.

Visualization requires nothing more than sitting in a quiet place, turning off your phone and getting comfortable. It typically only takes a few moments.

There are a few ways to easily create visualization opportunities:

- Memories
- Peaceful or safe space
- Guided imagery

Memories

Take a few moments without distractions and recall a favorite memory.

Remember the situation, people, colors, shapes and setting. Recall your feelings, smells, sounds and tastes, if applicable.

Breathe in the images and sensory experience.

Smile with the memory.

Peaceful and Safe Space

Create a few moments to think about a place that calms you. It could be a room in a museum, a favorite dinner place or a space in nature – a mountain top, beach, meadow or field of flowers.

Think about this place and picture yourself there. See and feel your surroundings. What are the images? Feelings? Senses?

Breathe in the peace, safety and calm you feel.

Smile with the calm and peaceful feeling.

Guided Imagery

Find recordings of guided visualizations and listen to them for connection.

I have included three from my book, *all about calm*, to give you an idea of a guided visualization.

Beach Visualization

If you want to close your eyes, feel free. If not, there's no requirement to do so. Just fix a soft gaze on an object a few feet in front of you.

Now, sitting comfortably in your chair, relax your arms with your hands resting on top of your thighs or whatever is most comfortable.

Take a nice full breath, inhaling deeply and as you exhale, fully relax your arms and legs. Continue breathing normally relaxing your entire body.

As you relax, imagine yourself sitting in a very comfortable beach chair. It fits your body perfectly and you don't have to worry about how you're going to get out of it because it's the perfect height.

As you continue breathing, feel the warm and soft sand on your toes as you burrow

Beach Visualization

them into the sand. The grains are smooth and filled with mild heat. You can envision moving your feet easily and gently around in the sand. It feels really good on the bottoms of your feet.

In your mind's eye, picture the beautiful turquoise color of the water. The ocean is gorgeous. The sun is glistening on the water and you see the iridescent colors its rays make along the ocean's surface.

You hear a few sea gulls and notice a couple of sandpipers at the edge of the water. The waves are lapping gently on the shore. You hear the surf- whoosh, whoosh, whoosh and you lift your face toward the sun. You feel its warmth radiate through you. You feel warm, relaxed and peaceful.

Whoosh, whoosh, whoosh...hmm...nice.

Take a few moments to relish the warmth of the sun, the glistening of the water, and the lapping of the waves.

Being at the beach is so soothing and relaxing. Take another deep breath and if you need to, open your eyes.

What a wonderful visit to the beach.

Meditation

More in depth than visualization, meditation is another way to find calm.

Meditation means:

> ➢ '*to think deeply or focus one's mind for a period of time… as a method of relaxation*'.

> ➢ It *can* be for a religious or spiritual purpose and it *may* be as a result of silence or chanting.

Meditation is fundamental to connecting to your inner life and making magic in your outer one.

Many people, however, have a difficult time meditating or developing a sustainable meditation practice.

If you don't have one, review the following types of meditation to find one that interests you.

Finding an appealing method will support you in developing a regular practice.

Types of Meditation

Here are the types of meditation in order of ease:

Moving

So, moving meditation is just that, it can happen while you're moving about doing something else. It could be while you're walking in nature, running, dancing, swimming, skiing, skating or doing yoga. It happens when you clear your mind and focus on the activity at hand.

Sometimes, you may become one with your body. You're completely focused on moving your body and not thinking about anything else at that moment.

Most times, when you finish one of these activities, you feel better, more centered and more alive. This is because you've just experienced a moving meditation.

Guided Meditation

There are many guided meditation experts who walk you through the steps for relaxation and help you clear or focus your mind by having your mind follow what's being said aloud by them and not by the tape forever running in your head.

Guided meditations may be prefect for you if you have trouble quieting your mind.

I've included one for you from my book, *all about calm*, to help quiet your mind. It's at the end of this section.

Mantra, Chanting or Transcendental Meditation

This type of meditation involves mantras or chanting that helps to quiet or focus the mind while the body relaxes and a meditative state is achieved. Also, if you say the mantra, the vibration of your voice and the mantra itself is said to lift you to a higher state of consciousness.

There's an entire movement called the Transcendental Meditation movement that employs a particular set of mantras. You can explore this or use other mantras, chant or songs.

Mindful

Here it is, the Holy Grail of meditation - that perfect image of sitting in that lotus position with a clear mind, full heart and connected soul.

To perform mindful meditation, you need to be open, accepting and forgiving all of your thoughts and feelings in a completely compassionate manner.

In approaching this type of meditation, practice sitting in quiet contemplation with soothing music, drumming or nature sounds in the background before getting into complete silence and full awareness.

If that's not needed, perfect. However, the complete quiet may be overwhelming, so ease into it with some soothing sounds.

So sit quietly, either with or without music *(Two easily accessible recommendations: Dave & Steve Gordon: Drum Medicine or Soulfood: Shaman's Way).*

Then, notice your breath.

You can use your breath to relax and soothe your body and connect with yourself. Then notice everything in your mind's eye. Pay attention to your thoughts and feelings.

Mindful meditation is not about clearing your mind of all thought. It's about letting your mind wander and welcome what comes. It's about connecting with yourself at a whole new level. It's about self-compassion and self-awareness.

It helps with spiritual connection.

Here is the guided meditation from my *all about calm* book:

Guided Meditation – Calm Your Thoughts

Get into a comfortable position and turn off your phone. You don't need to sit in lotus position on the floor – a comfortable cushion, couch or chair will do just fine. Settle yourself into your seated position.

Now, close your eyes and take a nice refreshing breath by inhaling deeply and exhaling gently, letting go of any distracting thoughts, events or happenings of the day or week. You deserve to be here doing something just for you and your peace of mind.

Take another breath by inhaling in and exhaling out. You're breathing easily and gently, allowing your body to relax as you do so. Continue to breathe. As you're breathing, feel the chair beneath you and against your back, supporting you beautifully.

Hear the normal sounds of your home. You're comfortable with these sounds. You know

---

you're completely safe, warm and content in your own environment. You are protected at all times as you surround yourself with protective white light directly from the source energy of the Universe.

As you continue to breathe in and out, notice there are thoughts still in your head. Your mind isn't empty. It's still creating thoughts about things that aren't part of this meditation. That's okay. It's totally fine. Your thoughts are always welcome. In fact, they're completely welcome.

Embrace them and give thanks. You're so thankful for your thoughts. Whisper to yourself, "Thank you, thoughts."

Now, picture these wonderful thoughts in front of your face, streaming from the top of your head, across your forehead and down your nose to form a line right in front of you.

See your thoughts. Really look at them. They're so beautiful. They're words made up of perfectly formed letters. Maybe these letters are black or white, perhaps a particular color or even many colors.

Look at your words dancing before you. They're so beautiful. As you see them, they start dancing together to form a shape. They are lining up and starting to swirl around each other.

See the shape. "Oh - it's a ball". This ball shape is getting more and more rounded as you comfortably sit and look at your beautiful words.

When you breathe in, the ball stays in place, but when you breathe out, the ball moves a little further away from you. So, breathe in again to see what happens and look - the ball doesn't move. It stays, just where it is. As you breathe out, however, the ball moves a little further away again. Do it one more time. Breathe in, oh it stays, and breathe out and it moves even further away.

Now, let's try something more. Let's breathe in and this time when you breathe out, you

Guided Meditation – Calm Your Thoughts

blow with your exhale to move the ball further and further away from you. Continue to do this three more times. Breathe in and then out to blow the ball further. Breathe in and again, on the exhaled breath, the ball moves even farther away. One more time, breathe in and out.

Notice the ball of words is very far in the distance. If you reach out with your hands, you can't touch it. With each gentle breath, your ball of words is floating away until it disappears from view.

Your gentle breath makes you relax even more and feel completely settled, centered and calm. How wonderful and how beautiful you feel with your thoughts having disappeared after floating peacefully away.

Sit silently for a few moments to savor the feeling of peace and calm. Breathing gently, you feel contented. Breathing easily, you feel relaxed. Breathing fully, you feel rejuvenated.

Take a few more breaths and come back into the room. Notice the seat beneath you and against your back. Notice the noises of your home and within the room. Take one more breath in and as you exhale, open your eyes.

Welcome back.

If you want more information on achieving calm, check out my book *all about calm.*

There are audio files of the guided meditations available on my website: *kecfreedom.com.*

"Just as a candle cannot burn without fire, man cannot live without a spiritual life."
— Buddha

You may not be attuned to the spiritual world and that's okay. This section helps you make connection to the spiritual realm.

To summon spirit, all you need to do is ask, but that may seem daunting at first. Before you ask spirit, employ other techniques to get you balanced, centered and grounded.

<u>Breath</u>

As always, breath is the easiest way to gain your center. Take 3 deep breaths.

Inhale. Exhale.

Inhale. Exhale.

Inhale. Exhale.

Visualization

Visualization is another way to get connected to yourself. Imagine yourself as a tree.

Close your eyes and imagine yourself in your safe place. Fill your body with calm and relaxing energy and imagine yourself as a tree. Feel your strong trunk, leafy branches and roots sinking deeply into the soil. Imagine your feet are the roots of the tree extending into the earth and delving fully into the ground.

As you breathe, feel your energy going into your feet and into the earth.

Take a few moments with this guided imagery.

Meditation

Meditation is the crucible for spiritual connection and this guided one balances your chakra system so you can go on to summon spirit.

Chakra Meditation

Get comfortable and remove any distractions.

Close your eyes and breathe deeply by taking a long inhale and exhaling fully. Take a moment to gather yourself. You're here for yourself at this moment. Continue to breathe and say hello to yourself. You're here to balance and align your chakras.

Welcome and open to the light within you. Integrate yourself with the pure crystalline light of all that is. Take a deep cleansing breath and envision the bright white pure light of Universal source coming down into your crown chakra as it balances your crown chakra opening it wide and connecting to the spirit world.

68

Next, this white light goes into your third eye, opening it to be all seeing. You can now see the unseen and know the unknown. Third eye wide open as it's balanced and stimulated. Now, the pure white light moves to your throat, activating your truth, intuition and instinct.

The bright Universal light then travels to your heart chakra. Your heart alights with this white, pure crystalline light, healing and opening it to all the love in the Universe.

Now the white light enters the solar plexus chakra in your mid-abdomen and stimulates your will power. You feel brave, alive and filled with action.

This pure white light now goes into your sacral chakra drenching it with love and joy. Your sacral chakra is activated, allowing it to spin in the correct direction.

This light shines on your root chakra - clearing and energizing it. It then flows down your legs through your feet and into Mother Earth. These roots of light burrow deeply into the earth to ground alighting it with Universal source energy.

You bring the light from Mother Earth up through the bottoms of your feet and into your being, filling yourself with light, and connecting you to the heavens above and the earth below. As above, so below. As within, so without. Heaven and earth.

The energy of the spirit world re-enters into your crown, traveling down your chakras and into the earth. You breathe through the movement from earth's core to spirit and back again. The ancient wisdom of the earth and the spiritual knowing of 'all that is' comes up from the earth, through your body, into the spirit world, from universal source and back down through your body.

You're deeply connected to the earthly and spiritual realms.

Chakra Meditation

Now, this light surrounds you in a gorgeous white and golden healing glow. See it swirling around you, gently, patiently, and serenely. You are glowing in and of this light.

You're surrounded by the pure light and unconditional love within and without.

As you breathe, fully connect to yourself, your physical, emotional, mental and spiritual bodies.

Feel your breath flow throughout your bodies. You're centered and grounded in this moment. Bask in the glory of your connection.

Now bring your awareness back to the room. Take a deep cleansing breath and feel the bliss of being connected. Take another deep breath and fill yourself with the energetic flow of life. As you take your next breath, take a moment to ground and center yourself. Close the energy.

When you're ready, open your eyes and gaze softly in front you – seeing nothing, yet aware of everything. If you would like, wiggle your fingers and toes and do any gentle stretching your body requires. Breathe in again and open your eyes fully.

Ask

When you want to summon spirit, all you need to do is ask.

It's that simple.

Ask spirit to come to you.

Ask for information.

Ask for a message to make your life better.

70

If you're wondering who to ask for or who to connect with, the first and best is always your higher self.

Higher Self

Who is your higher self?

Your higher self is also known as your *magical self* or divine self. Your higher self is the highest aspect of you that can be reached while in the physical body. It's the part of you that holds your highest potential of evolution here on Earth.

It knows how to assist you to live your very best life. It knows what's in your heart and the direction you should take to overcome your obstacles and to achieve the yearnings of your soul.

Your higher self is different than your intuition. Your intuition acts as your inner guide and lets you know when something should or shouldn't be done.

Your higher self is more than that. Your higher self connects you to your spirit and your divinity. It lifts you up, fills you with love and supports you in every way.

Your higher self is different than your *soul*. Your soul is vast and directly connected to universal source. Your soul has many dimensions across time and space, while your higher self stays connected to your physical body's experience here on Earth.

The higher self is also different than your guardian angel or spirit guides.

Guardian angels guide you with pure love, compassion and wisdom. They ensure you're surrounded with angelic energy. Guardian angels haven't incarnated on Earth and travel with you throughout your life.

A *spirit guide*, on the other hand, has incarnated on Earth and is now in the spiritual realm. The spirit guide assists you in the same way as a guardian angel.

Oftentimes, there's confusion about the divine or higher self and the divine feminine and masculine in relation.

The *divine feminine* is the matrix of creation. It's the wholeness of creation and destruction, birth and death, and then transforming to rebirth. The *divine masculine* is the seed of life.

The union of the divine feminine with the divine masculine creates heaven on earth. Each revolving around the other in perfect partnership – yin and yang, being and doing.

The higher self is part of you and you'll recognize the energy as part of you. The guardian angels or spirit guides will make themselves known to you in some way when you ask. They'll have differences from you – voice, tone, accent or gender.

Accessing Your Higher Self

Welcome your higher self by meditating and connecting to the spiritual aspects within you. In meditation, set the intention to welcome your higher self.

Set aside moments of quiet time throughout your days or weeks to create space for your higher self.

Open your heart to the idea of your higher self.

Find calm to quiet your mind and build on this calm with yoga, walking in nature, gardening or creating through art, music or dance. Welcome your higher self as you engage in these nurturing activities.

Meeting Your Higher Self

The most effective way to meet your higher self is through meditation. Here is a guided one.

Meeting Your Higher Self Meditation

You can amplify this meditation by choosing crystals that speak to you. You may also select energy cards to relay messages and information from your magical self. Grab a journal and pen if you want to make any notes about your experience.

You can also ask, "What do you want me to know today?"

Select and hold a crystal that speaks to you. Remove any distractions and get into a comfortable position.

Close your eyes and take a nice cleansing breath. Inhale deeply and exhale fully. As you breathe, feel yourself sink more deeply into the seat beneath you. Feel your body relax as you take a few moments to be present with yourself.

Now, imagine white light in your root chakra, clearing and energizing it. This white light travels to your sacral chakra and activates it, allowing it to spin in the correct direction. Now the white light enters to the solar plexus in your mid abdomen and stimulates your will power. Your heart alights with this white, pure crystalline light, healing and opening your heart chakra to all the love in the Universe. The pure white light moves to your throat, activating your truth, intuition and instinct. Now it goes into your third eye, opening it to be all seeing. You can now see the unseen and know the unknown. The white light goes to your crown chakra opening it wide and connecting to the spirit world. The white light travels from a few feet above your head through all of your chakras down into your hands, filling your palms with energy. You are activating your manifestation chakras and allowing reciprocity of support. You feel your hands swirl with energy. They pulse with electricity. You can feel the crystal in your hands vibrate.

Continue breathing and as you do, return your focus to the white light filling each of your chakras, connecting to the spirit world through your crown chakra. It fills your third eye,

---

throat, heart, solar plexus, sacral, root and going into the ground beneath you. The light travels deeply into the core of the earth.

As you breathe, there is a channel of energy going into the earth's heart, grabbing all of the ancient wisdom from the volcanic core, traveling up into your feet, along your chakras and connecting to the spirit world through your crown chakra.

The energy of the spirit world enters into your crown, down your chakras and into the earth. Breathe through the movement from spirit to the earth's core and back again. The ancient wisdom of the earth and the spiritual knowing of 'all that is' is traveling up from the earth, through your body, into the spirit world, from the universe and back down through your body.

Take a moment and a few deep breaths. Now say to yourself, "I am a spiritual being and I want to meet my higher self."

With your third eye wide open, your crown chakra connected to the spiritual realm and your root chakra connected to the earth's heart, see your magical self.

You can see your higher self. Where is he or she? What is he or she doing? Notice what he or she looks like. What colors surround him/her? How big is he or she? Does he or she have hair? If so, what color? Is he or she wearing anything? Is he or she holding anything? Notice each of the details, but see the overall picture.

Now, what does he or she feel like? Feel him/her love for you. Breathe it in.

Bask in his/her love and his/her energy.

Take a few moments seeing and feeling his/her energy.

Say thank you for meeting your higher self and for all of the love.

As you take your next breath, bring your awareness back to the room.

Meeting Your Higher Self Meditation

Close your energy by crossing your hands over your heart.

When you're ready, open your eyes and gaze softly in front you — seeing nothing, yet aware of everything. If you would like, wiggle your fingers and toes and do any gentle stretching your body requires. Breathe in again and open your eyes fully.

Make any notes about your experience.

Summoning spirit is as simple as asking. Your higher self is always with you at the ready with whatever guidance or information you require.

Simply ask.

"Spirituality is not a formula; it is not a test. It is a relationship. Spirituality is not about competency; it is about intimacy. Spirituality is not about perfection; it is about connection. The way of the spiritual life begins where we are now in the mess of our lives." – Mike Yaconelli

There are fun and easy ways to maintain connection to spirit. Inner guidance is the purest and most direct, however, sometimes your connection may not be clear or your mind not quiet. Using divination, vibrational or cyclical methods help you.

Divination, vibrational or cyclical tools provide assistance.

First, let's go through another connection to your higher self.

Then, I'll outline a few of the tools that can help you. Details about each are included in my *all about magic - beginnings* book.

Connecting to Your Higher Self

Now that you've met your higher self, you can make connections more easily.

Connecting to Your Higher Self Meditation

Remove any distractions, grab a journal and pen for notes if desired and get comfortable. (For purposes of this meditation, let's assume your higher self is female.)

Close your eyes and take a nice cleansing breath. Inhale deeply and exhale fully. As you breathe, relax as you take a few moments to be present with yourself.

Let's take another deep cleansing breath and envision the bright white pure light of universal source coming down into the room and filling it completely with light and love.

Now picture your crown chakra opening at the top of your head. The pure crystalline light of universal source pours into your crown chakra and travels through all of your chakras, filling them deeply and completely. The light flows from your crown, through your third eye, to your throat into your heart – filling it with love. The light then flows into your solar plexus, your sacral and then your root chakra. The pure crystalline light then flows down your legs through your feet and into Mother Earth. These roots of light burrow deeply into the earth to ground alighting it with universal source energy.

Bring the light from Mother Earth up through the bottoms of the feet and into your being, filling yourself with light, and connecting you to the heavens above and the earth below.

As the light fills your body, bring your awareness to your heart chakra. As you breathe, focus the light into your heart. As you inhale, the light fills your heart expanding it with love. As you exhale, the light nudges your heart to open up to the love and light in your body and in the room. Inhale and exhale and feel your heart opening.

As you breathe, feel your heart connecting to the light in your body and down into your solar plexus, sacral and root chakra and up into your throat, third eye and crown chakras. Continue breathing and feel your light and love connecting through your chakras and into the core of the earth and up into the spiritual realm.

> ### Connecting to Your Higher Self Meditation
>
> *Now, in your connection, ask to see your higher self again. Watch as she appears.*
>
> *Picture her again and feel her energy.*
>
> *Spend a few moments with your higher self. Ask her if she has a message for you. What does she have to say? Hear her answer in your mind or heart.*
>
> *Thank your higher self and close the energy by crossing your hands over your heart. As you take your next breath, bring your awareness back to the room.*
>
> *When you're ready, open your eyes and gaze softly in front you – seeing nothing, yet aware of everything. If you would like, wiggle your fingers and toes and do any gentle stretching your body requires. Breathe in again and open your eyes fully.*
>
> *Make notes of your experience and any messages you received.*

The more you connect with your higher self, the easier it becomes to connect again.

Working with Your Higher Self

You can work with your higher self to find peace and tranquility, lift your spirit, open your heart, enter into the universal flow and stay connected to spirit.

There are methods to help you connect to your higher self and these involve divination, vibration, cycles and seasons and group energy.

Divination

What is divination?

> ➢ *The practice of seeking the future or the unknown by supernatural means.*

Divination is a practice of delving into the spiritual realm in order to gain knowledge of the future, the present or the past. It's used by many to seek wisdom through omens, oracles, signs and symbols.

There are many ways to tap into the divine and using divination tools can give spiritual access to their users. It's an excellent way to receive messages from the spiritual realm.

When alone and at home, use the following *divination tools* to help you connect and receive messages:

- Pendulum
- Energy oracle cards
- Devas, fairies or elementals

Vibration

What is vibration? According to the dictionary, the definition of vibrate is to;

o *Move or cause to move continuously and rapidly to and fro,*

o *Quiver with (a quality or emotion),*

o *(Of a sound) resonate; continue to be heard.*

The entire physical universe is made up of pure energy and vibration. As light is vibration, the varying wave lengths or vibrations produce different colors along the light spectrum.

These colors have particular properties, comprise auras around the physical body and relate to chakras or energy centers in the body.

Sound also relates to light as the wavelengths have corresponding frequencies. These frequencies resonate or vibrate to form specific sounds.

Crystals also vibrate. They each have a different frequency depending on their type of matter, size, thickness and color.

Flowers have vibrational properties as well. Eckhart Tolle speaks to the ability of flowers to enlighten us in his *New Earth* book.

Increase your vibration with *vibrational tools*:

- Tuning forks
- Crystals
- Flower essences

Cycles and Seasons

The energy shifts with the lunar and solar calendar throughout a month and the year respectively. Knowing these cyclical energies help you connect based on the power of the celestial influences.

Harness your power using *cycles and seasons*:

- Full or New Moon
- Solstice
- Equinox

Group Energy

Additionally, group energy also makes it easier to connect to your spiritual side as the collective force allows for more concentrated energy. Leverage others with *group energy*:

- Healing circles
- Guided meditations
- Sound baths

Maintaining connection to your spiritual side may seem elusive at first, but the more you do it, the easier it becomes. Connect directly through guided meditation, get help from group energy or utilize magical tools to help you. There's no wrong answer, use whatever works for you.

Remember, your higher self is always with you.

Connect anytime.

"Always say 'yes' to the present moment... Surrender to what is. Say 'yes' to life - and see how life starts suddenly to start working for you rather than against you."
— Eckhart Tolle

As you make space, find calm and connect to the source of all that is, you're saying YES to yourself. You're saying yes to life. Yes, to a better way of living.

Yes, yes, yes.

When saying yes, you're:

- Making space
- Finding calm
- Summoning spirit
- Maintaining connection

Doing these things helps you create an awareness beyond your daily thoughts and habits. It gives you the perspective of the vastness and awesomeness of the universe.

It introduces you to its gifts.

Welcome spiritual connection into your life.

Fold it into your days.

Allow the magic of the cosmos to reveal itself to you in all of its glory.

Watch abundance unfold right before your eyes.

Let's continue down the chakras and elements.

Next, it's all about AIR.

Air: Clarity

"The key to abundance is meeting limited circumstances with unlimited thoughts."
— Marianne Williamson

When speaking of air, the third eye and throat chakras are called into action.

Also, air relates to the mental body, so it's about your mind and all of its thoughts, beliefs, perceptions, observations and intuitive knowing.

Air is impossible to capture and difficult to control. It's fast moving, active and unpredictable.

How do you manage air? How do you control your thoughts? How do you capture the energy of your mental being?

The short answer is – you don't.

The longer answer is you get into its flow, you honor its movement and you navigate its path.

This is where the figure 8 of infinity is most helpful.

Imagine moving along the figure 8. If you need to, use your index finger in front of you and follow the path of the figure 8 a couple of times.

There's a beautiful flow, a natural rhythm and a grace that doesn't include a still point. It's constantly moving – back and forth, back and forth, back and forth.

You can make the figure 8 bigger and wider or smaller and tighter. You can move along its path quickly or slowly.

The point is there's constant movement. It's hypnotic, soothing and engaging.

You can appreciate this movement and the elegance of the dance.

Back and forth, back and forth, back and forth.

While you're moving your finger and following it with your eyes, connect your mind to this pathway. Your thoughts flow back and forth, back and forth, back and forth.

Your breathing probably entrains to this as well. As you do this for a few more moments, you feel calmer, quieter and softer.

Now engage your mind – think of your thoughts and your beliefs about being in a meditative state. You probably picture your mind completely clear and coming to a total stop.

No movement. No action. No thoughts.

Why would your thoughts stand still? Why do you envision your mind stopping completely and ridding itself of all of its contents?

Can you feel the tension arising as you expect this to be true?

Your mind never stops, it never completely empties and it doesn't clear itself of its all of its activity.

Instead, your mind flows, it moves and it engages.

Your job?

Your job is to give your mind a job.

Have it follow the path of the figure 8.

Have it engage in its natural movement.

Have it concentrate on the give and take of the flow of infinity.

Just as air flows, your mind does as well.

Respect it. Allow it. Accept it.

In this section on air, you're going to use the figure 8 to welcome wishes and blessings by recognizing your wishes and expressing gratitude for your blessings.

You're then going to use the power of intentions and beliefs to realize the areas of your life you're grateful for and want to enhance and those you want to adjust or change.

Next, you're going to delve more deeply into any scarcity you may be traveling with and then release it to the universe for transformation.

Finally, you're going to expand your power to manifest your desires with the natural cycles of the universe.

The style and process of air works just as the element. It goes wide and far and comes close and fast.

You're going to respect that and allow yourself to go with the flow, keeping an open mind to the wonders it represents.

This openness clarifies your mind which in turn, helps you envision your future.

The purer your clarity, the bigger the possibilities.

You ask yourself, "What else is possible?"

You hear the answer, "EVERYTHING."

Wishes and Blessings

"A dream is a wish your heart makes." – Walt Disney

Story: The Blessing of Making Beds

When my first child's a baby, I start taking Pilates classes, because, hey I've just had a baby and am probably not in the best of shape. This Pilates teacher is connected to the spiritual world. She introduces me to the chakras and continues to blow my mind on a daily basis.

I'll never forget one of our conversations as I know it has tremendous impact and I also know I'm not ready. In fact, I won't be ready for the information for many years.

"True surrender to the universe and all of its blessings is knowing that everything is perfect. All is divine and the blessings flow to you every moment of every day. Each minute is perfection. Each minute carries the divine. Each minute is filled with total blessing," she says as I'm doing some heinous Pilates exercise and struggling to perform.

"Okay, I'm following," I gasp.

"As you're making the beds, ironing clothes or washing dishes, recognize each task is perfection, divine and filled with blessings."

"Okay?" I question and falter in one of the exercises.

She continues, "You're so grateful for these tasks. You see them as pure and wonderful blessings the universe has allowed you to…"

"Wait, what?" I interrupt and stop all physical movement.

"What?" I repeat.

I'm incredulous as I'm in the midst of more laundry, dishes and other household tasks than I can handle. I've just had a baby and you can imagine the mountains of activities I'm engaged in on a daily basis.

Being thankful for these chores is not something I can get behind.

"Soon, you'll see that with connection to the divine, everything becomes divine. You'll see all of the wonders of the universe before you and know of its splendor regardless of what you're doing in any given moment. Basking in the glory of a sunset or making a bed will become one and the same."

As I listen, I know she's speaking the truth, so I allow the words to wash over me.

I accept them as part of my future self, knowing I'm not ready yet.

I hold them in my sphere.

I know someday I will be ready and what a day that will be!

The first and easiest step to welcome abundance into your life is being grateful for everything. Express your gratitude. Thank the universe for the pleasure and the honor of being alive.

Blessings

The universe likes knowing it's helpful and appreciated. Showing gratitude opens your heart to receive from the Universe. It's literally the fastest and easiest way to clear your mind and allow the blessings to flow back to you.

Think of Thanksgiving while you're sitting around the dinner table with your family. What's the first question typically asked?

What are you thankful for on this day?

It's a wonderful exercise.

Yet, giving thanks is not only for Thanksgiving. It's for every day.

You can express thanks every single day.

So, express gratitude for the little daily things.

Count your blessings.

Think of things you're thankful for right now.

If you're having trouble, then enter a meditation to prompt you.

The following image may help you as you enter the following meditation on gratitude.

You may want a journal and pen to make any notes after you're finished with the meditation.

Gratitude Meditation

Close your eyes and take a nice cleansing breath. Inhale deeply and exhale fully. As you breathe, feel yourself sink more deeply into the seat beneath you. Feel your body relax as you take a few moments to be present with yourself.

You're here right now in this moment to quiet your mind, open your heart and express gratitude.

You're here to open to the abundance of the universe and to tap into your deep knowing of your role in the co-creation of your life. Welcome and open to the light within you. Integrate yourself with the pure crystalline light of all that is.

Take a deep cleansing breath and envision this bright white pure light of Universal source coming down into the room and filling it completely with light and love.

Now picture your crown chakra opening at the top of your head. The pure crystalline light of universal source pours into your crown chakra and travels through all of your chakras, filling them deeply and completely. The light flows from your crown and into your third eye. Third eye wide open. Third eye wide open. Third eye wide open. The light then flows into your throat – strengthening your voice and ability to be heard. You speak the truth. This light then goes into your heart – filling it with love.

You love and are loved. The light then flows into your solar plexus, your sacral and then your root chakra –grounding and centering you. The pure crystalline light then flows down your legs through your feet and into Mother Earth. These roots of light burrow deeply into the earth, alighting it with Universal source energy.

You bring the light from Mother Earth up through the bottoms of your feet and into your being, filling yourself with light, and connecting you to the heavens above and the earth below. As above, so below. Heaven and earth. As above, so below.

Now, this light surrounds you in a gorgeous white and golden healing glow. See it swirling around you, gently, patiently, and serenely. You are glowing in and of this light.

As you breathe in this glowing light, focus on your heart. Feel it beating within your chest and in your mind's eye, see it surrounded by the glowing white light. Imagine the beating of your heart synchronizing with this glowing white light. Your breath is in sync as well. As you breathe in, this glowing light flows inside your body and filters into your heart. As you breathe out, it expands beyond you, into the room and out into the world. Continue to breathe and notice the flowing pure light.

See it safely receiving beautiful loving energy back from the world. Now imagine your heart sending this glorious loving energy out into the world. See it opening to the love from the universe. Feel this love. Feel the compassion, kindness and support.

Open your heart to the universal source energy and to the heavens and earth. Connect to the love and support. Connect to the flow of the universe. Connect to all that is.

As you revel in your heart opening, direct your focus to the blessings in your life. What are you thankful for? What in your life sustains you? Your breath? Your body? Your mind? Food, water, shelter? Heat, air conditioning? Your car? Your arms, hands and legs? Your hearing? Your voice? Vitamins? Fruits? Vegetables?

What in your life supports you? Your job, career or business? Your partner? Your home?

What in your life makes you happy? Music? Art? Design? Fashion? Creating? Gardening? Biking? Nature? Dining? Entertaining? What in your life gives you joy? Your friends? Family? Loved ones? Children? Pets? Chocolate?

What in your life feeds you love? You? Spirit? Angels? Loved ones, including pets?

Feel all of the sustenance, support, happiness, joy and love in your life and from the universe. Count your blessings. Tell the universe you're grateful for all of the things and people in your life. Tell the universe you're thankful for your life.

Take a few moments to revel in the plenty and bounty of the universe in your life.

As you take your next breath, bring your awareness back to the room.

When you're ready, open your eyes and gaze softly in front you – seeing nothing, yet aware of everything. If you would like, wiggle your fingers and toes and do any gentle stretching your body requires. Breathe in again and open your eyes fully.

Now, take a few minutes to write down the blessings in your life.

What are you thankful for?

Contemplate each one.

Say thank you, either quietly in your mind, by whispering it or saying it out loud.

As you've expressed your thanks, you've given back to the universe. Imagine the path of the figure 8 and know you've traveled along the outward pathway.

Now, it's time to invite blessings in.

Blessings on the inward path are first known as wishes.

What do you wish for today?

Let's explore.

Wishes

Wishes lift your spirit and feel wonderful as they don't have any timeframe or basis in reality. They can be anything.

Remember with air and thoughts, you're going far and wide at times. This is one of those times to go far and wide.

What do you wish for today?

What seeds to do you want to send out into the universe right now?

Picture yourself as a child blowing on a dandelion and sending those seeds across the neighbor's lawn, into the fields and trees beyond.

In order to free your mind and have it travel far and wide, use magical tools to help you.

Connecting to Fairy Realm

Regarding magic, fairies clear your mind and lift your spirits faster than anything else.

If you're having trouble making wishes, connect to the fairies as this facilitates flow from the universe.

In order to connect, you may want to use energy cards, crystals or the fairy meditation in this section.

You can actually use all three.

Recommendations for energy cards, crystals and ways to connect to the fairies are listed below:

Energy Cards:

Each of these decks of cards relate to the fairy realm either directly or through the earthly elements.

- Butterfly: Life Changes by Doreen Virtue
- Earth Magic by Steven Farmer
- Fairy Tarot by Doreen Virtue
- Flower Therapy by Doreen Virtue

Choose a card and read its message.

Select a past, present and future or mind, body and spirit spread to read the information presented to you.

Ruminate on the information.

Journal any thoughts, dreams or wishes.

Crystals & Stones:

Fairies love everything sparkly.

Clear quartz, amethyst or rose quartz work just fine.

Other stones involve:

- Blue lace agate – Happiness and hope. Calming and strengthening spiritual communication.
- Bloodstone (heliotrope) – Grounding and centering. Brings energy to you.
- Fuchsite – Stone of health – friendliness, compassion and lightheartedness; attracts fairies and birds into your gardens.
- Green tourmaline – Happiness, joy and compassion - facilitates learning herbalism.
- Moss agate – Gardener's Stone – ensures a full crop. Brings general abundance and prosperity.
- Turquoise – Bridge between heaven and earth. Good protector and healer – good for attuning to spiritually and communicating between worlds.

Select a crystal or stone, hold is in your hands and feel its energy. Close your eyes, take a deep breath and ask to speak with the fairies.

See what happens.

Connecting to Fairies:

There are many ways to connect to the fairies in addition to meditating:

1. Believing in fairies. Saying, "Yes, I believe."
2. Reading fairy tales.
3. Singing, laughing and playing outside in nature.
4. Planting and gardening.
5. Doing anything creative or artistic.
6. Feeding the birds – keeping bird feeders full.
7. Being with children or animals in nature.
8. Using organic products and taking care of Mother Earth.
9. Putting crystals, stones and statues in your garden.

You may want to do this fairy meditation.

Connecting to Fairies Meditation

Pick a card.

Select a crystal.

Settle in. You're going to connect with the fairies.

Gaze softly at the card and crystal front of you. Take a few deep and full breaths. As you breathe, let your eyes lose their focus and then close them. Continue to breathe and as you do, open your heart to the universal source energy and to the heavens and earth. Just as you are, the heavens and earth are made up of all of the elements.

Connect to air with its cooling and energizing properties. Feel the wind stirring gently around you. The breeze is blowing your hair and on your body. Smile to welcome air,

---

the element of mental thoughts and concepts. The element of the crown, third eye and throat chakras. Third eye wide open. Third eye wide open. Third eye wide open.

Now, picture fire as it's the element of spirit, inspiration, creativity and passion. See the sun in your mind's eye. See it shining brightly in the sky and feel its heat on your face as you smile with the bright brilliant light and energy. Feel it opening your heart and stirring your passion and will.

Next, look up at the sky and see clouds filled with rain gathering on the horizon. Notice raindrops in the distance. See them sprinkling the trees, plants and flowers. The plants, flowers and trees drink this water as it feeds them life. Water is so nourishing. Feel the gratitude the plants, flowers and trees have for this water. Know the joy of it in your being. Sense your sacral chakra rejoicing.

Now feel the earth beneath your feet. It's stable, safe and secure. It's so affirming to have it around you and underneath you. Picture the trees, plants and flowers in the distance. Then, notice trees, plants and grass around you. You're standing in a meadow with flowers everywhere. You can see them and even smell them. Everything is fresh and alive. The sun is shining again and you begin to notice movement within the flowers. You think it's the wind and then realize it's more than that.

Hmmm…you see daffodils with their upturned yellow faces turned toward the sun. You know daffodils bring a connection to the fairies and are known for inner beauty. You can see fairies dancing around them. They are so beautiful.

You look to the left and see a field of lavender. The smell is so distinctive. It's calming and soothing. You see a number of fairies playing with elves in this healing and protecting field of lavender.

Then to your right, you see a bed of rose bushes. Oh, how gorgeous. There are pink, red and yellow blooms all through these bushes. The smell of the roses is so powerful – spicy and fresh. It smells of divinity. You feel the love emanating from the blooms.

The angels and the fairies smile at you from their perches within the branches.

You smile with love in return.

The fairies have made themselves known to you. Tell them you're feeling the love and healing of the flowers and would love to connect to them too.

Ask that they come out and play. As they do, say hello to the fairies in welcome. Offer them the crystal in your hand. They just love everything sparkly.

Now ask if the fairies are willing to grant you a wish. As you see them nodding, think of a wish. What do you wish? Think of the card you just pulled. Is this your wish?

Ask the fairies. If so, then ask for it to be granted. If not, think about a wish you have just for yourself. What do you wish? Wishes are dreams granted in love and dreams are wishes filled with heart.

Ask the fairies – is this my wish?

Hear their giggles. They are so joyful and playful and fun. They love helping you.

They typically grant any wish you desire. Whisper "I wish. I wish. I wish." Then say it aloud. Say, "I wish. I wish. I wish."

Take a few moments to play with the fairies. Feel their joy lift your spirit. Know they begin granting your wish.

Express gratitude to honor the fairies and elements.

Thank the crystals.

Continue to breathe and as you take your next breath, open your eyes to gaze softly around the room.

You're grounded and centered. Cross your arms over your heart to close the energy.

Wishing Moments

You can set wishing moments throughout your day to bring joy and abundance into your life.

<u>Set Wishing Moments</u>

Choose a few times a day you'd like to make wishes. Make these a time you do something daily like; take a shower, walk the dog or at a stop light as you drive to work.

While doing any of these activities, take a moment to connect to yourself and make wishes or amplify the energy of the wishes you've already made.

Breathe and smile.

You're helping make your wishes come true.

If you need reminders for wishing, you can purchase a fairy charm, make a mini-vision board or journal for your wishes.

Fairy Charms

You can buy a fairy charm at a toy or craft store or online at Amazon, Etsy or the Oriental Trading Company.

Once you have your charm, clear its energy.

You can do this by placing it in a bowl of crystals or rice or place it in the sun. Leave it there for a few hours.

Next, you may infuse it with heart energy to make your wishes into dreams.

Energize your Fairy Charm

To energize your fairy charm, you're going to engage your heart.

Hold your fairy charm in your open hand.

Simply enter a meditative state as you stare at your charm.

Once there, breathe deeply and fully. Focus your attention on your heart chakra and start breathing into it. As you inhale, expand your heart center and feel it opening. Feel it filling with love. As you exhale, feel your heart extend its love into the space in front of you and behind you. Continue to breathe, opening and extending your love.

Focus this heart energy from your heart and into your fairy charm. Imagine it forming a figure 8 from your heart and into the charm and from the charm and into your heart.

Take a few moments.

Thank your heart for its health in keeping you alive, for its passions, messages and all of its love. Thank the fairy charm as it's now infused with your heart energy.

When you're ready, take a nice full breath and bring your awareness back into the room.

Exit your meditative state and close your energy.

Mini-Vision Board

Typically, people make vision boards around the first of the year to capture their goals and desires for that year.

However, you can make a vision board anytime during the year. You don't have to make a big or comprehensive one.

You can make a miniature one.

Take a piece of paper or a portion of a journal.

Find a few magazines with words and images that relate to you and represent things you wish to bring into your life.

Cut out a handful of words, quotes and images.

Glue these onto your mini-vision board or portion of your journal.

Place the board or open the journal to pages so you can see them as reminders.

When you look at your images, set a wishing moment.

Journal Fun

When can you take a few moments in your day to journal?

Journaling can be fun. It doesn't have to be a complete capturing of your thoughts, emotions and dreams every time you write in it.

You can brainstorm, dream, color or draw.

You can take photos and place them in your journal.

You can look at memes online and write these down.

Make a wish and write it down.

Think of a few things you want to do in the next week, month or year.

Write these ideas in your journal.

Remember to have fun.

This is about wishes and dreams.

These first steps in this AIR section of expressing gratitude for the blessings in your life and then making wishes help create abundance.

These steps honor the movement of air and ease it into alignment by extending far and wide.

Intentions and Beliefs

"All that we are is a result of what we thought." — Buddha

Now that you've made wishes, you may want to solidify these into intentions.

An intention is an aim or a plan, while a wish is a desire or hope. A wish is like a dream and an intention is like a goal.

So, let's focus your mind to help set and then fuel your intentions.

Here are three exercises for you to do:

1. Set Intentions

2. Fuel Intentions

3. Amplify the Flow

Set Intentions

The following gratitude and intention meter exercise helps you set intentions as it highlights all of the areas of your life.

It involves the Kaleidoscope Wheel of Life™ of the aspects of your inner life and outer world.

There's a description of each segment of the pie along with an image.

The first exercise is to assess the areas of your life.

Area of Life Assessment Exercise

Refer to the circle diagram. There are eight areas depicting your life.

Inner Life:

- Create wellness | health & fitness – *physical/ earth - make it real*
- Spark mind | intellectual life – *mental/ air – calm*
- Satisfy heart | creativity & love – *emotional/ water – joy*
- Fill soul | spiritual life – *spiritual/ fire – passion*

Outer World:

- Improve living conditions | environment – *home, office, car, furnishings, clothing, finances, administration, second home, if applicable*
- Relish life work | career – *'work' is defined as job, career, business, volunteer positions, position & role in society*
- Boost fun with friends | family, friendships, relationships – *entertain, host parties & family events, celebrate holidays, relax throughout week, do fun things on weekends, gather with friends, see them regularly, stay in contact, connect intimately with besties and partner, go on dates, laugh, be frivolous, welcome levity*
- Expand your horizons | adventures & community - *adventure, travel, new discoveries and experiences, meet new people, cultural explorations, philosophy of life, establish community, be in service, engage actively to create a better world*

Calm, passion and joy in your inner life leads to magic, abundance and freedom in your outer world.

Striving for outer world possessions and material gain is a direct result of the health, strength and well-being of your inner life.

Each slice of the pie balances and helps facilitate growth in the other areas. The first part of this exercise is to assess your inner life. What do you feel are your strong points for each area? Where do you want to make more strides? Circle those you're pleased with your current status or are making progress. Underline those areas you want to improve.

Create Wellness - Health & Fitness	Spark Mind - Intellectual Life	Satisfy Heart - Love & Creativity	Fill Soul - Spiritual Life
▪ Daily regimen of fitness routine – strength, cardio, flexibility, balance and coordination ▪ Healthy organic diet ▪ Drink lots of water – daily: ½ of weight in ounces ▪ Sleep well and thoroughly every night ▪ Wake up without alarm every morning ▪ Feel vital, youthful and balanced every day ▪ Always feel sexy and alive ▪ Engage in sensual exploration ▪ Have active sex life ▪ Hair and nails are shiny and strong	▪ Plethora of reading: up-to-date on periodicals, current events & best seller list ▪ Explore new information continuously ▪ Currently, learning new skills ▪ Seeking cultural exploits ▪ Visionary mental abilities ▪ Constantly able to think critically ▪ Solve problems regularly ▪ Impeccable memory ▪ Decisive ▪ Insatiable curiosity ▪ Constantly aware of surroundings ▪ Connected intuitively ▪ Flexible thinking	▪ Live with open heart ▪ Trust self and others ▪ Surf emotional cycles smoothly and harmoniously ▪ Healthy connections with friends and family ▪ Welcome and provide intimate relationships ▪ Satisfy perceptions and senses ▪ Seek joy regularly ▪ Feel happy and content on a daily basis ▪ Nurturing and full of caring for self and others ▪ Nourishing and active self-love	▪ Meditate daily ▪ Visualize regularly ▪ Create and imagine as basis for life ▪ Receive messages from spirit on daily basis ▪ Highly developed intuition ▪ Pursue dream work ▪ Act on messages from spirit ▪ Feel calm and connected every minute ▪ Attune with universal flow of life ▪ Fully integrated with higher self ▪ Aligned with soul work ▪ Living your soul purpose ▪ Expanded state of consciousness and awareness ▪ Strive toward soul yearnings

Create Wellness - Health & Fitness	Spark Mind - Intellectual Life	Satisfy Heart - Love & Creativity	Fill Soul - Spiritual Life
▪ Complexion is clear and dewy ▪ At perfect weight ▪ Full of energy ▪ Feel beautiful every day	▪ Integrative philosophies/big picture life ▪ Facile with paradoxes ▪ Actively solve mysteries	▪ Balance between giving and receiving ▪ Engaged in harmonious intimate relationship ▪ Connected to soul mate ▪ Always allow heart to rule	

Next, refer to your outer world. Perform the same steps as above.

Living Conditions - *Environment*	Relish Life Work - *Career*	Boost Fun with Friends - *Family, Friends, Relationships*	Expand Horizons - *Adventures, Community*
▪ Love your car and it runs smoothly ▪ Home is your sanctuary ▪ House is cleaned regularly ▪ Spring cleaning is	▪ Have level of education necessary to work in your selected industry ▪ Have necessary certifications for same ▪ Passionate about your work	▪ Have healthy relationship with family ▪ Have soul brothers and sisters ▪ Create family of own – related or tribe ▪ Get together with family	▪ Invent ways to seek new adventures ▪ Find ways to travel and explore ▪ Seek out new material – books, classes, mentors, ideas, concepts ▪ Embrace new technologies

Living Conditions - *Environment*	Relish Life Work - *Career*	Boost Fun with Friends - *Family, Friends, Relationships*	Expand Horizons - *Adventures, Community*
done seasonally	▪ Seek to discover or learn more about your work	and friends on holidays	▪ Actively and frequently try new things – learn a new sport, craft or game
▪ Landscape design is to your liking and done regularly	▪ Actively strive to achieve more in your work	▪ Have intimate, trusting and supportive friendships	▪ Solve puzzles
▪ Space is clear and uncluttered	▪ Your work supports your livelihood	▪ Relax during the week and play during the weekends	▪ Love to meet new people in either large groups or intimate settings
▪ Everything is in its place	▪ Gain energy by doing your work, it stimulates your mind, feeds your heart and enlivens your soul	▪ Exciting daily activities	▪ Regularly go to different events – art exhibits, sports games, soup nights, musical concerts, barbeques, plays, kid shows
▪ Organized and practical		▪ Take vacations regularly	
▪ Have plenty of luxurious clothing and accessories		▪ Relish time off	
▪ Haircut, make-up and clothing maintained	▪ Your work is aligned with soul purpose	▪ Enjoy frivolity and laugh – often	▪ Engaged with like-minded people Volunteer for local charity – soup kitchen, animal shelter, library, children's
▪ Have appropriate outer wear & footwear for every season	▪ At the end of the day, your work makes you feel lucky & blessed	▪ Sink into own life, love the solitude of spending time alone	
▪ Do laundry on regular basis		▪ Healthy connection with ancestry	
		▪ Awareness and	

Living Conditions - *Environment*	Relish Life Work - *Career*	Boost Fun with Friends - *Family, Friends, Relationships*	Expand Horizons - *Adventures, Community*
<ul><li>Finances are in order</li><li>Taxes are done regularly</li><li>Have will, healthcare proxy, etc.</li></ul>		resolution of past lives	school, board room <ul><li>Expansive and inclusive life philosophy</li></ul>

Once you've gathered your circles and underlines, you want to emphasize gratitude and celebration for you on those areas you're pleased with your progress or current status. Look at your circles and be thankful.

Next, you want to set intentions around those areas you'd like to improve.

Refer to the exercise you've just completed and look at your underlines, where do you want to set intentions? Get a pen and paper as you're going to write out your intentions.

The next exercise reviews these areas, yet adds more punch to each. If you want to set an intention, why not make it big and bold?

For each area you've underlined, look at the examples below and determine which ones resonate.

Physical Well-Being:

- I am my perfect weight.
- My body is youthful and vital.
- I feel healthy, vibrant and alive.

110

Emotional Balance:

- I'm self-aware and can be objective about dramatic events in my life.
- My heart is open and trusting.
- I love healthily and happily.

Mental Clarity:

- I love to read —everything I can get my hands on.
- I listen intently and talk excitedly about many topics.
- My mind is open to the wonders of the world.

Spiritual Connection:

- I say 'Yes' to my intuition.
- I associate with my higher self regularly.
- I am living my soul purpose.

Living Conditions:

- My home is my sanctuary.
- I love my style – haircut, makeup, clothing and accessories.
- I feel I have the level of luxury I desire.

Money and Work:

- I love to make money.
- I have a lucrative and interesting job.
- I'm going to start a new and successful business.

Love Life:

- I attract my soul mate.

- I am in a loving partnership.

- I have a fulfilling, intimate and loving relationship with my soul mate.

Fun and Adventure:

- I travel and see the world.

- I have great friends who are interested and interesting.

- I love to entertain and host gatherings.

For each underline, state an intention, even if there isn't an example for it listed above.

Now, let's explore your intentions. Go through them and look at your phrasing.

- Each should be stated in the positive.

- Each should be stated in the present.

- Each should be as big as possible.

Let's do this now.

Take a litmus test for each intention and ensure it passes.

Is your intention stated in the positive, in the present and as big as it can be?

Litmus Test #1 – Positive.

You always want your intentions to be stated in the positive. The universe relates equally to the positive as to the negative. If you set an intention as I don't want, or I can't, the universe will focus on the objective, not the preceding wording.

Instead of, "I don't want any more debt" or "I want to be debt-free". Say instead, "I desire financial freedom" or "I have plenty of money". The focus is on the financial freedom and money versus debt.

Similarly, if you say, "I can't be late or deal with traffic", the universe focuses on lateness and traffic. You're actually creating both. Say instead, "I am on time" or "I drive smoothly and easily going to work every day".

Check your intentions. Are they in the positive? Are you emphasizing what you actually desire?

Litmus Test #2 - Now.

Are each of your intentions written in the present form – not the future or the past? The present.

> I am…
>
> I have…
>
> I feel…

Be careful of *I wish* or *desire*. These are not necessarily ineffective; however, they may push the intention into the future. If you want it in the future, perfect. If you want it now, you can add an intention or restate it.

Example; I wish to be the perfect weight.

This can be changed to "I am the perfect weight". If that doesn't feel right, you can add the two statements together.

I wish to be the perfect weight and I am the perfect weight.

Litmus Test #3 - BIG.

Are your intentions as BIG as possible? Are they infinite?

Think Bigger. Think INFINITELY.

- I am infinitely abundant.
- I'm in perfect health.
- I am loved and love unconditionally.
- My life is filled with new adventures and infinite possibilities.
- I am an infinitely divine being.

How can you make your intentions bigger? Infinite?

Fuel Intentions

Now that you've set your intentions, add punch to each.

You can fuel your intentions in a number of ways. The most straightforward is visualization and meditation. I've included a meditation that uses vibration to add more power. You can use you voice through chanting, tuning fork or singing bowl for resonance.

Intention Setting Mantras and Vibration
Write your infinite intention.
Stare at it. Absorb it. Own it.
If desired, select a tuning fork or singing bowl.

Intention Setting Mantras and Vibration

Gaze softly at your intention. Take a few deep and full breaths. As you breathe, let your eyes lose their focus and continue to gaze softly. Place your other hand near the base of your spine at your root chakra and say, "I live" and chant UUH. Breathe in your intention. Place your hand at your sacral chakra, say, "I feel" and chant OOO. Breathe in your intention. Place your hand at your solar plexus, say, "I will" and chant OH. Breathe in your intention. Place your hand at your heart, say, "I love" and chant AH. Breathe in your intention. Place your hand at your throat, say, "I speak — the truth" and chant EYE. Breathe in your intention. Place your hand at your third eye, say, "I see" and chant AYE. Breathe in your intention. Place your hand at your crown, say, "I AM" and chant EEE. Breathe in your intention and state it — loudly and clearly. UUH, OOO, OH, AH, EYE, AYE, EEE. Breathe in your intention and state it — loudly and clearly. UUH, OOO, OH, AH, EYE, AYE, EEE. Breathe in your intention and state it — loudly and clearly. UUH, OOO, OH, AH, EYE, AYE, EEE. Breathe all of your power into your intention. Welcome it. Embrace it. Embody it. Own it.

Continue to breathe and ease back into the room.

It's time to fuel your intentions with supportive beliefs.

- Look for signs.
- Take note of your response.
- Shift your focus.
- Fuel your intentions with positive beliefs.

How supportive are your beliefs? Check it out below.

Money:

When you've set your intention to have more money, the universe will send you signs.

115

Your next-door neighbor buys a new car.

A typical reaction is: *"How can they buy a new car? Their children are in college."* Or *"They have a new car…why can't I have one?"*

Your reaction could be: *"Oh, wow, how lucky are they to get a new vehicle? Prosperity is here for me too. I'm delighted."*

You read about the person winning the lottery.

A typical reaction is: *"How can they have won? The odds are unbelievable."*

Your reaction could be: *"That person must be thrilled. I'm so happy for him or her. I feel my worth increasing right now."*

Work:

A co-worker gets a promotion.

A typical reaction is: *"She doesn't deserve it. I bet she flirted her way to the top."*

Your reaction could be: *"The company is promoting people from within. I'm so ready for a promotion."*

Another business owner reveals a new offering.

A typical reaction is: *"How could he have created that? I bet he doesn't get that many clients."*

Your reaction could be: *"There's so much creativity in the universe. I create my own offerings and attract so many clients."*

Health:

Your friend announces she lost 10 lbs.

A typical reaction is: *"How did she do that? Why can't I? I never lose weight. She didn't have to work too hard for it. I bet she gains it back."*

Your reaction could be: *"How amazing! I'm at my perfect weight."*

You see an ad for a new spa opening up in your town.

A typical reaction is: *"I don't have the time or the money to go to a new spa."*

Your reaction could be: *"Oh, a spa. I've manifested the best place to relax and unwind. I'm calling right now to make an appointment."*

Love Life:

A friend tells you she thinks she's met the one.

A typical reaction is: *"I'm happy for her of course, but she always says that. I'll just have to pick up the pieces again."*

Your reaction could be: *"I'm so happy for you! How amazing is this? What else is possible?"*

You hear a couple in the neighborhood is getting a divorce.

A typical reaction is: *"Phew — that evens the odds. The statistics certainly support this. Thank goodness that's not us."*

Your reaction could be: *"I hope they find happiness. We're so happy, I hope that for them too."*

Balancing the Flow

Setting and fueling intentions is all outlay with respect to energy. As you set and fuel, you're pushing energy into the universe. This doesn't allow for acceptance or inflow of abundance as it's only one side of the figure 8.

The universe requires balance.

Using the infinite flow requires inflow as well as outflow.

As you're putting more energy into intentions, you need to balance that power with the 'other side' of it.

So, you need to balance this by powering up your inflow. There are ways to amp up the volume on the inward portion of the curve.

Notice how you receive. Are you good at it? Do you receive with grace or with struggle? Do you receive in a manner that allows for it or do you try to control it? Do you observe the ways you receive throughout the day? Do you welcome these with gratitude or with criticism?

Take Note

How do you receive in your life?

Here are a few examples. Take note of your actions. Be honest with yourself and your true reactions.

Grace versus struggle

A friend gives you a gift out of the blue.

Do you accept it by expressing gratitude and excitement and leave it at that?

- or -

Do you say thank you and immediately try to figure out what you can give them in return?

A friend offers to pay for lunch.

Do you smile, say "Thank you" and casually offer to pay next time?

- or -

Do you keep insisting it's your turn to pay or you can split the bill?

A group of you decide to purchase a present for a friend's celebration.

Do you buy the gift, split the amount evenly among everyone and easily collect the money?

- or -

Do you buy the gift, split the amount evenly among everyone and have difficulty collecting the money? Each time this situation occurs, you don't collect all of the money owed to you.

Allowance or control

A family member offers to host the next holiday.

Do you say "Great", allow it to happen without giving any advice and enjoy it thoroughly?

- or -

Do you say "Okay", give lots of advice and don't enjoy it as much as you would if you hosted?

Your spouse offers to go grocery shopping for you.

Do you say "Hooray" and let 'him' go? When he comes home, you put the groceries away and are thankful for it getting done without any effort from you.

- or -

Do you give him a list, remark on what he brings and all the while thinking if you had just done it yourself, it would have gone a lot more smoothly?

You're given a paid vacation with all of the plans made and timing coordinated. All you have to do is show up and enjoy.

Do you go and thoroughly enjoy your time?

- or -

Do you feel guilty about going away or complain about the choices?

Gratitude or criticism

Your spouse does all of the laundry one weekend.

Do you say "Thank you"?

- or -

Do you criticize the way he folded most of your clothing (even if the criticism is only in your head)?

Your children ask to help you make dinner.

Do you say yes and delegate some tasks according to their ability? Do you enjoy the time you're spending together?

- or -

Do you give them a few tasks and then comment in detail about how they should have done it differently?

A family member offers to assist at home.

Do you say, "Great, I could help with…"?

- or -

Do you say, "No thanks, I'm all set"?

What about the universe at large?

Do you notice the wonders of the world?

- Yourself
- Family
- Friends
- Community
- Nature
- Spirit

Are you open to the possibilities of abundance everywhere?

Notice the bounty and support from the universe in all of its forms including; sunrise, sunset, flowers, trees, birds or animals.

Soak it all in with an open mind and grateful heart.

Receive Compliments Exercise

Notice how you receive compliments throughout your days. Next time someone gives you a compliment, say "Thank you."

And then STOP.

Don't say any mitigating comment.

Don't say, "Oh, I woke up late, or this old thing or I only paid X for it."

When someone says something nice to you, say "Oh, thank you or thank you so much!"

Bask for a few seconds in how good it feels.

Receive the compliment.

Don't deflect it with an offhand comment.

Receive Visualization

Another way to receive is through this goblet visualization.

Abundance Goblets Visualization
Imagine holding huge brandy snifters in your hands.
Place your hands facing upward and balance on your thighs.
Breathe in deeply and fully.
Continue to breathe and envision your crown chakra opening and accepting the universal abundance of all that is.
Now picture hundreds of dollars coming from the universe and going into your crown chakra.
Next imagine them traveling from your crown, down your head, through the neck, over your shoulders, down your arms and into your hands.
See the dollars filling the goblets in your hands.
Continue to breathe, allowing and accepting the prosperity of the universe.
You are abundant, prosperous and wealthy.

Abundance Goblets Visualization
You are overflowing with the infinite supply of the universe.   *Thank the universe for its blessings.*   *Close the energy by crossing your arms over your heart.*   *Bow to the universe for its honoring of you.*

You may substitute anything in this visualization – love, support, health, travel or friends.

Do this as often as you'd like to bring in the bounty of the universe.

Recap

You've set your infinite intentions. Now what?

1. Stay open.
2. Remain positive.
3. In other words – Breathe. Let go. Breathe.
4. Continue to power your intentions.
5. Be alert for signs.
6. Receive.
7. Say yes when they arrive.
8. Take action.

"What I call my 'self' now is hardly a person at all. It's mainly a meeting place for various natural forces, desires, and fears, etcetera, some of which come from my ancestors, and some from my education, some perhaps from devils. The self you were really intended to be is something that lives not from nature but from God."
– C. S. Lewis

The former section covers intentions and beliefs and the power of fueling your intentions.

This section involves your beliefs and the conditioning of the generations, ancestors and past life influences.

You're given the opportunity to become aware of these and then surrender any beliefs or conditioning no longer serving you to the universe.

You'll be reviewing your beliefs about money, time and gender.

Surrendering scarcity involves reengineering the tapes in your head, letting go of ancestral programming and evolving beyond past life wounding.

Reengineering Tapes in Your Head

Abundant Money

Regarding money, you'll complete two exercises in the next moments and a handful you can do on a regular basis.

You'll need pen, paper and a $20 bill.

Numbers Exercise

Pick a number.

What is your dream revenue or salary?

Write down your dream # in your journal.

Next, double your dream #.

Double it again.

Money Gauge

Your money thermometer is set to a certain gauge. You need to change it.

Write down the highest amount of money you have ever made.

Now, compare these figures.

How far are they from each other?

The dream number is the figure you desire. However, the other number is your real number. The one you're use to experiencing.

Now it's time to change your money gauge – raise the temperature.

Choose to be a hero versus a victim.

Choose to be wealthy – to be in abundance. *No – if's, and's or but's.*

Commit to being wealthy – to being abundant.

Say it out loud.

"I am a hero. I commit to being wealthy. I commit to being abundant."

Money Energy Exercise

The following exercise allows you feel the energy of money.

Money Energy Exercise

Money energy is all-inclusive, it's creative, it's nurturing. It's warm, it's beautiful. In fact, it feels similar to the energy of a wise elemental.

Hold a $20-dollar bill between your hands in prayer position.

Don't ask for stuff – you're feeling the energy of money. You're going to meet the spirit of money. So, close your eyes and take a nice deep breath in and a long exhale. Clear your mind with your breath. Breathe in and out, in and out. Inhale and exhale.

Now, feel the note. Feel it in your palms. Allow it to be there. Accept it in your hands.

"Hi money – it's nice to meet you. I welcome you in my hands. I welcome you in my life. I welcome you with an open heart."

Now listen to what the money has to say to you. Listen and breathe.

Money Energy Exercise

Make a mental note of any messages, images or feelings you received if you desire to remember them.

Then release images or messages that come up for you and let go of any no longer serving you.

Your palms are probably getting warm and they may be tingling. Feel the money. Feel its energy. Once again, welcome it. Smile as you express your fondness for the energy – your fondness for money.

Allow the money energy to become warm, perhaps even hot.

Allow the warm feeling to grow – larger and larger. Allow the warmth to encompass you. Feel it surrounding you – above and below you. Allow the warm energy to come into your life, the flow of it and the love of it.

The signature, you will find, is extremely similar to that of Mother Earth because they are one and the same.

Welcome it, embrace it.

After you are done, say thank you to the elemental of money for having expressed itself fully to you. Open your eyes if they were closed, and put the money back onto the table.

Jot down any notes from your experience.

Collective, Family and Individual Beliefs

Unfortunately, many are fighting against collective, family or societal beliefs about money. These can revolve around either lack or greed.

<u>Money Lack</u>

"You can't have everything you want in life."

"There's no free lunch."

"Money is the root of all evil."

"Money is dirty."

"You don't get something for nothing."

"Spiritual people don't need money. If you're spiritual, you're beyond needing money."

"You must save for a rainy day."

"The rich get richer and the poor get poorer."

"Money doesn't grow on trees."

Oh, but it does.

Money is unlimited. Money is boundless. Money is infinite.

Money Greed

"Whoever dies with the most money wins."
"I want more. I need more."
"Greed is good."
"Keeping up with the Joneses."

Money is energy. Money is spiritual. Money is divine.

Practical Ways to Enjoy Money

- As you pay your bills - express appreciation. Be thankful, you can easily and joyfully pay your bills on time.

- When you check your bank balance, power your thinking - "Oh, look how much money I have."

- Keep your finances in order. Pay your bills on time and use the simplest system (for you).

- If you don't have cash in your wallet, don't say "I don't have any money." Say instead, "I don't have cash in my wallet right now."

- Keep your wallet neatly arranged – for easy access.

- As you pay for something at the cash register, breathe in peace and calm. You have plenty of money.

- Believe and know you always have plenty of money.

Feel the supportive energy of money. Be thankful for it. Believe you always have enough.

Magical Ways to Enjoy Money

- Include Chinese coins with red string under your front door mat.

- Make wealth vases during the Chinese New Year.

- Make prosperity bowls with crystals of aventurine, citrine, jade, pyrite and clear quartz, I Ching coins and little statues of Buddha.

- Perform rituals during the New Moon to manifest more money, prosperity and wealth in your life.

- Do ceremony during the equinox and solstice times to show gratitude for the abundance in your life.

- Make wealth bags for your purse or cash drawers with gold coins and abundance stones.

- Carry a placard with Archangel Michael to put into your wallet to protect your money.

You can have fun with money in both practical and magical ways.

Abundant Time

Some people create lack when it comes to time. They're constantly busy, running late for meetings and behind in returning calls, emails or texts, and don't have any time for leisure or vacations.

Time is an important commodity. Having plenty of it matters.

However, I bet you can hear these common sayings in your mind:

"There's never enough time in a day."

"Lost time is never found again."

"There are only 24 hours in a day."

"Time flies when you're having fun."

"I don't have time."

"Time is the most valuable thing a man can spend."

"If only I managed my time better."

"I need to take a time management course."

Yet, when thinking of time, there's another school of thought. Namely, that it doesn't even exist.

As Albert Einstein contends, *"Time is an illusion."*

If this is true, perhaps, time is flexible or bendable. You can create time.

Your new mantra may be:

I create time. I create time. I create time.

If you want to add power to your time creation, do a mini-visualization.

Time Exercise

Look at this picture of the clocks.

Look at it intensely.

Let your eyes focus until your gaze softens.

With your softened gaze, breathe deeply and fully. Continue to breathe and notice the different times on the clocks.

These times are not real.

Time is an illusion.

Time is an illusion.

Time is an illusion.

"I create time. I have plenty of time. My time is bountiful. I have all of the time in the world."

Abundant Women

Regarding the balance between the masculine and feminine, it's clear that women are undervalued, overlooked and even maligned.

Accordingly, it's beyond time to heal the divine feminine energy and bring it into wholeness with the divine masculine.

Recognizing this need and beginning the process is important work for both men and women.

Additionally, honoring the male while healing the female is required to bring these two energies into balance and harmony.

For the feminine, it's time for everyone to welcome the goddess.

For the masculine, it's time for honor, integrity and respect.

For both, it's time to be authentic, unapologetic and unstoppable.

Let's look at recent history and current events to highlight the pressures on the feminine.

Shining the light creates awareness. Awareness is the first step in healing.

133

Envision your grandmother following the advice from the Singer sewing machine manual in the following illustration.

> ## Advice from a Singer Sewing Machine Manual from 1949
>
> *Prepare yourself mentally for sewing. Think about what you are going to do. Never approach sewing with a sigh or lackadaisically. Good results are difficult when indifference dominates. Never try to sew with a sink full of dirty dishes or beds unmade.*
>
> *When there are urgent housekeeping chores, do these first so that your mind is free to enjoy your sewing. When you sew, make yourself as attractive as possible. Put on a clean dress. Keep a little bag of French chalk near your sewing machine to dust your fingers at intervals. Have your hair in order, powder and lipstick put on. If you are constantly fearful that a visitor might drop in or your husband will come home, and you will not look neatly put together, you will not enjoy your sewing.*

Can you picture yourself ensuring your home and hair, makeup and dress are camera ready before sitting down to be creative?

Can you envision your grandmother actually doing it?

Recent History

Women have been slighted throughout history. Here are a few highlights:

- Women got the right to vote in 1920. (It hasn't even been 100 years.)

- In 1963, Betty Friedan published a landmark book, *The Feminine Mystique*.

- Title VII of the 1964 Civil Rights Act was passed, prohibiting employment discrimination on the basis of sex as well as race, religion, and national origin.

- Education Codes of 1972, provided women equal access to higher education and to professional schools.

Do you realize that just 35 years ago married women were not issued credit cards in their own name? That most women could not get a bank loan without a male co-signer?

In 1972, the Equal Rights Amendment was necessary as Civil Rights Act of 1964 didn't clear the issues of sex-discrimination in the work place.

Today

Today women hold only 19% of the seats in Congress, and 21% of the state legislative seats.

Women make up 32 out of the 500 CEO seats in the Fortune 500 – that's 6.4%.

A woman is paid 77% of a man's salary. By race, Asian women make 85%, white women make 75%, black women make 63% and Latina women make 54%.

US economic gender equality is getting worse; falling from 3rd in the world in 2006 to 26th in 2016.

42% of the time women pay more than men for similar products.

10 million women a year are victims of domestic violence; 3 women are murdered every day by their husband or boyfriend.

Given all of this information, imagine the sayings running through your head.

"A woman over 40 has a better chance of being killed by a terrorist than getting married."

"You throw like a girl."

"Women should be barefoot and pregnant."

"She's too bossy, whereas he's a true leader."

"Girls should be sugar and spice and everything nice."

"She's just a little girl."

"Look at her, she thinks she can wear the pants in the family."

"Whining like a girl."

"She's so fickle. That's okay, she's just a girl."

"Women, you can never please them."

Knowing these statements are floating somewhere in your consciousness introduces awareness for changing them.

Awareness is the first step and integrating the Goddess to help create change is an excellent second one.

The Goddess

The Goddess helps you lean into a particular archetype. She helps you wear a certain energy. Once you begin to wear it, you can integrate it and call upon this energy whenever you need it.

Call on your Goddess archetype. Integrate her to make her part of you. Once you do, she becomes the Inner Goddess.

The Inner Goddess anchors the light of the skies, the energies of the world and the divinity of the universe.

The meditation below brings the energies of the archetypes for the phases of life: Maiden, Lover, Mother and Queen.

You're each at every stage of your life.

Inner Goddess Guided Meditation

Take a deep cleansing breath and expel anything that no longer serves you. You're here, present, centered and grounded. You are in a safe space, one of white light, pure intentions, clear thoughts, positive emotions and relaxed physicality. You're at peace in every part of you.

As you continue to breathe, and know you're going to be filled with the blessings of the Goddess.

Your heart expands as you know this to be true. You know the Goddess is part of you. The Goddess has been with you for your entire soul journey. You're intrinsically linked. You're intertwined. Your energies are enmeshed. Breathe in the Goddess' strength, power, love and support. You're already connected to the earthly and spiritual realms. You can feel your chakras spinning clearly and actively in the appropriate directions. You know you're an open channel of light traveling from the earth up through your chakras and connecting to the pure universal light of all that is.

Your chakras are wide open to expand the powerful energy of your inner goddess.

Diana the huntress, wearing bow and arrow, accompanied by many animals. She defends the sacred forest with her life. She is the call of the wild. She is the animal spirit within. She awakens nature within you. You can feel the winds rustling through your hair and hear the cries of the wolf. Be strong. Stand up for what you believe in. Defend those who are weaker than you or have no voice. Diana. Diana. Diana. Breathe in her strength and know it's yours. You are strong. You are defender.

As lover, be Oshun – the African goddess of love, beauty and the arts. She rules the waters and gives to the earth. She is sweet, courageous and a force of harmony. She loves – selflessly. She empowers – generously. She experiences ecstasy – regularly. Be the lover in her. In you. You are the lover. Be a lover to yourself – first and completely. Be generous, sweet, courageous and kind to yourself. Then, and only then, give your love to others. Be Oshun. Be love, beauty and harmony.

Next, the nurturer. Mother, lover, sister, teacher, rescuer. Ceres - of hearth and home. She lights the home fires and keeps them bright. She makes dinner and feeds all who travel from their journeys. She listens to the stories, hears the joy in their hearts and know she is an integral part of their lives. She likes to stay at home - providing, supporting and loving. She is the foundation of their worlds. She is the caregiver. Breathe in the caregiving aspects within you.

The Queen - Juno sits on the throne – surveying everything. Missing nothing. She reigns – with love, nobility and decency. She is regal. Powerful. Everything in her sphere is under her control. Her power. Her word. She is Queen. Tradition. She is the divine protector. She reigns with the divine force. You are queen. You reign. You are called regina or queen. Breathe in the bounty of your queendom. Be noble, regal and wise.

You are defender, lover, mother and queen. You are whole in your divinity. You are infinite. You are light. You are love.

Be authentic. Be unapologetic. Be unstoppable.

To repeat, be authentic, unapologetic and unstoppable in all of your glory and power.

As you take your next breath, bring your awareness back to the room.

When you're ready, open your eyes and gaze softly in front you – seeing nothing, yet aware of everything. If you would like, wiggle your fingers and toes and do any gentle stretching your body requires.

Breathe in again and open your eyes fully.

Make any notes in your journal about your experience or any messages you received.

Healing of the feminine energy begins with the Goddess.

Reengineering the tapes in your head is the first part of the process. There are ancestral and past life wound resolution still to come.

Diving deeper into conditional beliefs, ancestral and past life influences are reviewed next.

Ancestral Influences

Through the generations, your ancestors have been dealing with collective beliefs, world events and their own ancestral lineage.

These collective energies also affect the living generations today.

Recognize the current energies evolving and changing the consciousness of the country. These living generations are the only energies in the country today. As each generation passes, the energies shift toward the future ones.

Living Generations of America

As of 2015, the percentage of U.S. population for each generation is as follows:

Gen Z/Boomlets	22.6%
Gen Y/Millennials	24.3%
Gen-X	20.1%
Baby Boomers	23.1%
Silent	8.7%
Greatest	1.2%

140

The energies from the Gen Z, Millennials, Gen X and Baby Boomers are approximately the same. Those from the Silent and Greatest Generations are, as expected, waning.

Let's gain understanding of the energies presently available.

Generation	Impacts	Pop Culture and Advances	Attitudes about Money	Characteristics	Values
Generation Z/ Boomlets – 2001+ *(some data uses 1995)*	9/11; Afghanistan & Iraq Wars, Hispanics = 49% Larger generation than baby boomers	Smart phones Computers TV ads/shows targeted directly to them	Savvy consumers; conservative spenders; price-conscious; over saturated with brands	Foodies; Hard-working; Bright-eyed workers; Comfort-seeking travelers	Optimistic Self-assured Health-conscious
Generation Y/ Millennials 1981 – 2000	Age of Prosperity, Gulf War I, Falling crime, Falling teen pregnancies	Omni-present parents; Over-scheduled; Academic pressure	Don't like to work; overindulge in fancy living conditions; use credit cards for luxuries	Delayed adulthood Need lots of hand-holding & accolades Digital world	Feel special Respect authority Assertive Strong opinions Team players
Generation X 1965 – 1980	Latch-key kids, AIDS, parents disappoint-ed with government authority and Vietnam War	Space Age Civil Rights OPEC Disposable society; 7 jobs/career; late to marry	Designer labels & brand names; struggling to buy – deeply in debt	Desire to learn Explore Make a contribution Suspicious of organizations	Entre-preneurial/ self-reliant Individual-istic Cautious of authority Wary of commitment

141

Generation	Impacts	Pop Culture and Advances	Attitudes about Money	Characteristics	Values
Baby Boomers - 1946 – 1964	Peace & Prosperity; 2 subsets: Crusaders and "ME"	Defined by Korean & Vietnam Wars Rock & Roll TV Divorce	Buy it now – use credit – means for travel and adventure for retirement	Causes Free love or money Technology Self-righteous Self-centered	Driven Optimistic Innovative Team-oriented
Mature/ Silents – 1927 – 1945	Suffocating conformity; Fought in Korean & Vietnam War; Pre-feminism	Big Band/ Swing; Defined by WWII/ Great depression Job for life	Save for retirement, relax in retirement – pursue peace in retirement	Lifelong marriage Avid readers	Respectful Disciplined Cautious Sacrifice
Greatest – 1901- 1926	Young in Great Depression; Fighters in WWII; League of Nations; Federal income tax	Radio Car Air flight Labor Unions	Avoid debt, pay with cash; work throughout life – no retirement *"Use it up, fix it up, make it do, or do without."*	Saved the world Built the nation	Team loyalty Civic duty "Greatest generation"

Historical Eras

The past generational impacts also affect the belief systems of your ancestors and you too.

Evolving through the ancestral beliefs affects both past and future generations.

Era	Details
Post World War II: 1945 - present	Current Events Global Security Global Transformations Nationalist & Independence Movements Cold War Changes after WWII
World Conflicts: 1914 - 1945	World War II Post WWI Political Shifts Great Depression WWI
Imperialism: 1800 - 1914	Reactions to Colonization Spanish-American War Japan Modernizes Scramble for Africa Imperialism
Revolution & Enlightenment: 1500 -1865	Women's Movement – 1848 - 1920 Industrial Revolution – 1760 - 1850 American Civil War – 1861 - 1865 Nationalist Movements French Revolution – 1789 - 1799 American Revolution – 1775 - 1783 Monarch Rise in Europe Scientific Revolution & Enlightenment Enlightenment – Age of Reason: <ul><li>Adam Smith (1776) – *wealth of nations – laissez-faire -> capitalism*</li><li>Rousseau (1762) – *social contract = governed by general will*</li><li>John Locke (1690)– *own civil rights = life, liberty & property*</li></ul>
Exploration: 1400 - 1800	American colonies Europe explores Asia Europe sets sail

143

Era	Details
Renaissance & Reformation: 1350 - 1650	Renaissance Reformation

Ancestral Impacts

The cumulative impacts over the generations are listed below along with the related healing:

Negative Impacts	Healing
Sudden Violence: Anger, fear, shock - *Feuds/wars– tribal, geographical, religious beliefs, geopolitical, civil unrest*	Calm, joy, love, trust
Enduring Violence: Anger, bitterness, regret and perhaps shame - *Famine – sandstorms, potato famine, great depression; physical & sexual abuse*	Peace, calm, ease, innocence
Despair – trapped in hopeless situation – *loveless marriage; obligatory circumstances*	Faith, hope, amazement, intimacy, trust, love
Duties & Responsibilities – overwhelming – *sickness, too many children, family burdens*	Joy, freedom, independence, selfish enlightenment
Escapism – victimized by life situation	Skillful, practical, embodied, present, spiritually connected
Greed – gluttony - *royalty, entitlement, elitist, racist, narcissist*	Generosity, maturation, wisdom, inclusion, of service, healthy appetites
Lack – scarcity - *poverty, grueling, back-breaking work, working for others*	Luxury, travel, exploration, blessings, abundance

Negative Impacts	Healing
Outsiders – disassociation - *Them versus us, Ellis Island - not belonging – not being accepted*	Connection, passion, partnership, emotional ties, family, tribe
Servitude - *Tithing to exclusion of self-care, self-deprecation, too much humility, chaste life, erosion of self*	Natural authority, power, life mission, self-worth
Stoicism – *rose to challenges, gave up everything for others or situation, survived*	Play, feelings, desires, pleasure, softness, sensations

The overall healing involves the ability to receive and heal, self-forgiveness, self-acceptance, self-confidence, self-esteem, self-worth and self-love.

Ancestral Release Meditation

Get into a meditative state and deeply connect to your breath and the universal connection.

As you breathe, call on the universal pure white crystalline light of all that is. Call on Archangel Michael for protection and St. Germain as the keeper of the violet flame. Call on your higher self and request all healing occur for the highest good of all. You are a being of violet fire! You are the purity God desires! Say to yourself, "I AM a being of violet fire! I AM the purity God desires!"

Now imagine the violet flame transmuting all of your negative thoughts, intentions, will, emotions and physical manifestations into pure white crystalline light.

As you invoke the violet flame, visualize yourself surrounded by the violet-flame pillar about six feet in diameter and about nine feet high. It extends from beneath your feet to well over the top of your head.

Inhale and exhale. Breathing in the transmutation abilities of the violet flame. You are pure white light. Anchor this light. Open the channel.

Now as you breathe, ask your ancestral lineage – past and future - to release all that no longer serves you. Ask your ancestral lineage and your higher self for guidance, grace and ease as you release unwanted beliefs and emotions and replace them with the light and love of healthy ones.

Continue to breathe. Anchor the light.

Ask your ancestors to release the beliefs and emotions of anger, fear, shock and sudden violence and replace these with joy, trust and love. Inhale deeply and exhale fully. Anchor the light.

Ask your ancestors to release the beliefs and emotions of anger, bitterness, regret and chronic violence and replace these with ease, calm and peace. Inhale deeply and exhale fully. Anchor the light.

Ask your ancestors to release the beliefs and emotions of escapism and replace it with skill, embodiment, and present energy. Inhale and exhale. Anchor the light.

Ask your ancestors to release the beliefs and emotions of despair and replace it with amazement, hope, and faith. Inhale deeply and exhale fully. Anchor the light.

Ask your ancestors to release the beliefs and emotions of overwhelming duties & responsibilities and replace these with independence, selfish enlightenment, joy, and freedom. Inhale deeply and exhale fully. Anchor the light.

Ask your ancestors to release the beliefs and emotions of feeling of being outsiders or disassociated and replace these with connection, passion, partnership, emotional ties, family, and tribe. Inhale deeply and exhale fully. Anchor the light.

Ask your ancestors to release the beliefs and emotions of lack and scarcity and replace these with luxury, travel, exploration, blessings, and abundance. Inhale deeply and exhale fully. Anchor the light.

Ask your ancestors to release the beliefs and emotions of greed and gluttony and replace these with healthy appetites, maturation, and wisdom. Inhale deeply and exhale fully.

146

Anchor the light.

Ask your ancestors to release the beliefs and emotions of servitude and replace this with natural authority, power, life mission, and self-worth. Inhale deeply and exhale fully. Anchor the light.

Ask your ancestors to release the beliefs and emotions of stoicism and replace these with play, feelings, pleasure, softness, sensations and desires. Inhale deeply and exhale fully. Anchor the light.

Overall, ask your ancestors to release any unwanted beliefs and emotions and replace these with healing, self-forgiveness, and ability to receive all the light and love of the universe.

You are at peace, you are present, you are faith, you are freedom, you are tribe, you are abundance, you are wisdom, you are self-worth, you are desire and pleasure.

You are infinite. You are divine. You are love.

Continue to breathe and close this healing by thanking your ancestors, the violet flame, Archangel Michael, St. Germain and your higher self.

When you're ready, take a deep cleansing breath and wiggle your fingers and your toes. Close the energy by crossing your arms over your heart. Bow to your ancestors and your guides in respect.

Open your eyes.

Write in your journal about your experience if your desire.

Drink water to ground your energy.

Past Life Wounding

The wounding is similar in past lives as those for ancestral releasing. However, there's an additional layer to remove. The layer of vows. You may have taken a vow of poverty, chastity, self-sacrifice, celibacy/separation, silence, suffering/retribution and/or obedience.

Past life vows along the chakras are:

Root – vow of poverty or anti-materialism

Sacral – vows of chastity & sexual abstinence

Solar Plexus – vows of self-sacrifice & abnegation

Heart – vow of celibacy & separation

Throat – vow of silence & voluntary denial

Third eye – vow of suffering & retribution

Crown – vow of obedience & humility

The vow reversals are:

- Root Chakra – from *poverty* to **abundance**

- Sacral Chakra – from *chastity* to **creation**

- Solar Plexus – from *self-sacrifice* to **self-love**

- Heart – from *separation* to **union**

- Throat – from *silence* to **true expression**

- Third Eye – from *suffering & retribution* to **joyful living**

- Crown – from *obedience* to **trust**

The first vow to release is the vow of poverty.

Vow of Poverty Release

Close your eyes. Take a deep breath and reestablish your connection to the universal white pure crystallize light. Call on your higher self. Call on your soul connection to your past lives.

Now, imagine the pure white crystalline light in your root chakra, clearing and energizing it. This white light travels to your sacral chakra and activates it, allowing it to spin in the correct direction. Now the white light enters to the solar plexus in your mid abdomen and stimulates your will power. Your heart alights with this white, pure crystalline light, healing and opening your heart chakra to all the love in the Universe. The pure white light moves to your throat, activating your truth, intuition and instinct. Now it goes into your third eye, opening it to be all seeing. The white light goes to your crown chakra opening it wide and connecting to the spirit world.

Continue breathing and as you do, focus on this white light filling each of your chakras, and connecting to the spirit world through your crown chakra. It fills your third eye, throat, heart, solar plexus, sacral, root and going into the ground beneath you. The light travels deeply into the core of the earth.

Now, envision the white pure light coming out of your root chakra and forming a ball in front of you. It's a healing ball filled with light and love from all that is. It transforms everything into beautiful, abundant energy. It sparkles with white twinkles.

Vow of Poverty Release

Continue to breathe. Visualize the energy of the vow of poverty moving out of your root chakra and into this healing ball as you make a new vow. It is vital that you speak this new vow out loud for it is the sound of your voice that gives it power.

So, you're going to repeat after me. "In the past, I made a Vow of Poverty. (pause) I have learned much from this Vow. (pause) I learned practicality, humility, and the art of letting go. (pause) Yet in the present and for the future, I realize that this old Vow of Poverty now no longer serves me. (pause) I now release this old Vow from my energy field (pause) and my consciousness at all levels as well as all the limitations that it has created in my life now. (pause) I now embrace a new Vow of Abundance and incorporate it into my Being. (pause) I ask my guides to bring the new energies of this vow into my life. (pause) I embrace the needed learnings and the wondrous changes that this new vow will bring into my life. (pause) So be it, it is so."

Breathe and say "I am abundant. I am infinite. I am love."

Take a few more breaths and thank your higher self and your soul connection to your past lives. Thank universal source of all that is. Ground your energy.

Take a few more breaths and when you're ready, open your eyes and return to the room.

Make any notes about your experience.

Be vigilant about reengineering the tapes in your head. Pay attention to your thoughts on a daily basis.

Take time periodically to do the ancestral reprogramming and release of past life vow meditations.

You're creating space to allow abundance to flow toward you.

Welcome to the new abundant you.

150

"At the Summer Solstice, all is green and growing, potential coming into being, the miracle of manifestation painted large on the canvas of awareness. At the Winter Solstice, the wind is cold, trees are bare and all lies in stillness beneath blankets of snow." – Gary Zukav

After you've let go of some of your conditional programming, you have space to invite more energy for manifestation.

Tuning into the natural cycles of the universe help create power for you without extra effort.

Knowing the cycles and associated meanings of the Sun, Moon and seasonal energies brings influence to the things you want to manifest and those you desire to release.

The Sun and the Moon travel in monthly and yearly cycles according to the zodiac. Knowing your birth details leads to information on your solar and lunar signs. This in turn provides material for you to use to power up your intentions.

You most likely know your Sun sign and can figure your Moon sign at astrocal.co.uk/moon-sign-calculator. All you need is your date, time and time zone of birth.

Once you know your Sun and Moon signs, you can tune into the Goddess power related to your zodiac signs as the sun travels through the year and the moon rotates celestially.

Solar and Lunar Signs - Goddess Power

Look at the chart below for your Sun sign and note the Goddess and then look again for your Moon sign. You can use either to employ the power of the Goddess.

Alternatively, you can use the lunar power as the moon enters each sign. The Moon travels into a different sign approximately every 2 ¼ days. To determine where the Moon is on any given day, there are many websites keeping track. *Moontracks.com* or *Lunarliving.org* are excellent ones.

Moon Goddess – Harness the Power of the Moon

Referencing work from Simone Butler, Alaina Fairchild, Steven Forrest and Doreen Virtue comprises the information about the Goddess and the Moon.

The zodiac sign has characteristics as does the Goddess. Also, there are recommended activities relating to each lunar signature. See what resonates.

Zodiac Sign	Solar and Lunar Powers	Goddess	Monthly Lunar Cycles *(2 ½ days)*
Aries *(3/21 – 4/19)*	**Aries likes to lead.** **Spark of life.** (+) Authenticity, irresistible,	*Ancient Goddess:* Sekhmet *Origin:* Egyptian warrior goddess	*Things to do when the moon is in Aries:* ▪ Start a new project

152

Zodiac Sign	Solar and Lunar Powers	Goddess	Monthly Lunar Cycles *(2 ½ days)*
	independent, fierce, adventurous, resilient. Enthusiastic (-) Headstrong, impatient, impulsive, hot tempered, confrontational *Aim:* Courage *Strategy:* To go to one's limits, to seek stress in the form of adventure, acts of moral valor or risk. *Planetary Ruler:* Mars *Libras* can teach you harmony and balance.	and is depicted as a lioness. *Description:* She is the powerful one who protected and led pharaohs into war. She also can bring disease and heal it. *Message:* "Through passion you will dedicate yourself with an intensity and discipline that may surprise you. You can recover from any pain through the courage, commitment and bold, loving devotion to what matters most to you." *Crystals:* Fire agate, sunstone, pyrite	▪ Exercise or work-out ▪ Go hiking or horseback riding ▪ Light a fire, do a fire ceremony to release the past ▪ Take a trip ▪ Activate your inner child by playing with children, going to an amusement park or driving bumper cars ▪ Light fireworks ▪ Play loud music and dance
Taurus *(4/20 – 5/20)*	**Taurus likes stability. Grounds the spark into physical form.** (+) Earth Mama, steadfast devotion,	*Ancient Goddess:* Lakshmi *Origin:* Hindu goddess of abundance	*Things to do when the moon is in Taurus:* ▪ Spend time cleaning and beautifying your home

Zodiac Sign	Solar and Lunar Powers	Goddess	Monthly Lunar Cycles (2 ½ days)
	advisor, love material world, beauty, nature, and food (-) Overindulgence, gluttony, overspending, issues with debt *Aim:* Naturalness, ease, simplicity, silence. *Strategy:* To remain close to nature. To maintain stable relationships. To lose oneself in music. To touch & be touched. To establish one's position in world. *Planetary Ruler:* Venus *Scorpios* help by touching your emotions and soul.	*Description:* Wealth, health, blessings, fortune and prosperity. She clears obstacles in your path as she works with Ganesha. Sacred animal: elephant – matriarchal society, endurance and strength; removal of obstacles *Message:* "Call on me to bring abundance to you now." *Crystal:* Aventurine, malachite, jade	▪ Plant a garden ▪ Walk in nature ▪ Play with a pet ▪ Make love to your partner ▪ Spend time on a creative, money-making project ▪ Balance your checkbook ▪ Ask for a raise ▪ Look for a job or determine next steps for career or business ▪ Put $100 in your wallet to feel wealthy ▪ Set abundance intentions and put more money into your wealth vases
Gemini *(5/21 – 6/20)*	**Gemini likes communicating. Takes notice of surrounding environment.**	*Ancient Goddess:* Athena *Origin:* Greek warrior goddess, daughter of Zeus	*Things to do when the moon is in Gemini:* ▪ Socialize, entertain, gather friends ▪ Read or tell a story

154

Zodiac Sign	Solar and Lunar Powers	Goddess	Monthly Lunar Cycles *(2 ½ days)*
	(+) Perception, world speaks to you, inquisitive, intellectual, great writer and speaker, and flexibility (-) Aloofness, too active imagination -> anxiousness *Aim:* A radically open mind. *Strategy:* To seek the unexpected. To listen. To flood the senses with stimuli. *Planetary Ruler:* Mercury *Sagittarius* helps with faith, belief, commitment and mind-stretching experience.	*Description:* Goddess of wisdom and war, helps protect, creativity and intellectual pursuits. She strategizes and boosts ability to see both sides and big picture. *Message:* "Quiet your mind and call upon me for protection, wisdom and inner guidance. I remind you who you are – you too, are a warrior goddess!" *Crystal:* Azurite, lapis lazuli	▪ Write ▪ Speak in front of an audience, teach a class or communicate messages ▪ Learn a new skill, take a class or explore different information ▪ Travel or go somewhere you've never been ▪ Help others resolve any issues or challenges ▪ Make a plan or strategize ▪ Update your calendar ▪ Entice your senses of perception ▪ Meditate
Cancer *(6/21 – 7/22)*	**Cancer likes to experience emotions. Chooses its home in the environment.** (+) Nurturer, caregiver, heart-	*Ancient Goddess:* Hestia *Origin:* Greek Goddess of Home *Description:* Goddess of home, hearth and architecture.	*Things to do when the moon is in Cancer:* ▪ Cook, garden, create ▪ Host a dinner ▪ Go to the sea shore ▪ Take a bath

Zodiac Sign	Solar and Lunar Powers	Goddess	Monthly Lunar Cycles *(2 ½ days)*
	centered, protector of loved ones, strong, sensitive, intuitive, excellent gardener and chef, home creator (-) Moody, close heart too tightly, withdraw from world, lack self-confidence to have healthy boundaries with others, tendency to overeat and over-care *Aim:* An open heart *Strategy:* To feel, care, nurture, imagine, to acknowledge pain & sorrow. *Planetary Ruler:* Moon *Capricorns* help with self-discipline, integrity, and objective accomplishments.	Peaceful, content, introvert. Followed her own fate. Provides family meals and comfort to family. Calm, peaceful and caring personality. *Message:* "Follow your own path. Take care of yourself and others." *Crystal:* Fire agate, ruby, tiger's eye	▪ Spend time in your garden ▪ Spend time with your children ▪ Connect with family ▪ Explore your family tree ▪ Visit a cemetery to connect with your ancestors ▪ Watch family or romantic television ▪ Play with pets, childhood toys or your inner child
Leo *(7/23 – 8/22)*	**Leo likes to be in the spotlight.**	*Ancient Goddess:* Oshun	*Things to do when the moon is in Leo:* ▪ Be romantic

Zodiac Sign	Solar and Lunar Powers	Goddess	Monthly Lunar Cycles *(2 ½ days)*
	Expresses creativity from its center. (+) Joy, trust, open heart, creativity, passion, warm, love children, flair, panache, charisma, leader, charming, self-expression (-) Pride and ego, bossy, controlling, dismissive *Aim:* Joy, comfort, trust *Strategy:* To express oneself creatively. To perform. To earn appreciation & applause. *Planetary Ruler:* Sun *Aquarius* helps with individuation, unusual experiences, and escape from social constraint.	*Origin:* African Goddess of Love, Intimacy, Beauty and Diplomacy *Description:* Widely loved, known for healing sick and bringing prosperity. Beautiful, charming and cheerful. *Message:* "Lean into the sweetness of life. Find joy. Be cheerful and grateful for all of life's beauty." *Crystal:* Amber, aquamarine, watermelon tourmaline	▪ Spend time with your intimate partner ▪ Make love ▪ Get dressed up and go dancing ▪ Buy new clothes or jewelry ▪ Go to an art opening, theater or musical performance ▪ Host a party or go to one ▪ Get a spa treatment ▪ Be creative ▪ Pitch a creative idea ▪ Give a talk or presentation ▪ Tackle a big project ▪ Be vocal about accomplishments
Virgo *(8/23 – 9/22)*	**Virgo likes order and neatness.**	*Ancient Goddess:* Vesta	*Things to do when the moon is in Virgo:*

Zodiac Sign	Solar and Lunar Powers	Goddess	Monthly Lunar Cycles (2 ½ days)
	Adjusts Leo's expression to the physical conditions present. (+) Earthly sensuality, sexy, diligence, self-reliant, independent, excellent health regimens, discipline, practical, analytical, organic (-) Fault-finding, judgmental, critical, especially of self, perfectionist *Aim:* Perfection *Strategy:* To observe oneself with meticulous honesty. To log hours expressing helpful skills through good works. *Planetary Ruler:* Mercury *Pisces* helps with meditation, surrender and mystical experience.	*Origin:* Roman fire goddess of home and hearth *Description:* Helps with living conditions, improves your home or household. Adds warmth as necessary. *Message:* "Make a home. Create warmth and add your touch to your living space. Ensure it reflects you." *Crystal:* Fire agate, opal *Sacred animal:* cat	▪ Begin a fitness or health regimen ▪ Catch up on sleep ▪ Make healthy food ▪ Take an Epsom salt bath ▪ Buy vitamins or plant herbs ▪ Tidy, clean and clear your home and work spaces ▪ Weed or prune your garden ▪ Groom your pets ▪ Volunteer ▪ Do detailed work ▪ Make plans ▪ Schedule events (unless the moon is void of course)

Zodiac Sign	Solar and Lunar Powers	Goddess	Monthly Lunar Cycles *(2 ½ days)*
Libra *(9/23 – 10/22)*	**Libra likes fairness and justice. Meets others as equals.** (+) Collaboration, negotiation, harmony, peace-making, diplomacy, civil, graceful, elegant, good bargainer, advocate, socially just, balanced (-) Indecision, stay in unhealthy or unbalanced relationships too long, too loyal *Aim:* Serenity, peace. *Strategy:* To flood the mind with beauty. To seek common ground with others. To cultivate the refined, elegant and lofty dimensions of experience. *Planetary Ruler:* Venus	*Ancient Goddess:* Inanna *Origin:* Babylon Goddess of war and sexual love. Personification of Venus. *Description:* Divine feminine, feminine in fullness- creation and destruction. Give and receive. Take action and lay back and bask in the results. *Message:* "Don't be afraid to be fully feminine. All aspects of yourself are beautiful. Be authentic in your thoughts, intentions and deeds." *Crystal:* Astrophyllite, rose quartz, lapis lazuli *Sacred animal:* Lioness	*Things to do when the moon is in Libra:* - Host or attend a gathering - Have a heart-to-heart talk with a loved one - Spend time you're your intimate partner - Connect with friends - Go to an art exhibit, design show or musical performance - Write love poems, stories or songs - Send flowers to loved ones, including yourself - Beautify your home or office - Do yoga - Stand up for social justice - Attend a peaceful rally - Go to court

Zodiac Sign	Solar and Lunar Powers	Goddess	Monthly Lunar Cycles *(2 ½ days)*
	Aries helps with courage, directness and right use of force.		<ul><li>Hold important meetings and negotiations</li><li>Sign contracts (unless Mercury is retrograde)</li></ul>
Scorpio *(10/23 – 11/21)*	**Scorpio likes to live a secret life. Deepens relationships, transforming itself and others.** (+) Undying passion, legendary emotional strength, raw, direct power in spades, loyal when can trust, intense, intuitive, magical powers, powerful siren (-) Secretive, possessive, jealous, manipulative, controlling *Planetary Rulers:* Mars & Pluto *Aim:* Depth *Strategy:* To probe, suspect, risk honesty, to make eye contact.	*Ancient Goddess:* Hecate *Origin:* Greek goddess of witchcraft, magic, ghosts. Goddess of the earth, sea and sky. *Description:* She's a moon goddess and can see the other world. *Message:* "You are at a pivotal point in your life journey. This happens when you have mastered a cycle in life and are ready for the new. Listen to your heart." *Crystal:* Jet, mica	*Things to do when the moon is in Scorpio:* <ul><li>Research or make investments</li><li>Organize finances</li><li>Go shopping for occult items, garnets or rubies</li><li>Eat chocolate and drink red wine</li><li>Have hot, steamy sex</li><li>Practice kundalini breathing</li><li>Read a sexy book or watch a sexy movie</li><li>Share deep secrets with a trusted or loved one</li><li>Hold a confidential meeting or rendezvous</li></ul>

Zodiac Sign	Solar and Lunar Powers	Goddess	Monthly Lunar Cycles *(2 ½ days)*
	Taurus helps with calm, simplicity, and acceptance of that which arises naturally.		<ul><li>Get an astrology or tarot reading</li><li>Pay attention to dreams and insights</li><li>Visit someone in hospice</li></ul>
Sagittarius *(11/22 – 12/21)*	**Sagittarius likes to explore cultures. Seeks meaning through experiences.** (+) Generosity, good luck and fortune, philosopher, traveler, student, (-) Preachy, judgmental, pontificate too much, burn-out by overextending, *Aim:* Faith *Strategy:* To break up safe routines, to escape the tyranny of the familiar, to risk, to venture, to stretch one's horizons.	*Ancient Goddess:* Diana *Origin:* Roman moon goddess, daughter of Jupiter *Description:* Helps with childbirth, animals and connecting with nature, particularly the elementals. Aligned with oak tree for strength and focused intention. *Message:* "Be tenacious, yet patient. You're giving birth to something vast and need to be unwavering. Stay strong."	*Things to do when the moon is in Sagittarius:* <ul><li>Take a trip, explore other cultures or go on an adventure</li><li>Enroll in a class</li><li>Find a mentor</li><li>Read a book</li><li>Visit the library</li><li>Learn a new language</li><li>Write down your dreams and hunches</li><li>Throw a last-minute party</li><li>Get together with friends</li><li>Have a truth-telling session</li><li>Help out a friend</li></ul>

Zodiac Sign	Solar and Lunar Powers	Goddess	Monthly Lunar Cycles *(2 ½ days)*
	Planetary Ruler: Jupiter *Gemini* helps with curiosity, open-mindedness, conversation.	*Crystal:* Amethyst, moonstone *Sacred animal:* Dog	▪ Give generously to a cause ▪ Buy a lottery ticket ▪ Talk to trees ▪ Spend time with animals
Capricorn *(12/22 – 1/19)*	**Capricorn likes to succeed through work.** **Builds structures to support that meaning.** (+) Determined, capable, shrewd, ambitious, leader, tenacious, mastery, performing great works, warm, witty and fun (-) Rigid, inflexible, stoic, cold, workaholic. *Aim:* Integrity. *Strategy:* To define basic values & live up to them. To accomplish Great Works. To let will rather than appetite shape life.	*Ancient Goddess:* Matangi *Origin:* Hindu goddess of transcendent knowledge. *Description:* One of the 10 goddesses and she grants power to gain control over others, manifest one's wishes and attract people. Already there is value. *Message:* "In your enthusiasm, to move forward in life, don't forget to take the value that already exists in your world along with you." *Crystal:* Heliotrope	*Things to do when the moon is in Capricorn:* ▪ Initiate a work project ▪ Make a 5-year plan ▪ Do your taxes ▪ Refinance your house ▪ Meet with your financial planner ▪ Delegate to others ▪ Start a home remodel ▪ Redecorate or reorganize your home or office ▪ Climb a mountain ▪ Start a new fitness regimen ▪ Have earthy sex

Zodiac Sign	Solar and Lunar Powers	Goddess	Monthly Lunar Cycles *(2 ½ days)*
	Planetary Ruler: Saturn *Cancer* helps with gentleness, nurture and acceptance of human frailty.		
Aquarius *(1/20 – 2/18)*	**Aquarius likes to learn every day. Sets higher ideals for the society.** (+) Open-minded, friendly, even-keeled, inclusive, brilliant, ahead of your time, honest, uplifting, spiritual guide and healer, prophetic, revolutionary (-) Aloof, eccentric, withdrawn, seek independence at cost of relationship *Aim:* Individuality *Strategy:* To question authority. To overcome need for approval. To seek out unusual experiences or people.	*Ancient Goddess:* Rhiannon *Origin:* Welsh goddess of the sun and inspiration. Divine Queen of sovereignty and governance. *Description:* Accumulated wisdom, create order, love of people, and supernatural will. *Message:* "Integrity is the harmony between intention, word and action. You can express your integrity absolutely and yet with kindness and compassion. Integrity is the gift that will bring you a powerful piece of	*Things to do when the moon is in Aquarius:* ▪ Make a vision board ▪ Invent something ▪ Build or expand your website ▪ Brainstorm solutions ▪ Send out resumes or mailings ▪ Go to a networking event ▪ Join a meetup group ▪ Set important changes in motion ▪ Buy a new computer (unless Mercury is in retrograde) ▪ Buy a new trend-setting outfit

Zodiac Sign	Solar and Lunar Powers	Goddess	Monthly Lunar Cycles *(2 ½ days)*
	Leo helps with forthrightness, creativity, spontaneous self-expression and a sense of theater.	mind and loving self-respect." *Crystal:* Amazonite, danburite, howlite	▪ Anticipate surprises ▪ Have friends over for a party or dinner ▪ Share your heart with your best friend or lover
Pisces *(2/19 – 3/20)*	**Pisces likes to imagine and create.** **Connects to divine inspiration out of which new life is born again in Aries.** (+) Imaginative, creative, spiritual, magical, dreamy, psychic, visionary, sensitive, deep (-) Play the victim, delusional, escapist, irrationally emotional Aim: Self-transcendence *Strategy:* To relax in solitude. To meditate, imagine, create. To open	*Ancient Goddess:* Sedna *Origin:* Inuit and Alaskan goddess of the sea *Description:* Helps connect with all of the sea's inhabitants, particularly dolphins and whales. Balances the seas and supplies abundance to the seas. *Message:* "Flow like the ocean – expand and contract. There is a natural balance to everything. No need to worry, all of your needs are provided for – always."	*Things to do when the moon is in Pisces:* ▪ Work on creative projects ▪ Write down dreams ▪ Create vision board ▪ Make music, paint or dance ▪ Write poetry ▪ Take an acting or dancing class ▪ Have a romantic date ▪ Attend a meditation group or healing circle ▪ Avoid addictive measures ▪ Get a healing treatment

Zodiac Sign	Solar and Lunar Powers	Goddess	Monthly Lunar Cycles *(2 ½ days)*
	heart to other people's realities. *Planetary Rulers:* Jupiter and Neptune *Virgo* helps with service, groundedness, and skill.	*Crystal:* Aquamarine, selenite	▪ Confess your feelings ▪ Have a good cry ▪ Turn your bedroom into inviting temple

Make a note of your Sun and Moon Goddesses.

Void of Course Moon

Every few days, the Moon doesn't aspect any other planet in the cosmos and is about to enter a new sign. This is known as being void of course. When this happens, the energies you want to use for manifestation will fall flat. There's nothing the Moon is reflecting upon.

Don't issue anything you'd like to manifest during a void of course Moon.

Instead, during a void of course Moon, issue things you'd like to release. It's a great time for letting go.

Lunar Cycles

Monthly Lunar Cycles

In addition to the dance around the zodiac, the Moon is reflecting the light of the Sun as it orbits around the Earth. The most common Moon phases are full and new, however, there are actually eight lunar phases. These include:

- New
- Waxing crescent
- First quarter
- Waxing gibbous
- Full
- Waning gibbous
- Third (or last) quarter
- Waning crescent

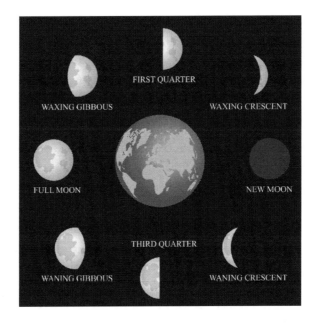

When the moon is waxing toward full, it's a great time to set intentions. The energies are getting bigger and bigger.

The full moon is a great time to show gratitude and celebrate the harvest of life.

When the moon is waning toward new, it's a great time for releasing or letting go.

The new moon is the still point of maximum potential. It's an excellent time for manifestation.

Your Moon Phase

You were born under the Moon, so have a particular phase of the Moon. Your lunar phase may be used to describe your placement or role in life.

To find out your lunar phase, simply type moon phase and then the date of your birth into the search bar on your internet connection. The *Calendar 12* website will display the Moon phase on your date of birth. Simply enter *moon phase for (your birth date)* in the search bar.

Refer to that moon phase in the table below.

Lunar Phases	Lunar Phase Description
New Moon *New beginnings.*	*Archetype:* **The Living Symbol (The Legend)** *Key Concepts:* Charisma, star quality, presence, nurturing qualities, leadership, guidance, seductive vagueness, innocence & naiveté, becoming symbolic to others, making others into symbols, a bringer of gifts. *Secret of Happiness:* Trusting the dictates of the heart more than those of reason. You are about passion and commitment to something that feels bigger than yourself.
Waxing Crescent Moon *Set intentions.*	*Archetype:* **The Extremist** *Key Concepts:* Drive to accomplish and experience, hunger, imbalance, success and its costs, presence, natural authority, radiant, infectious hope in the face of darkness

Lunar Phases	Lunar Phase Description
	Secret of Happiness: Have a mission, a worthy cause, effort reflects the best part of yourself and is somehow bigger than you.
First Quarter Moon *Take action.*	*Archetype:* **The Crusader** *Key Concepts:* Tension between self and group, concern with justice, battles, group efforts, organizations, sacrifice for group, abstract, idealistic principles of the archetypal realm collide with reality. *Secret of Happiness:* Learn to work with other people to successfully bring something important into manifestation. To have one's values felt in the world. To leave a mark. To have made a difference – working with others.
Waxing Gibbous Moon *Refine and hone.*	*Archetype:* **The Helper (Lover)** *Key Concepts:* Service, identification with group ideal, sexual energy, joint expression of creativity, creator-audience synergy, support offered to a person or principle, generosity, teamwork, partnership. *Secret of Happiness:* Lively, surprising and meaningful relationships, need to feel loved and appreciated.
Full Moon *Harvest endeavors.*	*Archetype:* **The Human Being** *Key Concepts:* Committed or inescapable involvements of all sorts, familial complexities, divorce, life-long bonding, wedlock as deadlock, caregiving, art & creativity made manifest, nurture, outward expression of light and dark, drama. *Secret of Happiness:* Jump wholeheartedly into life, be bold enough to love as if it never hurts, live dreams and aspirations, require mechanism for self-expression. Recognize stuck situations and end them.
Waning Gibbous Moon *Introspection.*	*Archetype:* **The Shaman** *Key Concepts:* Deep inner work, acceptance and surrender, caring, poignant sense of life's brevity, psychic intervention in other's lives, assistance around death, dying and crisis, loving relationships, attunement to primitive wisdom, death and rebirth, gratitude, loss of self-importance, mature perspectives.

Lunar Phases	Lunar Phase Description
	Secret of Happiness: Live everyday as if it were the last. Power of now.
Last Quarter Moon *Release and let go.*	*Archetype:* **The Pilgrim** *Key Concepts:* sensing the smell of home, sweet sorrow, longing, romantic tragedy, solitude, art as an inner search, service, theater, ritual, graceful endings, art of saying goodbye, air of death and finality. *Secret of Happiness:* Inner life. Mechanisms of transcendence. Clean endings. Energetic release, creatively effective ritual.
Waning Crescent Moon *Surrender.*	*Archetype:* **The Ghost, Mystic Wanderer** *Key Concepts:* deep psychic sensitivity, possible imbalances, alternative descriptions of reality, anthropologist, observing, hypersensitivity, ghosts and spirit visitations, creative, visionary imagination, awareness of ancestors and the dead, clean, definitive endings. *Secret of Happiness:* Psychic landscape, need rich, active solitude, time spent in mediation, yoga and spiritual practice, detach from past – go deeply into ourselves and come out into the universe.

Seasonal Energies

The annual cycles involve the movement of the Sun through the zodiac signs, the signs of the Full and New Moon each month, the semi-annual eclipses and the equinox and solstice energies.

The Earth travels around the sun in 365 days and each zodiac sign lasts approximately 30 days.

The Moon rotates around the earth every 28 days and travels through the 12 zodiac signs each month. Therefore, the Moon moves through each sign approximately every 2 ½ days.

Month	Sun Sign (until the 20th ish)	Full Moon (every 28 days)	New Moon (every 28 days)
January	Capricorn	Cancer	Aquarius
February	Aquarius	Leo	Pisces
March	Pisces	Virgo	Aries
April	Aries	Libra	Taurus
May	Taurus	Scorpio	Gemini
June	Gemini	Sagittarius	Cancer
July	Cancer	Capricorn	Leo
August	Leo	Aquarius	Virgo
September	Virgo	Pisces	Libra
October	Libra	Aries	Scorpio
November	Scorpio	Taurus	Sagittarius
December	Sagittarius	Gemini	Capricorn

Additionally, there are multiple sets of eclipses as well as equinoxes and solstices every year.

Eclipses

There are two main eclipses – solar and lunar.

A solar eclipse occurs during a new moon as the moon moves between the earth and the sun.

A lunar eclipse occurs as the earth casts a shadow on the Full Moon. The Moon does not project light, it reflects the Sun's. Therefore, a lunar eclipse happens when the Earth blocks the Sun's rays.

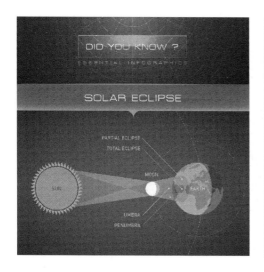 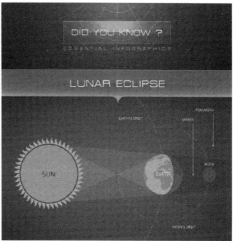

Types of Eclipses

There are three types of solar eclipses:

- o Total - Occurs when the Moon completely covers the Sun, as seen from the Earth.
- o Partial - Occurs when the Moon only partially covers the Sun.
- o Annular – Occurs when the Moon appears smaller than the Sun and passes in the center of it to form a ring of sunlight around the Moon.

There are three types of lunar eclipses:

- o Total – Occurs when the Earth obscures all of the Moon's surface.
- o Partial – Occurs when the Earth obscures part of the Moon's surface.
- o Penumbral - Occurs when the Earth's shadow obscures part of the Moon's surface.

Energies of Eclipses

Total eclipses are more intense than partial or penumbral.

The time of the year matters as the zodiac signs become factors in the energies of the pull of the Sun and Moon.

Solar eclipses act as Super New Moons and lunar eclipses act as Super Full Moons.

Eclipse Schedule for Next Few Years

Date	Eclipse	Type	Phase of Moon	Sun Sign	Moon Sign
2018 Eclipses					
Jan 31	Lunar	Total	Full	Aquarius	Leo
Feb 15	Solar	Partial	New	Aquarius	Aquarius
Jul 13	Solar	Partial	New	Cancer	Cancer
Jul 27/28	Lunar	Total	Full	Leo	Aquarius
Aug 11	Solar	Partial	New	Leo	Leo
2019 Eclipses					
Jan 5/6	Solar	Partial	New	Capricorn	Capricorn
Jan 20/21	Lunar	Total	Full	Aquarius	Leo
Jul 2	Solar	Total	New	Cancer	Cancer
Jul 16/17	Lunar	Partial	Full	Cancer	Capricorn
Dec 26	Solar	Annular	New	Capricorn	Capricorn
2020 Eclipses					
Jan 10/11	Lunar	Penumbral	Full	Capricorn	Cancer
Jun 5/6	Lunar	Penumbral	Full	Gemini	Sagittarius
Jun 21	Solar	Annular	New	Cancer/ summer solstice	Cancer
Jul 4/5	Lunar	Penumbral	Full	Cancer	Capricorn

Date	Eclipse	Type	Phase of Moon	Sun Sign	Moon Sign
Nov 29/30	Lunar	Penumbral	Full	Sagittarius	Gemini
Dec 14	Solar	Total	New	Sagittarius	Sagittarius

Equinox Energies

The equinoxes are about balance as day equals night and night equals day.

The Vernal or spring equinox occurs around March 20th as the Sun enters the sign of Aries. In pagan circles, it's known as Ostara. It's about new life and beginnings.

The Autumnal or fall equinox is around September 22nd as the Sun enters the sign of Libra. In pagan circles, it's known as Mabon. It's about harvest, gathering together and celebration.

Solstice Energies

In the northern hemisphere, the longest day is the summer solstice and the shortest is the winter solstice. The days get longer between the winter and summer solstice indicating the growth and manifestation of life. The days get shorter between the summer and winter solstice representing letting go or releasing.

In the northern hemisphere, the summer solstice occurs around June 21st as the sun enters the sign of Cancer. In pagan circles, it's known as Litha. It's about celebrating home, family and tribe.

The winter solstice occurs around December 21st as the sun enters the sign of Capricorn. In pagan circles, it's known as Yule. It's about honoring the reflection and depth of night and the life and joy of light.

Solar & Lunar Meditation

Connect to the solar and lunar energies.

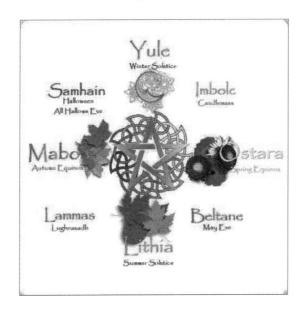

Solar and Lunar Meditation

Close your eyes and take a nice cleansing breath. Inhale deeply and exhale fully. As you breathe, feel yourself sink more deeply into the seat beneath you. Feel your body relax as you take a few moments to be present with yourself.

You're here right now in this room to enhance your connection to the cosmos. To connect to your eternal life force through the Sun and your deepest heart's desires through the Moon. The Goddess supports both.

You're here to recognize and dance with the infinite flow of the universe – giving and receiving, doing and being and manifesting and letting go.

You're here to connect to the abundance of the universe and deepen the knowing of your role in the co-creation of your life. Welcome and open to the light within you. Integrate yourself with the pure crystalline light of all that is.

As you continue to breathe, imagine the sun shining high in the sky. Feel its heat on your face. Feel its energy feeding everything on Earth, including you. The Sun is the center of the universe and everything gravitates around it. Everything in our known universe. The Sun is life, vitality, energy and tied to your identity. Think of your Sun Goddess. Picture her now. Invoke her strengths and power.

Breathe her in.

Now, you see the Moon in your mind's eye. She hangs high in the sky. She is clear of any tree line or clouds in the night sky. You picture her full and robust, effervescent and luminous. You revel in her fullness.

Hello Bella Luna.

You say to yourself, "I honor and celebrate you." You celebrate her fullness, her creativity, her expansiveness and her fecundity.

The Full Moon enhances your fullness, your creativity, your expansiveness and your fecundity. You are luminous. You are effervescent, mysterious, and passionate.

You now envision the Moon waning through her phases of waning gibbous, waning quarter and waning crescent.

The Moon's waning energy allows for releasing and letting go. Allow yourself to let go, forgive and accept yourself and others for anything no longer serving you.

Exhale and release. Exhale and allow. Exhale and accept.

The Moon wanes completely to her new status. She is a New Moon. She is black in the night sky. She is full of infinity, potential and ability to manifest. She stands still in the moment of all that is.

Think of your Moon Goddess. Breathe in her powers. Feel them in your heart.

Breathe in the divine, the infinity and the potential of all that is.

Inhale and accept. Inhale and allow. Inhale and receive.

The Moon continues her journey by waxing through her phases of waxing crescent, waxing quarter and waxing gibbous – back to full once again.

This monthly dance is elegant.

It's graceful.

It's divine.

As you breathe in and out, notice the similarities between your breath and the dance of the moon. You expand to full and exhale to new, inhale and exhale, inhale and exhale.

The dance is elegant.

It's graceful.

It's divine.

Now connect to the divinity within you. Divine creation flows through you into the room and flows back into you in perfect unison with all that is. Take a few moments and continue to breathe.

To close the energy, cross your arms over your heart.

As you take your next breath, bring your awareness back to the room.

When you're ready, open your eyes and gaze softly in front you – seeing nothing, yet aware of everything. If you would like, wiggle your fingers and toes and do any gentle stretching your body requires. Breathe in again and open your eyes fully.

Once you've brought in power from the celestial bodies and seasonal energies, revisit your intentions from the set your intention exercises.

Do you have them at the ready?

Can you recall them with relative accuracy?

Have you powered these through heart activation, ritual or ceremony?

If not, do so now.

Record your information in the space provided to capture the cosmic power and your dreams and passions.

You have the material at your fingertips to empower your desires.

Possible rituals or ceremony:

- Journal your intentions during one of your solar or lunar times.
- Perform a New Moon meditation and state your intentions.
- Do a heart activation with your intentions anytime.
- Beautifully write your intentions and then place them on your altar.
- Activate your intentions through meditation by sending them into the universe.
- During an eclipse, equinox or solstice, write your intentions and place them into a ginger or spice jar with a lid. Sprinkle glitter or small crystals into the jar. Take a moment to charge your jar filled with intentions. Put it in a special place.

There are many ways to power your intentions, choose one that speaks to you.

Remember to have fun!

	Manifestation Power
	Sun:
	Moon:
	Phase of Moon:
	Goddess(es):
	Notes:

My Intentions: Be positive. Be present. Be BIG.   *"I am…"*

Wishes –

_____

Blessings –

_____

Money –

_____

Health –

_____

Love –

_____

"Our intention creates our reality." – Wayne Dyer

Air gives you space – internally and externally.

It allows for growth – exponentially.

Air offers loft, faith and possibility.

Yet, it's tricky to work with – it defies logic and reason.

How best to work with air?

The key is to go with its flow through its twists and turns and to honor its vapor-like quality. The only downside of air occurs when you attempt to control or keep it still.

The natural state of air is movement. When you honor this, you honor air and then it works tirelessly for you.

It gifts you wishes and allows for bountiful blessings.

It fuels your intentions and alters your beliefs.

It surrenders limitations and scarcity.

It powers your intentions into manifestations.

As you do, you gain clarity.

With clarity, your wishes have space to blossom.

With clarity, your intentional seeds can be spread out into the universe.

With clarity, your future is bright.

Enjoy the beauty of riding air.

"My mission in life is not merely to survive, but to thrive; and to do so with some passion, some compassion, some humor and some style." – *Maya Angelou*

What is fire?

Fire is inspiration and creativity. It's tapping into the divine flow of life to capture the creative flow of the universe.

It's yang.

It's direct.

It's the sun.

It's your soul.

The vast movement of air continues with fire as its flames leap and flicker, yet the movement isn't as sizeable. The movement becomes slightly smaller and ironically, only grows with the influx of air.

So, the weaving and dancing continues, but fire adds punch and power. It lends an element of substance and heat. It gives desire, inspiration and passion.

As the upper chakras give way to the heart and solar plexus, air gives way to fire.

There's still the yang energy of action and movement, but the oomph comes with the intensity, power and magnificent ability for creation and destruction.

Harnessing fire involves understanding its relationship in your life to your heart and its desires, and your solar plexus and its will.

This yang energy requires openness and faith in the divine to tap into its inspiration and also needs action and willpower to actualize this creativity into manifestation.

Like the motion of air, fire utilizes movement. Going back and remembering who you are and moving into your future allows for heart opening, seeing with your heart and allowing yourself to be drenched with desire.

Leaning into the creation cycle and integrating its spiral of creativity and destruction allows you to burn away anything no longer serving you to make space for renewal and rebirth.

Tapping into divine creativity requires an open heart and faith in the universe.

Passion, desire and willpower come together to bring substance to your dreams.

Let's begin by opening your heart with gratitude.

Let's tap into your special essence.

Let's remember who you are.

"Every great dream begins with a dreamer. Always remember, you have within you the strength, the patience, and the passion to reach for the stars to change the world." – Harriet Tubman

Remembering who you are requires quietening your mind and dropping your focus into your heart to remove the conditioning and beliefs brought on by society and others.

There are a few quick ways to bring energy into your heart:

- Begin to breathe and then focus on your heart. Once you do, you'll find you breathe more deeply.

- Act in gratitude.

- Go out into nature and hug a tree, smell a flower or pet a friendly animal.

- Place your hands on your heart as you turn your attention to it. Take a few deep breaths.

- Laugh.

- Do a quick chakra meditation into your heart center.

- On your heart space, tap your fingers or rub in circular motion for a few moments.

- Lay down and place a cleansed rose quartz onto your heart space. Relax for a couple of minutes.

- If you do yoga, do a cobra pose.

- Visualize your heart being filled with the white light of the divine.

- Perform a heart opening meditation.

The easiest way to open your heart is through gratitude. You can start by doing a gratitude meditation.

Gratitude Heart Opening Meditation

Close your eyes and take a nice cleansing breath. Inhale deeply and exhale fully. As you breathe, feel yourself sink more deeply into the seat beneath you. Feel your body relax as you take a few moments to be present with yourself.

You're here right now in this moment to quiet your mind and open your heart. You're here to express thanks for all of your blessings.

You're here to open to the abundance of the universe and tap into your deep knowing of your role in the co-creation of your life. Welcome and open to the light within you. Integrate yourself with the pure crystalline light of all that is.

Take a deep cleansing breath and envision this bright white pure light of Universal source coming down into your crown chakra as it opens to receive it at the top of your head. The pure crystalline light of universal source pours into your crown chakra and travels through all of your chakras, filling them deeply and completely. The light flows from your crown, through your third eye, to your throat into your heart — filling it with love. The light then flows into your solar plexus, your sacral and then your root chakra.

The pure crystalline light then flows down your legs through your feet and into Mother Earth. These roots of light burrow deeply into the earth to ground alighting it with Universal source energy.

You bring the light from Mother Earth up through the bottoms of your feet and into your being, filling yourself with light, and connecting you to the heavens above and the earth below. As above, so below. As within, so without. Heaven and earth.

Now, this light surrounds you in a gorgeous white and golden healing glow. See it swirling around you, gently, patiently, and serenely. You are glowing in and of this light.

As you breathe in this glowing light, focus on your heart. Feel your heart opening to accept this beautiful pure loving white light. Feel its love. Feel its compassion, kindness and support.

Open your heart to the universal source energy and to the heavens and earth. Connect to the love and support. Connect to the flow of the universe. Connect to all that is.

As you revel in your heart opening, direct your focus to the blessings in your life. What are you thankful for? Are you thankful for the wellness you have created in your life? Do you love your body for its strength, endurance, flexibility and coordination? Are you grateful for its balance? Do you love your body for its ability to know of its hunger, thirst and sleep requirements? Do you love to nourish it and allow for its rejuvenation?

Are you grateful for your mental acuity? Your ability to remember, to solve problems, to perceive all of your senses? To pursue and absorb new information? To live strategically? In paradox? With infinite possibility?

Are you thankful for your beating heart? All of its love, support and compassion? Are you thankful for allowing the balance between giving and receiving in your life? Do you feel blessed as you welcome intimacy? Are you thankful for letting your heart rule?

Are you thankful for your connection to spirit? For your intuition? For the messages you receive from spirit? Are you grateful for universal support? Do you feel blessed for the abundance and bounty in your life?

Take a few moments to revel in the plenty and bounty of your life.

As you take your next breath, bring your awareness back to the room.

When you are ready, open your eyes and gaze softly in front you – seeing nothing, yet aware of everything. If you would like, wiggle your fingers and toes and do any gentle stretching your body requires. Breathe in again and open your eyes fully.

Journal any thoughts or messages you'd like to remember.

The next step to use fire energy and tap into your passion is to begin listening to your heart. With your heart's desires, listening to your heart is key.

Listening to your heart takes practice. At first, it seems fake and your mind fights to take over. Your mind thinks it's in control, but is really an administrator.

It administers to protect and process, but it can only do so with information or experience you've already had. This is good as it intersects with your heart's memories. However, your mind may have forgotten or dismissed relevant pieces.

Your mind has intelligence, but your heart has wisdom.

It's this wisdom you're to tap into through the various exercises in this section.

Moving the focus from your mind to your heart is a process. One you want to begin as your heart knows.

It knows and it remembers.

Listen to your heart.

Let's see what it remembers by recalling your hidden talents, retelling childhood stories and using numerology to determine your destiny and heart's path.

Hidden Talents

Story: What's Your Talent?

"What's your talent?" my daughter asks me a handful of years ago while watching a Disney fairy movie.

"My talent is animals," she continues, "and I wish I had flying as a talent too."

The Disney fairy movies are very cute and I love how they highlight each fairy's special and unique talent. These talents include extraordinary Pixie Hollow ones such as: leaf-curling, butterfly-herding and spider-web untangling. However, they also include more mainstream ones such as: gardening, singing and weaving.

I think about my daughter's question for several moments and respond, "My talent is creating. I create things – out of thin air."

She giggles and says she would like to see a butterfly.

Hmmm…that would be cool.

I let her linger in her laughter and don't attempt to explain the specifics of my creativity. Books, classes and new offerings cannot compare to a butterfly!

In using the fire element, inspiration and creativity are at the core. Part of this is remembering you have special talents, perhaps even a particular one. One that is uniquely yours and one you should leverage to gain purchase on your passion.

So, what's your talent? Take a few moments and think about the course of your life. Then make note of the things that stand out for you as you review the following questions.

What stands out?

Are you always helping others? Do you nurture? Are you a natural caregiver?

Do you tend to collaborate? Compromise? Communicate? Negotiate?

Do you surround yourself in beauty? Do you often redesign your home? Embark on new fashion styles? Do you like hair, makeup and design?

190

Are you creative, artistic, skilled in certain crafts? Do you love music, sound, or vibration? Do you like gardening, cooking, baking or entertaining?
Are you spiritual? Do you believe in the energetic flow of the Universe? Would you like to harness and work with it? Do you find yourself wanting to facilitate the healing of others?

Do you like to teach, inform, educate? Do you like working with adults or with children? If children, what age group?

Do you think in pictures or words? Do you learn by reading or listening? Are you a writer, author or speaker? Are you a natural public speaker?

Are you happier working alone or with others? Do you want to work for yourself or someone else?

Do you approach things from the bottom up or top down? Do you synthesize? See patterns? Seek out new information?

Are you attracted to travel? Are you comfortable with change or do you prefer routine?

Do you gain energy by being with others or by being alone?

Do you need lightness and humor or seriousness and depth? Do you need both?

Make notes in your journal. Record what stands out.

Your natural talents can help lead you along your pathway to your passion.

These are just jotted notes at this point as there are other exercises to add definition.

Childhood

The expressions of yourself during childhood are much more impactful and powerful than you realize.

You're so connected to spirit for the first few years of your life and the youthful yang energies are so strong.

Remembering aspects of your childhood is significant to learning the whispers of your heart.

Your heart continues to tell you as you grow older, but do you listen to it?

Do you hear its desires?

Do you know its passions?

Do you remember your gifts?

Let your heart rule as you remember who you are.

Remember and Imagine Who You Are Meditation

Remember who you are. You're going to go deep inside to consciously and intimately remember who you are through guided meditation. You're then going to take some notes and return to meditation to imagine the very best version of yourself.

Close your eyes and take a nice refreshing breath by inhaling deeply and exhaling gently. Take another deep breath in and gently breathe out, slowly expelling all of the air out of your lungs. Now take one more breath as you feel calm and relaxed in this space.

Continue breathing – in and out, in and out, and as you continue breathing, focus your attention on the floor beneath you. If you're sitting in a chair, feel the bottoms of your feet touching the floor. If you're sitting on the floor, feel the rug underneath you.

Remember and Imagine Who You Are Meditation

Now imagine roots growing out from the bottoms of your feet. They're strong, rugged and pulsating with energy. They peek out of your feet searching for the ground beneath you. They're alive, vital and searching to plant themselves deep into Mother Earth. As they continue to grow from your feet, they reach the floor and pierce through the boards to the ground beneath the house. They plow through grass, dirt and mud to penetrate into the earth. They continue reaching deep within the earth, going through rocks and crevices, until they reach its center. They plant themselves there and feel deeply satisfied to reach their destination. You become aware of them as they start sipping all of the nutrients Mother Earth has to offer. You feel these nutrients seep from the core of the earth into the bottoms of your feet. You feel deeply centered, rooted and nourished by Gaia.

As you feel nourished and rooted, you return your attention to yourself. You're breathing gently and fully. You're contented and satisfied. You feel really, really good to be alive. Now it's time to explore yourself fully and deeply. It's time to remember who you are.

Let's go back a bit in time, shall we? Let's first remember who you **were**. *Let's meet your younger self at a time you felt full of life, full of optimism and potential. You're so, so full of exuberance and enthusiasm. You can take on the world. You're ready!*

How old are you? What are you doing? Why are you so full of life and vigor? Take a few moments to capture the essence of yourself at this moment. Breathe it in. See it, sense it and feel it. Tuck it away in your memory. You will remember this.

Now let's explore your experience. What are you really good at doing? What has come easily to you? What abilities did you come in with and which ones have you nurtured lovingly? We are each a sum of our experiences. Let's absorb them once again, being grateful for them and knowing we can grasp those we want to take with us going forward. Take a few moments to savor those experiences that serve you. You will remember this.

Let's reacquaint ourselves with some of your most influential people. Who touched you – deeply and profoundly? Who has had impact on your life? Who has supported you? Who has affected your pathway forward? Who has propelled you beyond your own confines? Search your memory. The people are not important – leave them behind. Their effect on you is what's significant. The focus is purely on you. What did these people teach you? What message or messages do they have for you? Take a few minutes to remember. Tuck it away. You will remember this.

As you take your next breath, become aware of the seat beneath you and return to the room. When you're ready, open your eyes and gaze softly in front you – seeing nothing, yet aware of everything. If you would like, wiggle your fingers and toes and do any gentle stretching your body requires. Breathe in again and open your eyes fully.

Now, jot down a few notes in your journal.

Meeting your younger self – what are you doing? How do you feel?

What experience are you really good at doing?

Write down some of your natural abilities.

What messages do significant people have for you?

What do they want you to do?

Growing Up Exercise

Now you're going to remember what you wanted to be when you grew up. Do you remember? If so, you may skip this exercise. If not, then please continue.

Story: Coloring CEO's

I'm standing in a room full of CEO's explaining my business model to them. Preparing for this moment has been a challenge. You see, my husband and

I started a strategic consulting firm and I've determined I want to incorporate holistic methods into my approach. However, it's circa 2005 and being holistic in business is unconventional for its time, especially in New England where tradition, convention and conservative customs reign.

So, this moment is incredibly important to me as it's one of the first and only times I'm invited to explain.

The lead up to this moment has been frenetic. My administrators leap to make change after change to my presentation, give feedback and analysis and then make even more changes.

Finally, they go off to gather tools once I realize a demonstration will go much farther than any explanation.

You see, one of the components of holism is involving the heart with the mind and refocusing energy from the mind into the heart is new to the mainstream and foreign to business leaders.

However, I've pushed these CEO's in prior months as I've read children's stories, played the telephone game and had them solving easy puzzles to illustrate particular points.

Now, though, I'm passing out crayons and coloring books and this is no game, it's a business presentation.

And, this is at least a decade before coloring books hit the adult world.

So, as I'm talking, I hand out little boxes of crayons and spread the coloring pages around for each CEO to select one that appeals.

Oh, the looks and the reaching for phones.

They're looking for any distraction to allow them to disregard the activity in front of them. They're commanders in their industries, lead lots of people and have standing in their communities.

What will people think if they see them coloring like children?

I remind them the door's closed and they're off-site. No one's watching and this may just give them a moment of peace and quiet. They like that – no distractions, no questions and no decisions.

Just a moment for them.

They tentatively begin picking up a crayon and coloring. At first, they're talking to each other, to further distance themselves from this activity.

After a few moments, the talking quiets and a hush falls over the room.

After four or five minutes, each CEO is actively engaged in his or her coloring. Each selects more than one color and begins to enjoy the moment.

Now, I ask them a few easy, yet pertinent questions about their childhood dreams.

They answer from their hearts and surprise themselves.

Ah, the demonstration is successful and goes much deeper than any explanation of holistic methods in business.

Now, for you, take a few moments to quiet your mind and focus energy on your heart.

I've continued using coloring books for this exercise quite successfully over the years. You may want to do so as well.

There are three Q&A sections to this exercise:

1. *What did you like to do as a child? (It's more detailed than the prior listing in the previous exercise).*

2. Who did you want to be when you were 4 or 5 and then 9 or 10 years old?

3. Review the underlying themes of each question to determine what elements to incorporate into your life now.

What activities did you like to do as a child?

Circle your favorites.

• Draw, color or paint	• Play in mud
• Play on swing sets	• Swim in water
• Be outside	• Play with dolls and stuffed animals
• Ride a bike	
• Play dress up	• Read books
• Play house	• Play board games
• Cook in Easy-Bake® oven	• Climb trees
• Play with Legos®, trains, cars, trucks	• Set up forts
	• Play sports

Who did you want to be when you were 4 or 5 years old?

Circle the ones you remember wanting to be.

• A firefighter, police officer, super hero	• Circus performer
	• Astronaut

• Princess, a queen or a king	• Chef
• Ballerina or dancer	• Artist
• Actor/actress	• Race car driver
• Fairy	• Olympian or famous athlete
• Unicorn	• Just like Mom or Dad
• Horse, cat or dog	• Santa Claus

What about when you were 9 or 10 years old?

Circle the ones you remember wanting to be.

• Pilot	• Engineer
• Doctor or nurse	• Farmer or gardener
• Teacher	• Fashion designer
• Singer or rock star	• Architect
• Swimmer	• Graphic designer
• Skater	• Mother/Father
• Gymnast	• Playwright
• Video gamer	• Archeologist
• Zookeeper	• Lawyer
• Chef	• Actor or actress
• Scientist	• Artist
• Bus driver	• Chef
• Conductor	• Wife and Mother

• Dentist	• Husband and Father
• Sailor	• Gym teacher
• President	• Be own boss
• Acrobat	• Real estate agent
• Hair stylist	• Reporter or news anchor
• Yoga instructor	• Travel agent
• Writer	• DJ
• Veterinarian	• Coach
• Military	• Interior designer
• Athlete	• Judge
• Author	• Rocket Scientist
	• Mechanic

Review the following tables to look beneath the activities and roles to get to the elements you want to keep in your life.

Childhood Activities

Circle the corresponding elements in the right-hand column.

Childhood Activity	Element to Incorporate into your Life
Draw, color, paint Cook in Easy-Bake® oven	Create
Play with Legos®, trains, cars, trucks Set up forts	Construct, build
Play house Play with dolls Stuffed animals	Give care, nurture Give care, nurture

Childhood Activity	Element to Incorporate into your Life
Read books Play board games	Discovery, intellectual stimulation, quiet time
Be outside Play in mud Swim in water	Outdoors, nature
Play on swing sets Ride bike Climb trees	Movement, reach further, push yourself
Play dress up	Fashion, beauty, perform

Be When You Grew Up at 4 or 5 Years Old?

Take note of the corresponding elements in the right-hand column.

When you were 4 or 5?	Elements
A firefighter, police officer, super hero Astronaut Race car driver	Take risks, help, save, Adventure Recognition
Chef Artist	Create, feed, express
Princess, a queen or a king Ballerina, dancer Actor or actress Circus performer	Perform, stage, expression, accolades, audience
Fairy Unicorn Santa	Fantasy, magic, mystical
Horse, cat, dog	Animal lover
Just like Mom or Dad Giving presents like Santa Claus	Caregiver, nurturer
Olympian or famous athlete	Movement, physical, recognition

When you were 9 or 10 years old?

Again, circle or take note of the elements in the right-hand column.

When you were 9 or 10?	Elements
Be own boss President Military Judge Lawyer	Leading, being the boss, autonomy, form and structure, negotiating, debating, decision-making
Swimmer Skater Gymnast Athlete	Physical movement, stretching yourself, discipline, focus, strive to be better
Teacher Coach Gym teacher Yoga instructor	Teaching, instructing, molding minds, imparting knowledge, sharing expertise
Doctor or nurse Veterinarian Dentist Zookeeper Wife and Mother Husband and Father Farmer or gardener	Care giving, helping others, being in service, could be either people, animals or nature that's your priority
Interior designer Fashion designer Hair stylist Artist	Creating beauty, expression through beauty, creating
Singer or rock star Reporter or news anchor DJ Acrobat Actor or actress Conductor	Performing, being on stage, audience

When you were 9 or 10?	Elements
Pilot Real estate agent Travel agent Sailor Bus driver	Discover new places, travel, create new experiences, explore, new adventures, changing venues
Architect Graphic designer Chef Video gamer Writer Playwright Artist	Creating, producing, sharing expression in world: flavor could be images, buildings, technology or words
Scientist Mechanic Engineer Archeologist Rocket Scientist	Intellectual stimulation, discovery, details, building constructs, developing new ideas, watching and taking part in ideas to manifest in the physical

Putting It All Together

I'll use myself as an example of putting this all together.

Childhood activities

I liked to draw and color. I also liked to read books.

What to be at 4 or 5 years old?

I wanted to be a unicorn and a ballerina.

<u>What to be at 9 or 10 years old?</u>

I wanted to be a doctor.

<u>What are the elements of each?</u>

Answer	Element
Draw and color	*Create*
Read books	*Discovery*
Unicorn	*Magic*
Ballerina	*Perform*
Doctor	*Helping people*

<u>Bottom line?</u>

My intuitive business involves helping people discover their truth, potential and magic as I weave practical solutions with magical ones. Additionally, my approach of writing books, conducting workshops, speaking engagements and online programs involves creating, performing and helping others.

How About You?

o Use your journal to note your childhood activities.

o What did you want to be at 4 or 5 years old?

o What did you want to be at 9 or 10 years old?

o Copy a table in your journal and fill in the categories.

Answer	Element

What's the bottom line for you?

Destiny and Heart's Desire

Aligning your passion with your destiny is helpful to associate with the abundantly creative flow of the universe. Tapping into your heart's desire helps you live your passion.

There are fun magical tools to help you along the way and one of them is numerology.

Let's use it to determine your destiny and heart's desire.

What's your destiny?

Exercise: Destiny

Materials:
Pen, paper
Calculator, if desired

Your name equates to your destiny. Use your original name – the one on your birth certificate.

Letter Table:

1	2	3	4	5	6	7	8	9
A	B	C	D	E	F	G	H	I
J	K	L	M	N	O	P	Q	R
S	T	U	V	W	X	Y	Z	

Exercise: Destiny

Find your name's meaning:

Example:

Jane   Ann   Smith
1,1,5,5   1,5,5   1,4,9,2,8

Add each word of your name to get a sum of the numbers.

Jane = 1 + 1 + 5 + 5 = 12
Ann = 1 + 5 + 5 = 11
Smith = 1 + 4 + 9 + 2 + 8 = 24

Add these 3 totals together = 12 + 11 + 24 = 47

Add the digits together = 4 + 7 = 11

Reduce again, if applicable. Remember do not reduce either 11 or 22.

<u>Your Name's Meaning</u>:

First Name   Middle Name   Maiden Name

_____   _____   _____

Number for each letter

_____   _____   _____

Add the numbers together.

First Name: _____ = _____

Middle Name: _____ = _____

Last Name: _____ = _____

Exercise: Destiny

Add three totals together: _____ + _____ + _____ = _____

Add the digits together: _____ + _____ = _____

Reduce again, if necessary: _____ + _____ = _____

Interpret the meaning of your destiny number based on the following descriptions.

Destiny Number	Key Words	Meaning
1	Self-reliant, unique, innovative, powerful, quick, rebellious	You lead others. You work best alone. You like the appreciation of others. You naturally direct and delegate. You have tremendous integrity, honor and sense of pride. You hope to be the best and the first. Your destiny is to break up the existing order and rebel against tradition.
2	Delicate, caring, friendly, artistic, listener, tactful	You value relationship, aesthetics and community. You take care of things. You hope everything turns out all right for everyone concerned. Your success comes from persuasion, tact and waiting for the right moment.
3	Sanguine, inventive, creative, fun loving, dramatic, generous	You bring joy and friendliness to life. You're spontaneous, generous and love to gather friends. You like the good life – luxuries in art, food and material goods. You're lucky in fortune and friends.

Destiny Number	Key Words	Meaning
4	Realistic, trustworthy, diligent, serious, level-headed	You put your ideas to work with serious effort, focus and determination. You love routine and the rhythms of the earth. You like security and stability. You're a builder, worker, manager.
5	Daring, bold, persuasive, extroverted, rash	You love adventure, travel and new experiences. You may have many occupations and seem to live like a bohemian. You may be a 'jack of all trades'. You're strong, energetic and healthy. Your goal is personal expansion.
6	Dependable, loving, conventional, pragmatic	You create comfort and offer good advice. You're a nurturer and teacher. You value traditional methods of attaining goals such as; hard work and planning. People come to you for advice. You're supportive of family and friends. Your life task is to be of service.
7	Tranquil, sophisticated, careful, intellectual and deep	You're the researcher, analyzer, thinker, or inventor. You seek quality, value and depth. You love solitude and quiet contemplation. Your mission is to understand, accept and grow in life.
8	Strong, aspiring, poised, effective, dependable, discerning	Your work is of the highest quality. You make excellent decisions, solve problems and remove obstacles. You restore balance, increase speed and efficiency. Your goal in life is exercising power over your world. You may bring spiritual awareness to daily life.

Destiny Number	Key Words	Meaning
9	Idealist, universal, expressive, evolved, philanthropic	You're imaginative, artistic, sensitive and philosophical. You gain power through the nine by keeping the bigger picture in mind at all times. Your mission in life is fostering tolerance and compassion. You may have a humanitarian mission.
11	Inspirational, driven, spiritual, imaginative, enthusiastic	You need to put ideals into practice and in doing so, you can transform others' lives. Your imagination and powerful impression on others can transcend to higher knowledge. You envision new methods of healing, inventions and psychic knowledge. Putting these into practice is your quest.
22	Masterful, visionary, leader, builder, powerful, accomplished	You make things happen. You're capable, efficient and successful. You blend the spiritual with the practical. You're an expert in your chosen field. You're a leader and master.

Second, what's your heart's desire?

Exercise: Heart's Desire

Materials:
Pen, paper
Calculator, if desired

The vowels in your name equates to your heart's desire. Use you're your original name – the one on your birth certificate.

Exercise: Heart's Desire

Letter Table:

1	2	3	4	5	6	7	8	9
A	B	C	D	E	F	G	H	I
J	K	L	M	N	O	P	Q	R
S	T	U	V	W	X	Y	Z	

Find your name's meaning:

Example:

Jane   Ann   Smith
1,5   1   9

Add each word of your name to get a sum of the numbers.

Jane = 1 + 5 = 6
Ann = 1
Smith = 9

Add these 3 totals together = 6 + 1 + 9 = 16

Add the digits together = 1 + 6 = 7

Reduce again, if applicable. Remember do not reduce either 11 or 22.

Your Name's Meaning:

First Name   Middle Name   Maiden Name

_____   _____   _____

Number for each letter of vowels

_____   _____   _____

Add the numbers together.

Exercise: Heart's Desire

First Name vowels: _____ = _____

Middle Name vowels: _____ = _____

Last Name vowels: _____ = _____

Add three totals together: _____ + _____ + _____ = _____

Add the digits together: _____ + _____ = _____

Reduce again, if necessary: _____ + _____ = _____

Use the following descriptions to figure your heart's path.

Heart's Desire Number	Key Words	Meaning
1	Leader, dominant, rebellious, will, power	You're independent. You work best alone. You like the appreciation of others. You' have determination and willpower. You're self-reliant, highly idealistic, and generous. You love challenges. You like anything new. You appreciate equality in relationships. Your heart's desire is to take the lead.
2	Sympathetic, kind friendly, quiet, tactful	You value relationship, aesthetics and community. You take care of things. You like to work in the background. You love the details. You're easily influenced by others.

210

Heart's Desire Number	Key Words	Meaning
		Your heart's desire is to be understanding.
3	Psychic, inventive, creative, fun loving, dramatic, generous	You bring joy and friendliness to life. You are spontaneous, generous and love to gather friends. You like the good life – luxuries in art, food and material goods. Your heart's desire is fun and optimism.
4	Practical, cautious, diligent, serious, level-headed	You have a tremendously strong work ethic. You love routine and the rhythms of the earth. You like security and stability and defend home and family. Your heart's desire is security through conservative and tangible elements.
5	Freedom, adventure, persuasive, extroverted, rash	You love adventure, travel and new experiences. You may have many occupations and seem to live like a bohemian. You may be a 'jack of all trades'. You're strong, energetic and healthy. You are curious about everything life has to offer. Your heart's desire is to live life to its fullest.
6	Stable, reliable, loving, conventional, pragmatic	You're a nurturer and teacher. You value traditional methods of attaining goals such as; hard work and planning. You love unusual people as they live life differently than you. Your heart's desire is to be of service.

Heart's Desire Number	Key Words	Meaning
7	Questioning, analyzing, intellectual and deep	You're the researcher, thinker, or inventor. You seek quality, value and depth. You love solitude and quiet contemplation. Your heart's desire is inner wisdom.
8	Strong, aspiring, poised, effective, dependable, discerning	Your work is of the highest quality. You make excellent decisions, solve problems and remove obstacles. You restore balance, increase speed and efficiency. Your heart's desire is to be an advisor to others and have them follow your advice!
9	Warm, generous, universal, expressive, evolved, philanthropic	You're imaginative, artistic, sensitive and philosophical. You gain power through the nine by keeping the bigger picture in mind at all times. Your heart's desire is creativity.
11	Intuitive, driven, spiritual, imaginative, enthusiastic	(Look at 2 first) You need to put ideals into practice and in doing so, you can transform others' lives. Your imagination and powerful impression on others can transcend to higher knowledge. Your heart's desire is to yearn for the unattainable.
22	Masterful, visionary, leader, builder, powerful, accomplished	(Look at 4 first) You make things happen. You are capable, efficient and successful. You blend the spiritual with the practical. You're an expert in your chosen field. Your heart's desire is to integrate everything.

Putting it all Together

To tap into your heart center and your passion, let's review.

- What are your hidden talents?

- Childhood activities?

- Messages from childhood?

- Elements from childhood?

- Destiny?

- Heart's desire?

- Do you see any tie-ins, commonalities or overlap?

Going back to remember who you are requires stepping out of your mind and into your heart.

There are other ways to align with the creative flow of the universe. Let's continue by revealing your future self.

Welcome Your Future Self

"Your vision will become clear only when you can look into your own heart. Who looks outside, dreams; who looks inside, awakes."– Carl Jung

There's a relaxation and tranquility that occurs as you step into your future. All of the daily tasks and minutiae disappear. It's another way to move your focus from your mind and into your heart.

Take a few deeps breaths to become present in this space. You're going to step right in with a quick visualization.

Train Visualization
Close your eyes and take a nice refreshing breath by inhaling deeply and exhaling gently, letting go of any distracting thoughts, events or happenings of the day or week. You deserve to be here spending time contemplating your passion, your dreams and desires, your vision of the future. Nothing is more important at this moment.   *You picture yourself five years from now and find yourself waiting in a train depot for a train to take you to a wonderful destination. It's a destination where you'll be sharing*

your passion with others. You're so excited. This is an opportunity you've being working toward. Your dreams, desires and hard work have paid off.

Your family is all home, tucked in, and comfortable. You're traveling alone and relishing the adventure and freedom of it. There's nothing to concern yourself with, as you're completely safe. There are no worries. You're excited about the potentiality and secure in your travel activities.

You hear the first class boarding call and calmly and smoothly enter the train. You find your seat near the front of the car, stow your bag on the overhead rack. You put a few things next to you for easy access and look at your surroundings. Everything's perfect. You take a deep breath and smile to yourself. You're very satisfied. Things are going so well for you.

A gentleman, very attractive and vaguely familiar, enters the train car. You see that he is heading directly toward you and you smile in welcome. Yes, he's taking the seat across from you with a returning smile. He's very friendly looking and is he familiar? Yes, why yes he is! In fact, he's famous. You just saw him on television this week. You feel a little giddy, but in command at the same time. You look forward to spending this time next to him and hope he opens the conversation.

He does, in fact. He's very friendly. You speak about the weather and start a light conversation as strangers do as they're getting to know one another.

Then he asks about your family, you reply. He asks where you're going, you reply. He asks about your work, you reply. You reply that you're so excited and are traveling to share your passion. He asks about your passion and you reply.

My passion is…

I love to…

I am inspired by…

<table>
<tr><td align="center">***Train Visualization***</td></tr>
</table>

I am meeting with… to…

You smile and feel the excitement and satisfaction flowing through you. You deserve this. You've worked for it and it's paid off.

Breathe this in – fully and deeply. Exhale.

Now come back into the room, open your eyes.

Write your responses.

Jot a few notes in your journal.

My passion is…

I love to…

I am inspired by…

I am meeting with…to...

Astrology for Your Future Self

There are two primary ways to get a glimpse of your future self through astrology. You'll need your birth chart as described in previous sections. Once you have it, you'll want to look at your 11th house and the planet Uranus. Some look at the Sun for the future and the Moon for the past, but you're not going to do that here. You're going to stick with the 11th house and Uranus.

Firstly, you need to have at least a cursory understanding of the houses, signs and planets. The next three tables include information about each.

The houses are what you do. The signs are who you are and the planets are the energies of challenges and opportunities you've set up to overcome and integrate into your life.

House Descriptions:

House	Area of Life
1	**House of Self-Image and Outlook** This is the house of personal identity, self-image, physical appearance, body and awareness. It covers the way you operate, how others see you, and your general outlook on life.
2	**House of Money and Resources** This is the house of money and values, value systems, resources, connections, skills, competences, self-confidence, self-esteem and self-worth.
3	**House of Learning and Communication** This is the house of information, communication, concrete ideas, teaching, writing, and the practical mind. It's also one of siblings, early environment, neighbors, and short trips.
4	**House of Home and Family** This is the house of home, family, roots, bonded relationships, nurturing, instinctive behavior, family, and domestic life. It also represents security, connection to our past, and your ancestors. It's at the bottom of your chart, so signals who you are in the deepest part of your soul.
5	**House of Creativity, Pleasure and Romance** This is the house of creativity, fun, pleasure and entertainment. It's the one of self-expression, falling in love, affairs of the heart and romance. It also represents children.
6	**House of Service and Health** This is the house of duty, routines and responsibilities. It also covers health and service to others. It's the house of mentors.
7	**House of Partnership and Marriage** This is the house of intimate relationships, partnerships, and contracts. It's where you understand another.

House	Area of Life
8	**House of Intimacy & Death** Intimacy, sexuality, sex, transformation and crisis, letting go, death & endings, rebirth, healing or regeneration, occult, inheritance, shared resources, attachments, psychology, or partner's resources, other's money and what you need from others.
9	**House of Exploration** Personal world view or belief system, higher education, exploration, long journeys, spirituality, search for truth and meaning, philosophy, ideas, travel, teachers, cultural exchange, connection with the divine, exotic and wanderlust.
10	**House of Life Mission and Standing** Career and profession, vocation, reputation, position in society, ambition, public image, responsibility, authority, attainment, vocation and recognition
11	**House of Future and Tribe** The future, plans, aspirations, goals, hopes, wishes, groups, friends, associations, organizations, leaving a legacy, community ties, humanity and humanitarianism.
12	**House of Soul Growth and Undoing** Behind the scenes, privacy, inner Self, secrets, karma, dreams, soul growth, hidden strengths and weaknesses, private affairs, spiritual life, the past, spiritual insights, channeling.

Zodiac Signs:

Sign and Symbol	Characteristics
♈ Aries	**Ruled by Mars | 1st House** *Aries likes to lead.* *Archetypes:* Warrior, Pioneer, Daredevil, Survivor *Description:* Natural leader, ambitious, passionate, confident, fiery spirit, competitive, brave, energetic, straightforward, pioneer, adventurer, 1st to create something new, innovator, initiator, move quickly, help others in profound ways, courageous, daring, bold, enthusiastic, strong-willed, concerned with self; impatient, willful,

Sign and Symbol	Characteristics
	aggressive, angry – need to find inspiration and enthusiasm and act on it to lead others to do so as well.
♉ Taurus	**Ruled by Venus | 2ⁿᵈ House** *Taurus likes stability.* *Archetypes:* Earth Spirit, Musician, Silent One *Description:* Traditions, determined, dignified, protector of art and beauty, simply "be", steady, stable and grounded home, seek comfort, attached to possessions, gifted artistically, loyal, dependable, embodying; stubborn, materialistic – need to find ability to simply be.
♊ Gemini	**Ruled by Mercury | 3ʳᵈ House** *Gemini likes communicating.* *Archetypes:* Witness, Teacher, Storyteller, Journalist *Description:* Versatile, communicative, problem solver, multi-dimensional, quick-witted, lively, inquisitive, explore everything, gathering knowledge, messenger, inquiry, curious, adaptable, interpret lots of data quickly, wander & explore, hold two-sides of an issue and believe both to be true, remain young; non-committal, unstable, fearful – need to live life without expectation.
♋ Cancer	**Ruled by Moon | 4ᵗʰ House** *Cancer likes to experience emotions.* *Archetypes:* Mother, Healer, Invisible Man or Woman *Description:* Intuitive, easy going, sensitive, feminine/mother, patient, affectionate, emotional, how to feel deeply, nurturing, protective, longs to be accepted, empathic, absorption, mirror what you need to work on in yourself, , connected to Source energy; moody, over-sensitive, smothering, very vulnerable and easily hurt – need to feel accepted in order to feel deeply.
♌ Leo	**Ruled by Sun | 5ᵗʰ House** *Leo likes to be in the spotlight.* *Archetypes:* King/Queen, Performer, Clown, Child *Description:* King of the Jungle, natural leader, cheerful, magnetic, dominant, self-assured, creative, faithful, entertaining, proud, expression of will & power, celebrate life, generosity, regal, drama, heart, drive to be the best, confident, romantic, warm, inspiring,

Sign and Symbol	Characteristics
	hero; fragile egos, self-centered – need to develop personality and need pure expression of the vital heart in order to be content.
♍ Virgo	**Ruled by Mercury	6th House** *Virgo likes order and neatness.* *Archetypes:* Servant, Martyr, Perfectionist, Analyst *Description:* Service, responsible, practical, intelligent, organized, tidy, humble, hard-working, untouched, untainted, independent, discriminating, detailed, analytical skills, skillful, discerning, helpful, dependable friend, kind, pure, seek perfection by honing craft, deeply connected to spirit, put back into wholeness, healers; overcritical, tend to worry too much, forget to take care of themselves – need to give themselves permission to let go of perfection.
♎ Libra	**Ruled by Venus	7th House** *Libra likes fairness and justice.* *Archetypes:* Lover, Artist, Peacemaker *Description:* Compassionate, peaceful, diplomatic, romantic, charismatic, fair, balanced, friendly, gracious, attentive, right & wrong, freedom fighters, justice seekers, teamwork, getting people together, creating beautiful & harmonious spaces; people pleaser, indecisive - need to set boundaries to stay in balance themselves.
♏ Scorpio	**Ruled by Mars and Pluto	8th House** *Scorpio likes to live a secret life.* *Archetypes:* Detective, Sorcerer, Hypnotist *Description:* Perceptive, intuitive, determined, intense, sensual, mysterious, powerful, loyal, live every moment as if it's the last, passionate, judge what truth is, can see what is underneath, truth tellers, purify, penetrating, secretive, transformers, constant state of death & rebirth, comfortable with taboos such as: sexual, occult, & our subconscious desires, take leaps of faith, powerful healers; can be jealous, possessive, paranoid – need to forgive other people and let go of the past.
♐ Sagittarius	**Ruled by Jupiter	9th House** *Archetypes:* Gypsy, Student, Philosopher *Description:* Communicative, adventurous, entertainer, intelligent, optimistic, traveler, outgoing, independent, hope, faith, expansion,

Sign and Symbol	Characteristics
	constantly grow & expand through higher learning, travel or exploring new ideas, need to go beyond limitations, spiritual knowledge to practical level, outgoing, cheerful, lots of laughter, freedom; may take too many risks, too idealistic, lack commitment, careless with details – need to grow and expand to be happy.
♑ Capricorn	**Ruled by Saturn | 10th House** *Archetypes:* Hermit, Father, Prime Minister *Description:* Successful, logical, determined, faithful, loyal, striving, ambitious, persevere through circumstance, practical vision, sober, orderly, powerful, endurance, responsibility, committed, cheerful, well organized, knows how to create own personal boundaries, discerning, funny, deep intuitive awareness, find the light in any situation; can become rigid, controlling, bossy, overly ambitious - need to discover solitude to know thyself.
♒ Aquarius	**Ruled by Uranus and Saturn | 11th House** ***Aquarius likes to learn every day.*** *Archetypes:* Genius, Revolutionary, Truth Sayer, Exile, Scientist *Description:* Original, individualistic, liberal, idealistic, intellectual, friendly, kind, creative, independent, freedom, inventive, aspiring, radical, express own truth, nonconformist, creates own rules & structures, visionary, lots of mental activity, higher mind, lightning bolt of truth, leaders; impersonal, can be too stubborn – to be happy need to fully individuate.
♓ Pisces	**Ruled by Neptune and Jupiter | 12th House** ***Pisces likes to imagine and create.*** *Description:* Imaginative, spiritual, artistic, dreamers, gentle, intuitive, empathetic, consciousness looking at itself, individuality & togetherness at same time, compassionate, inspiring, understanding, fluidity, must be observer, develop a healthy detachment, highly psychic, fluid, flexible; lacks boundaries, easily overwhelmed by vastness, depth & severity of everything, avoid escapism – need to develop objectivity with connection, meditation or deep awareness.

Planetary Energies:

Planet and Symbol	Description
☉ Sun	**Shining Light** *Highlights:* Sense of identity, what we consider important, what we are proud of, what we seek to put our heart into. Vitality. Importance. Pride. Illumination. Recognition. Our will, purpose, future goals. Describes the core. *Sun Traditional:* Identity, ego, personality, shines forth easily, vitality, authenticity and psychological truth in life. Leader or conductor of life. We are most aware of in our conscious moments. Take care of your sun for a sunny disposition.
☾ Moon	**Heart and Nurturance** *Highlights:* Feelings, reaction, response, mother, home, food preferences, domestic habits generally. Where we retreat to. Our place of safety. How we feel nurtured and how we nurture others. Accommodation. *Moon Traditional:* Heart, cosmic mirror of soul, reflection of your light, emotional drives, soul desires, what nurtures your soul & how your emotions are conveyed to world, Mother, feminine, trans-rational feelings, intuition. Be true to moon, you will be happy, qualities you need in people, carries your inner child.
☿ Mercury	**Mind and Communication** Thought, perception, senses, messenger, how you communicate & how you process your thoughts, quick, intelligent, curious, open-minded, speech, language, teaching.
♀ Venus	**Love** Cooperation. Giving. Sharing. Compromise. Beauty. Love. Value. Comparison. Art. Taste. Means of exchange. Money. How we seek to make ourselves happy. Harmony, connection-builder, ease-bringer, heart-softener, love, truth, beauty, art, relationships, what you love, how you love, how you receive love, justice, staying connected with all levels of awareness, inner female, serenity, connect, wisdom from others, discernment in relationship, soul contract.

Planet and Symbol	Description
♂ Mars	**Action and Initiative** God of War, claim territory, will and action, hunter & prey, assertiveness, how you stand up and act in the world, highly spiritual, passion, drive, enthusiasm, extraversion, sexual drive, seeing Goddess energy, expressing zeal, tension, edge, right to use force, defender of innocence.
♃ Jupiter	**Guide and Guru** King of Gods, lucky, happy, faith, triumph, richness and goodness in life. Blessings, abundance, benign protection. Optimism, self-confidence, hope. Enormous and expansive, areas of your life that also expand you and push you forward into your biggest expansion, luck, friendly, generous, see bigger picture.
♄ Saturn	**Responsibilities and Mastery** Elder, Father, maturity through effort – increase in one's acceptance of what is real and actual; greater integrity, wisdom, and tolerance for defeats and compromise. Massive efforts and acts of will breeds dignity, self-respect and quality of natural authority. Boundaries, traffic cop, create form & structure that really supports you, tough teacher, hard work, discipline, gives you ability to do what you don't feel like doing. Builds character. Teaches mastery.
♅ Uranus	**Breakthroughs and Revolution** The future. Guardian of true individuality, rebellious, choosing self over society, true nature versus conditioning, rule breaker, follow own path, be unapologetically yourself, feisty, independent, shocking, sudden, wild, unpredictable, go against the grain, fierce individuation, channel electricity through our bodies and healing energies.
♆ Neptune	**Ideals and Imagination** God of Sea, consciousness, blank slate, mind without thought, pure being, be aware of everything, mysticism, dreams, spirituality, heartbeat of religion, delicate sense of intuition, connecting to everything that is, mystics, shamans, artists, also escapists.

Planet and Symbol	Description
♇ Pluto	**Transformation** Lord of Underworld, God of Hell, gives you the ability to go to places you don't want to go within yourself, great intensity, retrieve your soul, afterlife, wealth & riches, how to use your power in this world, agent of transformation, death & rebirth, catalyst for change, honesty.

Finally, the future.

When looking at the future through astrology, there are many ways to accomplish this with a professional reader. You may want to reach out and have your progression and transit chart done.

For this purpose, however, you'll simplify this process and look at two primary energies. The first is the 11th house – the house of the future. Then, you'll look at Uranus, the planet that brings the future into the present.

The 11th House of Future and Tribe

The future, plans, aspirations, goals, hopes, wishes, groups, friends, associations, organizations, leaving a legacy, community ties, humanity and humanitarianism.

What sign do you have in the 11th house? It's the one that intersects at the beginning of the house. In the following example, the sign of Aries ♈ is the sign that begins at the 11th house. Any sign in the 11th house will get stronger and stronger as the life progresses.

Therefore, in this case, Aries is getting more energetic as the life continues. Refer to the chart of signs to see which sign is in your 11th house.

Remember it's the one that BEGINS the house, not one that is further into the house.

In this case, Taurus doesn't have 11ᵗʰ house energy due to its not being in the beginning of the house. Aries is at the beginning, so it's the sign to use.

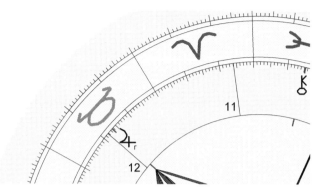

Due to Aries being in the 11ᵗʰ house, this person is gaining energy for leadership, ambition, passion and bravery. This person will want to demonstrate courage, enthusiasm and innovation more in later life than in the early years. Therefore, the future has more of this energy than the past holds.

Next, you're going to see if you have any planets in the 11ᵗʰ house. In this case, the person has Jupiter here in Taurus. Therefore, this life has Jupiter's influences gaining energy in the sign of Taurus. So, Taurus comes into play only due to the planetary energy.

This person has both Jupiter and Taurus growing stronger. Jupiter's energy involves luck, good fortune and happiness. It's expansive and pushes forward in big and bold ways. It allows for seeing the big picture. Taurus is determined, steady and stable. It's grounded, seeks comfort and embodies silence. It simply wants to just be.

These energies seem to contradict each other, thereby adding complexity to their integration into the life as it moves forward. Perhaps one way would be to explore the spiritual aspects of life more fully than the realistic ones. This could speak to the bravery *(coming out of the spiritual closet)*, seeing the big picture in bold ways *(weaving the practical and the magical)* and embodying groundedness and silence *(embracing meditative and spiritual practices)*. Hmmm…I wonder what this person does for a living (I ask cheekily).

Use your journal to answer the following questions:

- What's your sign in the 11th house?

- What does it mean? *(Refer to the sign table).*

- Do you have a planet here? What's its energy? *(Refer to the planet table).*

- If so, what sign? *(Refer again to the sign table).*

- Do you have other planets here? What's the energy? *(Refer to the planet table).*

- Can you put the information together?

If you have more than one planet here in different signs, it gets really confusing very quickly. You may want to refer to an astrologer or a reputable online interpretation.

Another look at the future involves the planet Uranus with the glyph of ♅.

Uranus ♅ – Breakthroughs and Revolution

The future. Guardian of true individuality, rebellious, choosing self over society, true nature versus conditioning, rule breaker, follow own path, be unapologetically yourself, feisty, independent, shocking, sudden, wild, unpredictable, go against the grain, fierce individuation, channel electricity through our bodies and healing energies.

Where is Uranus in your chart? What house? What sign? Are there other planets right next to it? In the following example, Uranus is in the 4th house in Virgo ♍ with Mars ♂ and Pluto ♇ right next to it. That means the energies of Mars, Uranus and Pluto are blended together. If this were my chart (and of course it is), I would refer to an astrologer to help with the interpretation as it gets complicated. (I did until I studied it myself). I am, however, going to persevere in the explanation as it could help you by reviewing complexity instead of simplicity.

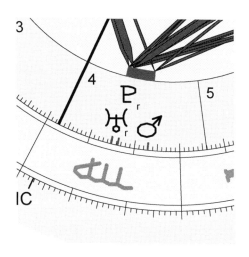

Look at the description of the house to determine the energy of the future with Uranus. In this case, it's the 4th house and its description involves home, family, roots and connection to the past and ancestors. It also signifies who you are at midnight, deep inside of your soul.

Then you look at the sign, in this case, Virgo and its description of service, practical methods, skillful ways and helpful manner. It also symbolizes a connection of spirit in purity and the need for perfection. Virgo can be nervous, anxious and tense and at the bottom of the chart, where it lies, can lend an undercurrent of tension throughout the life. With Uranus here, it could get stronger as the life continues.

Now, refer to the other planets, if any that are close to Uranus. In this case, Mars and Pluto. Mars represents action, will and claiming your power. It's how you stand up for yourself and asks you where you need to be brave in your life. It also lends drive, vitality and passion. Pluto signifies transformation. It gives you the ability to go to places you don't want to go within yourself with great intensity. It provides honesty as a catalyst for change.

So, how to combine all of this information that is the energy of the future. There will be a bid for freedom and independence in the home life, roots and family for this individual. There will be a strengthening of assertiveness and personal power in the family life and home. This individual will strive for transformation of the past, roots, ancestry to bring honesty and change to the life and deep soul yearning. The Virgo influences of service, spiritual pursuit in practical ways will be employed as calm and mindfulness will be integrated to decrease the tendencies of tension and anxiety. All of this is true as the life advances into the middle years.

Now for you, where is Uranus? Which house?

- o What does it mean? *(Refer to the house table).*

- o What flavor does it have – what's its sign? *(Refer to the sign table).*

- o Do you have another planet close to Uranus? What's the energy? *(Refer to the planet table).*

- o Can you put the information together?

Again, if you have more than one planet blending with Uranus, it gets really confusing very quickly. You may want to refer to an astrologer or a reputable online interpretation.

For your future self, you've visualized yourself on a train five years from now, you imagined your best self and you referred to the astrological influences of your future.

Each piece of information you've gleaned may be combined with those energies you reviewed of your past. Does anything overlap? Converge or blend? Are these elements diverging? Can you turn the box on its side to make sense of the information you've gained so far?

Don't think about this too much. If you have either tremendous clarity or are in a complete fog, both are perfect.

Remember this is about your heart, not your mind.

The mind doesn't need to latch on and the heart already knows.

So, let's continue.

"The most powerful weapon on earth is the human soul on fire."
~ Ferdinand Foch, French Military Strategist

Incorporating passion and creativity into your life involves leaning into the energies of fire.

Fire is both creative and destructive. From a physical standpoint, fire is a transformer, using dry material, ignition and air to produce warmth and a source for cooking. It's active, filled with color, motion and light.

Fire also is a manifestation of power. It fuels passion, energizing in more than the physical sense.

It's also destructive as it may consume everything available to it. Therefore, fire needs to be controlled.

When working with this element, you may utilize both the creative and the destructive aspects of it to your advantage.

Esoterically, the creative aspects involve opening the heart and awakening your connection to the universal flow of inspiration.

The destructive aspects may be used for releasing, purification or healing.

Using Fire

You can tap into the divine flow of creation through the element of fire.

Fire is the physical manifestation of spirit - one of creativity and inspiration.

The following are ways you can tap into fire for passion and creativity:

Astrology

Perform a similar exercise as the 11th house and Uranus for the areas of fire in your chart. You'll need your natal or birth chart as well as the tables in the previous section. Look at the following signs, planets and houses.

- Aries – bravery, courage, taking risks, innovation
- Mars – where do you want to be brave?
- 1st house of individuality
- Leo – theater, performance, creative flow
- Sun – who are you at the core?
- 5th house of creativity
- Sagittarius – philosophy, travel and learning
- Jupiter – how can you take big and bold action in your life?
- 9th house of exploration

Crystals

There are crystals and stones that magnify the creative passion for you. You can meditate with the stones before pursuing creative endeavors or carry these with you for periods of time.

- o *Apatite* – stimulates intellect and creativity as it clears confusion and promotes self-expression.

- o *Carnelian* – promotes courage and taking action. Can give you inspiration and align you with creativity to pursue your dreams.

- o *Celestite* - helpful with creative expression of thought and speech. Excellent for music and art.

- o *Citrine* – fires the imagination and carries the power of the Sun. It's used for awakening the imagination and bringing dreams into the physical realm.

- o *Garnet* – utilizes the forces of creative energy as it grounds the creative spirit to work lovingly on the physical plane. It represents primordial fire, the creation of the world.

- o *Herkimer diamond* – powerful creativity-enhancing crystal. Stimulates connection to higher self and imprints its energies into itself for continued access.

- o *Iolite* – sets your imagination free and boosts creative artistic abilities.

- o *Kunzite* – Awakens the heart and increases the connection to the divine flow of creativity.

- o *Lapis Lazuli* – Reveals inner truth and encourages self-expression. Brings clarity and attunes with life force.

- o *Rhodochrosite* – Encourages creativity and enhances dreams. Integrates new information.

The Goddess

The Goddess represents the archetypal expression of your life. There are Goddess exercises further in this section. However, for a quick connection, use the energy of Sarasvati, a creative Goddess. Bring her energy into your life by asking her to help you.

Seasons

Each season aligns with a natural element and summer is the fire season.

- o It signifies growth.
- o It represents passion.
- o Its symbol is the sun.
- o It's aligned with fire – creation and destruction.

During the summer season, unlock your passion and creativity by doing summertime activities, growing flowers and fruits and vegetables, spending time in nature, celebrating the solstice and seasonal harvest times.

Choose other summer activities:

- o Lie on the ground in the sun and observe the clouds passing by. Play the game of interpreting the clouds shapes.
- o Watch the leaves blowing in the gentle winds. Use this energy to let go of anything no longer serving you.
- o Take time to smell the flowers and bask in the slower movement of the season.
- o Make a bonfire (safely) and burn any notes you'd like to release. Watch the fire take the paper and energy away.
- o Go for a boat ride and feel the warmth of the sun. Release any tension or blocks.

- Spend time in your garden and lose yourself in creative ecstasy.
- Dine al fresco and connect with friends.
- Leisurely go for a bike ride and let your mind wander.
- Search for sea shells on the beach and clear your thoughts.

During other seasons, employ fiery activities:

- Sit in front of the fireplace and watch its flames.
- Perform a tea ritual.
- Hang twinkle lights along a curtain rod, bannister or the mantle.
- Draw or paint with bright colors.
- Do a candlelight ceremony.
- Cook anything warm and hearty.
- Get sexy.
- Diffuse warming essential oils.
- Make hot chocolate and sprinkle with cinnamon.

Tarot

Use your Tarot cards and ask about your passion, inspiration and creativity. Wands represent the spirit body and fire element. Look at the cards represented. See what's contributing or blocking your passion and creativity.

These are simple and accessible ways to use fire. There are deeper ways as well and are explored through destruction, creation and rebirth.

Destruction

The full creation cycle of fire involves both destruction and creation to bring about new life.

As always, you want to create space before you amplify energy into your life. The destructive force of fire is perfect to do this quickly and easily. There are a few exercises to help you.

Let Go through Fire

You may use fire to actually get rid of unwanted thoughts, feelings or obstacles. Simply write these onto a piece or pieces of paper, light a match and burn them over the sink.

Be careful with your smoke detectors as you don't want to set off your alarms.

Burn Sage or Palo Santo

Sage and Palo Santo are great negative energy releasers and you can use these to rid yourself of unwanted energy. Simply light a bundle at one end, blow out the excess fire and wave the smoke throughout the space you'd like to clear.

Violet Flame for Transmutation

The violet flame transmutes energy from lower to higher expressions as well as from negative to positive. It transforms and heals all negative and lower vibrational energies into positive higher ones.

When using the violet flame, surround yourself with the pure, white crystalline light of universal source.

Call on Archangel Michael for protection and St. Germain as the keeper of the violet flame.

Call on your higher self and God, if you desire. Ask that all healing occur for the highest good of all.

Invoke the preamble:

"I AM a being of violet fire! I AM the purity God desires!"

Imagine the violet flame transmuting all negative thoughts, intentions, will, emotions and physical manifestations into pure white crystalline light.

Close any healing by thanking the violet flame, Archangel Michael, St. Germain and your higher self.

Say silently, the transmutation is now closed.

Violet-Flame Image

When you invoke the violet flame, you can visualize yourself surrounded by a violet-flame pillar about six feet in diameter and about nine feet high. It can extend from beneath your feet to well over the top of your head.

See the violet flame come to life as if you're looking at a movie. The flames rise and pulsate around you in different shades of purple, pink and violet.

Around this violet-flame pillar, you can see your tube of light, an even bigger pillar of white light that protects and seals the violet flame.

See it transmuting everything into white pure light.

Remember to close the energy by thanking the protectors and keepers of the violet flame as well as your higher self.

Vow of Separation Removal

As a soul spirit inhabiting body, you've most likely brought past life experiences into this one. Some may have given you incredible traits and talents, while others may link to obstacles in your current circumstances. One type of link is a past life vow. You want to release these vows and for passion, any vow of separation will need to be cleared. Perform the ritual below.

Vow of Separation Release
Close your eyes. Take a deep breath and reestablish your connection to the universal white pure crystallize light. Call on your higher self. Call on your soul connection to your past lives.   *Now, imagine the pure white crystalline light in your root chakra, clearing and energizing it. This white light travels to your sacral chakra and activates it, allowing it to spin in the correct direction. Now the white light enters to the solar plexus in your mid-abdomen and stimulates your will power. Your heart alights with this white, pure crystalline light, healing and opening your heart chakra to all the love in the Universe. The pure white light moves to your throat, activating your truth, intuition and instinct. Now it goes into your third eye, opening it to be all seeing. The white light goes to your crown chakra opening it wide and connecting to the spirit world.*   *Continue breathing and as you do, focus on this white light filling each of your chakras, and connecting to the spirit world through your crown chakra. It fills your third eye,*

throat, heart, solar plexus, sacral, root and going into the ground beneath you. The light travels deeply into the core of the earth.

Now, envision the white pure light coming out of your root chakra and forming a ball in front of you. It's a healing ball filled with light and love from all that is. It transforms everything into beautiful, abundant energy. It sparkles with white twinkles.

Continue to breathe. You're going to visualize the energy of the vow of separation moving out of your heart chakra and into this healing ball as you make a new vow. It is vital that you speak this new vow out loud for it is the sound of your voice that gives it power.

So, you're going to say aloud: "In the past, I made a Vow of Separation. (pause) I have learned humility, practicality, and the art of letting go. (pause) This Vow of Separation served me then and no longer serves me now or in the future. (pause) As of this moment, I release this old Vow from my energy field through all dimensions of time and space. (pause) It no longer exists in my consciousness at any level. (pause) Any limitation is also released. (pause) Now, I embrace a new Vow of Union, Connection and Love and incorporate these energies into my Being. (pause) I ask my guides to bring the new energies of this vow into my life. (pause) I embrace the needed learnings and the wondrous changes that this new vow will bring into my life. (pause) So be it, it is so."

Breathe and say "I am blessed. I am infinite. I am love."

Take a few more breaths and thank your higher self and your soul connection to your past lives. Thank the element of fire and universal source of all that is.

Take a few more breaths and when you're ready, open your eyes and return to the room.

Creation

To utilize the creative forces of fire, you have fun exercises to bring about a connection to the energy. The first involves playing with the element in the palm of your hand, the second invokes a candle and the third activates your creative chakras.

Fire Energy in Palms

You need nothing other than yourself and a quiet place without distractions for this exercise.

Fire in Palms Exercise

Rub your palms together. Place your hands open palm up on your thighs. Take a few cleansing breaths. You may close your eyes, but you don't have to – just gaze softly in front of you.

Now, take a deep cleansing breath and expel anything that no longer serves you. You are here, present, centered and grounded. You are in a safe space, one of white light, pure intentions, clear thoughts, positive emotions and relaxed physicality. You are at peace in every part of you.

As you continue to breathe, welcome yourself into this space – you are here for you and only for you. You are going to be filled with the forces of fire this evening.

You rub your palms together once again as you call on the element of fire.

Imagine it shimmering, dancing and alive with magic as you're sitting comfortably in front of a beautiful stonework fireplace.

You see the flames dancing within the logs. The orange, red, yellow and blue flames crackle and leap into the air.

As the flame leaps, you turn your palms upward to catch it. You see small yellow, orange and blue flames dancing in your palms. You feel the heat. It's warm, but not hot.

Fire in Palms Exercise
As you continue to breathe, you imagine your fire leaping a little higher as you ask it to do so. Now take it down again. Raise it. Bring it down.
Add a spark or two. Watch it flow and crackle.
You have complete control.
Take a few moments.
Return to the room.

Journal any thoughts on your experience.

Candle Invocation

For this exercise, you'll need a candle and an intention you wish to energize with the creative force of fire. You can use any size from votive to pillar.

Candle Invocation
Hold your candle in both hands. Feel its smoothness and coolness against your palms. Close your eyes. Take a few deep breaths as you surround yourself with the loving white light of spirit. Imagine this light filling you completely as it travels into your crown chakra, into your head, chest, stomach, hips, arms, legs, hands and feet. You're completely filled with the magnificent white light of spirit.
You can feel it glowing within you. Now imagine your intention swirling in your mind. What is it? See it in your mind's eye.
Continue to breathe and feel your intention. Feel it in your heart. See yourself as you'll be once you integrate your intention into your being.
Now whisper your intention to yourself. Whisper it again.
See the words of your intention moving from your throat chakra into this beautiful white light of spirit. See it traveling within the white light surrounding you. Imagine it going

down your throat, over your chest, down your arms, into your hands and into your beautiful white candle.

Whisper it again holding your candle. Feel the words permeating the candle.

Continue to breathe for a few moments feeling your intention flow within you and into your candle.

When you're ready, open your eyes.

Every time you light your candle, you're invoking your intention.

Creativity Chakras

To activate your creativity, there's an inner aspect and an outer one. The inner aspect involves quieting your mind and opening your heart. The outer one involves activating your creativity chakras.

Creativity Chakra Visualization

Rub your palms together. Place your hands open palm up on your thighs. Take a few cleansing breaths. You may close your eyes, but you don't have to – just gaze softly in front of you.

Imagine a rainbow of beautiful, vibrant light coming down into your crown chakra. It's a ribbon of intertwining purple, indigo, blue, green, yellow, orange and red. The colors are alive and filled with the love, abundance and creative flow of the universe.

Visualize this rainbow threading its way through all of your chakras – from your crown, into your third eye, through your throat, into your heart and then bursting into your solar plexus. Next into your sacral one and finally into your root chakra and then onto the ground beneath your feet. The Earth fills with this gorgeous rainbow of spiritual color.

241

Journal any thoughts on your experience.

Rebirth - Fire Cycle of the Phoenix

Now that you know the creative and destructive elements of the creation cycle, you need to know how to combine them. The full creation cycle involves you being like the phoenix. You burn yourself up and then rise out of the ashes rebirthed and newly formed.

242

The phoenix represents transformation and rebirth. In ancient times, it's said the phoenix would build a nest high in a cypress tree and go there to die. It would set itself on fire, burning to ash. Three days later, it would come back to life. Three days, sound familiar? The phoenix is also one of the symbols for Jesus Christ.

In Chinese medicine, the phoenix images always carry two to symbolize the yin and yang, the divine feminine and masculine – always together in perfect union.

The mythical creature of the phoenix is linked to the peacock in real life. The peacock represents integrity and showing your true colors. A few key words of peacock involve glory, vision, awakening and immortality. The colorful peacock can remind you to rise out of the darkest moments.

Connect to the energy of the phoenix through the peacock. Refer to the image of peacock to imagine fluffing out your plumes.

Peacock Meditation

Close your eyes and breathe deeply by taking a long inhale and exhaling fully. Take a moment to gather yourself.

Imagine the peacock standing in front of you in all of its glory. The plumes are extended fully and you can envision the beautiful blues and gorgeous greens with specks of brilliant yellow on the feathers. They look like eyes and through these eyes, you see yourself. Reflected and mirrored back. You're in full glory as well.

You're beautiful, gorgeous and brilliant.

Spend a few moments basking in this feeling of the peacock. She stands in front of you and you feel her energy of awakening, vision and immortality. You feel electric and full of life. You want to use this energy to expand your passion.

As you breathe, think of your passion. Imagine living your dream. Envision embodying your heart's desire. Start to feel it in your body. Feel your passion whispering. Feel the quickening in your belly. Feel it stirring.

Imagine your passion starting at your root chakra and planting a new seed of physical manifestation. See the red glowing roots of your passion as they plant themselves into the world and light up with energy.

Peacock Meditation

Notice the red passion moving up your body into your sacral chakra and gathering emotion to generate even more feeling and desire. Notice as the orange desire swirls and moves into your solar plexus where it builds power and conviction. See the yellow power of your passion blending into green as it touches your heart. Smile as the passion fills your heart with joy.

Your joyous heart is singing with love as it spreads your passion into your throat chakra to give it voice. The blue of your throat moves the vibrational passion into your third eye, opening it to peer out at the indigo creation of your magnificent passion. Your crown chakra is waiting with bated breath to receive your passion and sing it into the spirit world and the Universe.

Your passion lights your chakra body from the red glow of the newly planted seeds through the rainbow of your body out the crown of your head connecting it to the flow of the Universe.

Feel it gaining momentum. Feel your rainbow passion flow throughout your body. Feel it build in energy and desire.

Feel your passion fill you to the brim and spill over to flow out of you and into the room.

See it swirling in front of you and all around you. It fills the entire room and needs to burst forth.

If you're ready, envision your passion opening the doors and windows and flowing into the streets. It flows through the city night, gathering love and support. It dances and sings and swirls. It's a beautiful rainbow of your passionate energy.

It swirls and sings and dances into the night. Waiting for others. When you're ready, it will whisper to them and they will hear its call. They'll be ready when it calls them again.

Peacock Meditation
You bring your awareness back to yourself. You feel your passion stirring into your body to become fully part of you.
Your passion quickens as you're asking it to quiet itself so you can carry it with you from this point forward. It breathes, it tries to push against your skin, but you contain it. Your passion is yours — now and forever.
It's part of you and part of the Universal flow. It's ready to serve you whenever you call it. You smile with the knowing that you've tapped into your passion.
Now bring your awareness back to the room. Take a deep cleansing breath and feel the bliss of being alive. Take another deep breath and fill yourself with the energy of life. As you take your next breath, take a moment to ground and center yourself.
When you're ready, open your eyes and gaze softly in front you — seeing nothing, yet aware of everything. If you'd like, wiggle your fingers and toes and do any gentle stretching your body requires. Breathe in again and open your eyes fully. Welcome back.

Grab a journal or notebook and make any notes about your experience.

Fire is an element of energy in its purest form and is closely tied to spirit.

Tapping into it regularly is useful to create abundance of love, passion, joy and creativity in your life.

Tap into Divine Creativity

"Creativity takes courage." – Henri Matisse

Creativity is an aspect of abundance. Being in the divine flow of the universe also means being in the divine flow of creativity.

Why Creativity?

Why do you care about creativity if you're here to increase your abundance?

Think of all of the ways creativity may help you in being abundant:

- Juggling schedules
- Planning fun activities
- Holiday and birthday shopping
- Making vacation plans
- Shopping

- Investing
- Giving advice to your spouse, children or friends
- Completing work
- Planning next business or career steps
- Working with others
- Wellness
- Learning new skills
- Decorating your home
- Entertaining
- Gardening
- Cooking

How to be Creative

In order to be creative and inspired, you need the passion of fire and an open heart. You also need to use the solar plexus chakra for your will power to claim your creativity to make it real in the physical realm.

So, to be creative, you also need to be brave.

- Brave enough to believe in your creativity.
- Brave enough to open your heart to accept and allow it.
- Brave enough to wrap your arms around it to act on it.

> Magic happens when
> you do not give up,
> even though you
> want to.
>
> The universe always
> falls in love with a
> stubborn heart.

From – the Smart Witch

Igniting your passion, opening your heart and engaging your courage is a winning combination for tapping into the divine flow of the universe.

Bravery Exercise

You can use astrology to figure out where you need to be brave. You'll be looking for the sign of Aries ♈ and the planet Mars ♂.

You will be looking at the house placement of Aries and the house and sign placement of Mars. You'll also be looking for planets in the sign of Aries.

Here's an example to follow similar to the exercise you completed for the future.

In this case, Aries is located in the 10th, but is not initiated by it. This sign has energy due to the Sun ☉ and Mercury ☿ being in Aries in the 10th house.

249

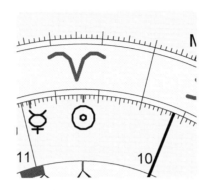

The 10th house represents life mission, authority, public image, role in society and recognition. The 10th house in this case is given energy due to the two planets placed here in Aries. The Sun is the most significant element of the chart. It signifies identity, life force and vitality. It's what is considered important and who you are at the core. Therefore, the 10th house is key to this person. Mercury affects speaking, listening, teaching and learning. It signifies travel and technology. It's how an individual perceives, observes and communicates. This person wants to claim his or her voice for the purpose of life mission.

As for Mars, it's located in the 7th house in the sign of Capricorn ♑. Mars asks directly where you want to be brave. It gives you vitality, passion and sex appeal.

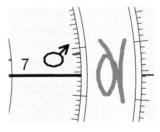

For this person, Mars is in the 7th house – the house of marriage and partnership. The plus side is the passion and sex appeal, the more difficult integration is the bravery piece. This person needs to be brave in close relationship. He or she needs to stand up and claim power. The sign of

Capricorn lends tradition, authority and leadership, so this person's significant other could hold these qualities making the task of assertiveness more difficult. This person really wants to stand up.

Bravery arises in this chart in both the areas of partnership and life mission. This individual needs to be brave in both areas. The life mission area actuates the identity and ability to communicate. Leaning into this area can lend energy to the individuation of the person and assist in the area of partnership. Additionally, Capricorn is tied to the 10th house as it's natural in this house further tying these two areas.

Now, where does bravery lie in your chart?

- o In which house does Aries lie?

- o What does it mean? *(Refer to the house table).*

- o Do you have a planet here? What's its energy? *(Refer to the planet table).*

- o Where is Mars in your chart? *(Refer again to the house table).*

- o What sign in Mars in? What is its energy? *(Refer to the sign table).*

- o Do you any other planets here? What's the energy? *(Refer to the planet table).*

- o Can you put the information together?

If you have more than one planet here in different signs, it gets really confusing very quickly. You may want to refer to an astrologer or a reputable online interpretation.

Another method to tap into bravery is through the Goddess. Her archetypal energy gives you a way to weave bravery into your being.

Connect to the Goddess

Creativity is not exclusively a feminine activity, but the feminine dominates in the creative process.

As humanity has become separate from the feminine, creativity has relied on the masculine methods of focus, discipline and production. This is linear and may eliminate the most powerful forces for creation.

Using fire and passion involves a more chaotic, circular and heart-based approach. Connecting to the energy of the Goddess helps you drop into your heart. The next exercise involves reviewing the meaning of the various Goddess archetypes to see what resonates and then calling on your Goddess to foster creativity into your life.

These Goddess meanings are based on Doreen Virtue's Goddess cards. See what calls to you.

Goddess	Goddess Meaning
Goddess Abundantia *Abundance*	*Origin:* Roman & Norse goddess of prosperity, success & abundance. *Description:* She brings good fortune and prosperity when called upon. She bestows all kinds of abundance – money, time, health, fun, friends, and support. *Crystal:* Emerald
Goddess Aeracura *Becoming*	*Origin:* Celtic and Germanic goddess – Earth Mother & Fairy Queen. *Description:* Multitasks as deity, Earth Mother & Fairy Queen. Assists artists and inventors. Helps eliminate needless stress. Welcome your creative gifts in harmony with the universe. *Crystal:* Blue lace agate
Goddess Aine *Faith*	*Origin:* Celtic goddess and Fairy Queen *Description:* Assists in farming and gardening. Helps give you courage and faith. Communes with the fairy realm. *Crystal:* Moss agate

Goddess	Goddess Meaning
Goddess Aphrodite *Inner Goddess*	*Origin:* Greek goddess of love and passion, associated with Venus. *Description:* Divine feminine. Beauty, joy, passion and pleasure. Explore your sexuality without inhibition. Bask in your inner goddess. *Crystal:* Rose quartz
Goddess Artemis *Protection*	*Origin:* Greek goddess, twin of Apollo. *Description:* Archer, huntress, protectress. Provides clarity of mind and focus of your intentions. *Crystal:* Amethyst, garnet
Goddess Athena *Inner Wisdom*	*Origin:* Greek warrior goddess, daughter of Zeus *Description:* Goddess of wisdom and war, helps protect, creativity and intellectual pursuits. She strategizes and boosts ability to see both sides and big picture. *Crystal:* Azurite, lapis lazuli
Goddess Bast(et) *Independence*	*Origin:* Egyptian goddess, daughter of sun god Ra *Description:* Cat goddess – moon and sun goddess. She is the sacred and all-seeing eye. Sensual pleasure, protector of household and bringer of health. Prevents the spread of disease and protects women and children. *Crystal:* Cat's eye, tiger's eye
Goddess Brigid (t) *Truth*	*Origin:* Celtic triple goddess – maiden, mother and sage; feminine counterpart to Archangel Michael. *Description:* Celebrated on Imbolc. Get in touch with your feminine power; speak your truth and be unwavering in your convictions. *Crystal:* Angelite, sodalite
Goddess Butterfly Maiden *Transformation*	*Origin:* Hopi spirit – springtime goddess *Description:* Brings new beginnings to nature and individuals. Symbolizes transformation. *Crystal:* Jade, moonstone, watermelon tourmaline
Goddess Cordelia *Natural World*	*Origin:* Celtic fairy goddess – spring and summertime *Description:* Helps bring warmth to situations. Urges rest and play in nature. Represents natural world.

Goddess	Goddess Meaning
	Crystal: Citrine
Goddess Coventina *Purify*	*Origin:* Celtic water goddess *Description:* Wishing wells are made in her honor. Purifies water, including inside of us. Helps strengthen our bodies and clears our thoughts and words. *Crystal:* Ocean jasper, opal
Goddess Damara *Guiding Children*	*Origin:* Celtic goddess – fertility, peace & harmony *Description:* She helps bring peace and harmony to families. Assists children in their innocence and faith. Helps guide parents for children's highest good. Celebrated in month of May. Gentle, sweet energy. *Crystal:* Jade
Goddess Dana *High Priestess*	*Origin:* Ancient Celtic goddess – magic & power *Description:* Ancient wisdom, magical powers, way-shower. Spiritual teachings – written or oral. *Crystal:* Labradorite, lapis Lazuli
Goddess Diana *Strength*	*Origin:* Roman moon goddess, daughter of Jupiter *Description:* Helps with childbirth, animals and connecting with nature, particularly the elementals. Aligned with oak tree for strength and focused intention. *Crystal:* Amethyst, moonstone
Goddess Eireen *Peace*	*Origin:* Greek goddess representing peace. Of three sisters – of peace, lawfulness and justice. *Description:* Peace. Be playful and relaxed – no need to worry. All will be well. *Crystal:* Blue chalcedony, peridot
Goddess Freya *Bold*	*Origin:* Norse goddess of beauty, love and destiny. *Description:* Friday is named after her representing time to celebrate. She had many lovers, unbridled sexuality and unyielding passion. Boldness. Bravery. Risk-taking. *Crystal:* Amber, aquamarine, cat's eye
Goddess Green Tara *Support*	*Origin:* Hindu and Buddhist goddess, meaning star *Description:* Reach out for support in accomplishing great things. Assistance. Support. Delegating. Cooperation. *Crystal:* Aventurine, jade

Goddess	Goddess Meaning
Goddess Guinevere *True Love*	*Origin:* Celtic triple goddess of fertility and bridge to afterlife. Avalon – wife of King Arthur, although she loved Lancelot. *Description:* True love, healthy intimate partnership. Soul mates. Romance. *Crystal:* Rhodonite, rose quartz
Goddess Hathor *Receptivity*	*Origin:* Egyptian goddess of mother; sun and sky goddess *Description:* Feminine energy of receptivity. Helps with receiving from the physical as well as spiritual worlds. Brings abundance once blockages are removed. Be thankful for all of the gifts you receive. *Crystal:* Malachite, turquoise
Goddess Ishtar *Boundaries*	*Origin:* Babylonian representation of Divine Feminine in all of her aspects *Description:* Goddess of love and war. Love, passion, sexuality and the Moon. Healing, protection and wisdom. Her animals are the lion and dove. *Crystal:* Garnet, moonstone, quartz crystal
Goddess Isis *Past Life*	*Origin:* Egyptian goddess of magic and giver of life, married to Osiris, mother of Horus. *Description:* Divine goddess of magic and alchemy. She taught her people practical and reading skills. She is also known as the goddess of medicine and wisdom. *Crystal:* Apophyllite, azurite, carnelian, lepidolite, malachite.
Goddess Isolt *Undying Love*	*Origin:* Celtic goddess who loved Sir Tristan, but was married to King Mark of Cornwall. *Description:* Heal your heart and love again. Be kind to yourself. Take your time. Rejuvenate your spirit. *Crystal:* Chrysoprase, rhodochrosite, rose quartz
Goddess Ixchel *Medicine Woman*	*Origin:* Mayan moon goddess - Lady Rainbow *Description:* Powerful healer and medicine woman who connects you to your roots of spiritual healer. Command your spiritual power and reconnect to your ancient roots. *Crystal:* Opal

Goddess	Goddess Meaning
Goddess Kali *Endings and Beginnings*	*Origin:* Hindu goddess of the cycles of life: Mother earth *Description:* She liberates souls. Rebirth, cycles, joy and courage are her themes. *Crystal:* Black obsidian, pietersite
Kuan Yin *Compassion*	*Origin:* Eastern goddess of compassion – ascended master as she wanted to stay close to earth to help healing *Description:* Compassion, love and mercy for all things. Gentle, nourishing, and loving kindness. *Crystal:* Amethyst, jade, rose quartz
Goddess Lakshmi *Bright Future*	*Origin:* Hindu goddess of abundance *Description:* Wealth, health, fortune and prosperity. She clears obstacles in your path as she works with Ganesha. *Crystal:* Aventurine, malachite, jade
Goddess Maat *Fairness*	*Origin:* Egyptian goddess of integrity, fairness and justice *Description:* Regulating stars, seasons, set order to the universe. Adherence to divine order, tradition, bound all things together. *Crystal:* Diamond, clear quartz
Goddess Maeve *Cycles and Rhythms*	*Origin:* Celtic goddess of femininity. Queen of the Fay. *Description:* Cycles, rhythms, fertility, sexuality, phases of a woman's life, go with emotional flow. Powerful magic, very wise, warrior goddess, balances white and black magic. *Crystal:* Black moonstone
Mary Magdalene *Unconditional Love*	*Origin:* Temple Priestess, Wife of Jesus *Description:* Love, lover of Jesus, disciple, wife. Loyalty, commitment, comrade, lover in arms. *Crystal:* Rhodochrosite
Mawu *Mother Earth*	*Origin:* West African Moon Goddess *Description:* Created all life. Helps you learn to live in harmony with nature. Needs abundantly supplied without hurting the planet. Supports environment and all of its inhabitants. *Crystal:* Moss agate, ocean jasper, green calcite

Goddess	Goddess Meaning
Mother Mary *Expect a Miracle*	*Origin:* Mother of Jesus Christ; Queen of the Angels *Description:* Miracles, spiritual healings, divine guidance. Divine Mother. *Crystal:* Blue lace agate
Goddess Nemetoma *Sacred Space*	*Origin:* Ancient Celtic Goddess of sacred sites *Description:* Watches over sacred sites, especially ones with nature. She'll assist with medicine wheel or labyrinth ceremonies. *Crystal:* Petrified wood, kyanite, dendritic quartz
Goddess Oonagh *Ease*	*Origin:* Ancient Celtic goddess of love, nature and relationships *Description:* Loves to dance and move her body. Transitions, creative and magical guidance. Movement, exercise, motivation. *Crystal:* Ruby fuchsite
Goddess Ostara *Fertility*	*Origin:* Germanic goddess of spring and fertility *Description:* Maiden goddess – full of potential. New beginnings, springtime, fertility. Lengthening days, warmth and light. *Crystal:* Agate, garnet, rose quartz
Goddess Pele *Sacred Passion*	*Origin:* Hawaiian Goddess of Creation and Fire – volcanoes. *Description:* She is fiery and stormy. She represents lightning, dance, wind, and volcanoes. She is a creator and destroyer. She created Hawaii. She is passionate and volatile. *Crystal:* Lava
Goddess Rhiannon *Sorceress*	*Origin:* Welsh goddess of the sun and inspiration. Divine Queen of sovereignty and governance. *Description:* Accumulated wisdom, create order, love of people, and supernatural will. *Crystal:* Amazonite, danburite, howlite
Goddess Sarasvati *The Arts*	*Origin:* Hindu goddess of knowledge, music, arts, and embodies the wisdom of Devi.

Goddess	Goddess Meaning
	Description: She dispels darkness of ignorance. She embodies the pure and sublime in nature. *Crystal:* Ammonite – fossil, fluorite, blue calcite
Goddess Sedna *Infinite Supply*	*Origin:* Intuit and Alaskan goddess of the sea *Description:* Helps connect with all of the sea's inhabitants, particularly dolphins and whales. Balances the seas and supplies abundance to the seas. *Crystal:* Aquamarine, selenite
Goddess Sekhmet *Be Strong*	*Origin:* Egyptian warrior goddess and is depicted as a lioness. *Description:* She is the powerful one who protected and led pharaohs into war. She also can bring disease and heal it. *Crystal:* Fire agate, sunstone, pyrite
Goddess Sige *Quiet Time*	*Origin:* Gnostic Goddess – Mother of Sophia *Description:* words create duality – find your true self in the silence. Our roots are with the silent void of all that is. *Crystal:* Blue lace agate
Goddess Sulis *Bodies of Water*	*Origin:* Celtic Sun Goddess *Description:* Oversees bodies of water used for healing – Bath, England is named in Sulis' honor. *Crystal:* Iolite, magnesite
Goddess Vesta *Home*	*Origin:* Roman fire goddess of home and hearth *Description:* Helps with living conditions, improves your home or household. Adds warmth as necessary. *Crystal:* Fire agate, opal
Goddess White Tara *Sensitivity*	*Origin:* Buddhist mother of liberation through success in work and achievements. *Description:* Enlightened activity, compassion, power and prosperity. *Crystal:* Tibetan Quartz
Goddess Yemanya *Golden opportunity*	*Origin:* African and Brazilian goddess of the sea *Description:* Mother goddess, protector and provider. *Crystal:* Ocean jasper, moonstone, turquoise

Once you've figured who calls to you, do a guided meditation to connect to the Goddess to bring in creative pursuits.

Make note of the Goddess and any words that jumped out. Refer to this at the beginning of the meditation.

Alternatively, if you have the Goddess deck by Doreen Virtue, you may pull a card and feel its energy and message.

Creative Goddess Meditation

Before you begin, look at your notes or card. Read the name, any wording or message. Say the name in your head. Envision the image of the Goddess who is showed up to help you tap into your abundant creativity.

Now, take a deep cleansing breath and expel anything that no longer serves you. You're here, present, centered and grounded. You're in a safe space, one of white light, pure intentions, clear thoughts, positive emotions and relaxed physicality. You're at peace in every part of you.

As you continue to breathe, welcome yourself into this space — you're here for you and only for you. You're going to be filled with the blessings of the goddess this evening.

Your heart expands as you know this to be true. You know the goddess is part of you. The Goddess has been with you for your entire soul journey. You're intrinsically linked. You're intertwined. Your energies are enmeshed. Breathe in the Goddess' strength, power, love and support.

As you breathe, you're going to clear yourself in the form a bright white pure loving light and picture it entering your root chakra. This cleansing illuminates and heals your root chakra and then your sacral one. Next, your solar plexus and your heart. You can feel your heart chakra expand with all of the love of the universe. It swells in the glory of the strength and support of all that is. Your throat chakra brightens as this pure white light clears your voice to allow you to speak your authentic truth without apology. Now it goes into your third eye, opening it to be all seeing. You can now see the unseen and know

259

the unknown. Third eye wide open. Third eye wide open. Third eye wide open. Next, it goes to your crown chakra opening it wide and connecting to the energy of all of that is. You are connected to the divine. You are connected to you. You're also connected to your Goddess.

See her name, image and message from your notes or card.

Imagine her coming to life out of your notes or card to stand in front of you. She is beautiful, powerful and so happy to be here helping you right now.

As you breathe, you can feel her energy.

Feel her support.

Feel her love.

Your Goddess is waiting to speak to you. She smiles and awaits your question(s).

Ask her anything you'd like to know.

She answers. Hear her answer.

Take a few moments with your Goddess.

As you take your next breath, bring your awareness back to the room. Close your energy by crossing your arms over your chest. You're centered and grounded.

When you're ready, open your eyes and gaze softly in front you — seeing nothing, yet aware of everything. If you'd like, wiggle your fingers and toes and do any gentle stretching your body requires. Breathe in again and open your eyes fully.

Make notes of your meditation, if you desire.

o   Her energy feels like…

o   Her messages to me are…

o   I will call on her when…

Divine Feminine

The Divine Feminine is your inner goddess. She needs to be awakened. Let's do so now.

Awaken Divine Feminine

Close your eyes and reenter your connected space. You're already connected to the earthly and spiritual realms. You can feel your chakras spinning clearly and actively in the appropriate directions. You know you're an open channel of light traveling from the earth up through your chakras and connecting to the pure universal light of all that is.

Your third eye and crown chakras are wide open to receive the powerful energy of the Universal Light of all that is. Your heart and solar plexus are activated to receive the creativity of the divine. Your sacral and root chakras are rooted to the earth — centering and grounding you.

Now, you're going to tap into your divine feminine and divine masculine energies that reside within you at all times.

By taking a deep breath into your crown chakra, direct your breath to go down the left side of your body. You can feel it going over your left shoulder, down your left arm, along your hip and continuing down your left leg and out of your foot. As you move your breath up and down your left side, feel your yin energies stirring. You feel receptive, relaxed, and supported. You sense your infinite being and recognize your wholeness. You lie back and survey the world before you - knowing, always knowing. You are grateful for your divine femininity.

Now we're going to see your divine feminine. What is she doing? How does she look? Imagine her coming to out to play. Does she have anything to say to you? Picture her in all of her fullness, power and strength. Imagine her filled with love and support. See her connected to the divinity of all that is.

As you continue to breathe, your breath renters your body, and you now direct it to go down your right side. You can feel it going over your right shoulder, down your right arm, along your hip and continuing down your right leg and out of your foot. As you move your breath up and down your right side, feel your yang energies building. You feel like doings something, producing, going, directing. This is your masculine energy — wanting to take action. As you breathe, say hello to your divine masculine self and thank your masculine nature for all of its energy, ability to take action and its strength. Bring your breath back up to your head and out through your crown chakra.

Now you're going to see your divine masculine. What is he doing? How does he look? Imagine him coming to out to play. Does he have anything to say to you? Picture him in all of his fullness, power and strength. Imagine him filled with love and support. See him connected to the divinity of all that is.

Picture your divine feminine and divine masculine meeting each other — smiling and blending into the perfection of all that is.

Take a few moments.

Take a final deep breath — breathing in all of your wholeness.

As you take your next breath, bring your awareness back to the room.

When you're ready, open your eyes and gaze softly in front you — seeing nothing, yet aware of everything. If you'd like, wiggle your fingers and toes and do any gentle stretching your body requires. Breathe in again and open your eyes fully.

Make any notes about your experience.

Become a Magnet for Passion and Creativity

Invoking the Goddess and awakening the divine feminine attracts passion and creativity into your life. However, you may want to clarify the elements of passion and creativity you wish to attract. If this is the case, perform the I AM exercise. If not, skip to the next section.

To continue, you'll want to elucidate your intentions, know your specific passions, realize your best self, utilize the energies of your future, enhance your bravery elements and lean into a Goddess archetype.

You may refer to any of the exercises noted above in order to make your I AM statements.

Collate your notes in your journal.

- o My intentions are…

- o My passions are…

- o My best self is…

- o The energies of my future are…

- o The elements of my bravery are…

- o My Goddess archetype is…

Refer to your notes and choose a few things to highlight in I AM statements.

I AM Exercise

The most powerful statements are I AM statements. The Universe doesn't understand time. It doesn't care about the past or the future. It only understands the present. It only understands now. I AM is a now statement.

It also doesn't know what to do with things we don't want. I AM NOT doesn't work. It switches to an I AM statement. So be positive and affirmative.

Use the mantra to start each day:

I AM ... *(intention)*

I AM ... *(passion)*

I AM ... *(best self)*

For this exercise, you may also choose a value, an occupation you desire, a skill you want or an essence you wish.

Now, imagine yourself.

Who are you? What do you desire? What do you wish to enhance?

I AM

I AM

I AM

Make a note to say this every morning in the shower.

Fire: Passion Closing

"Passion is energy. Feel the power that comes from focusing on what excites you."
— Oprah Winfrey

Igniting your passion and creativity requires you to quiet your mind and bring your energy into your heart. It also needs an open heart and an energized willpower center.

Using the element of fire helps you do these things. By reviewing the past and carving out key elements and diving into your future and bringing it forth, you stretch yourself and your creative possibilities.

By going with the full flow of creation, you expand space and activate creativity into your life.

By tapping into the Goddess and your divine feminine, you awaken yourself at your core.

So far, you've cleared your thoughts and heightened your vision to move into clarity as well as firing up your passion and creativity. You're primed to begin in the creative flow of the universe to bring abundance into your life.

If you want to also find joy, explore the following WATER section. There you'll discover renewal and rejuvenation that you'll need to avoid burn out with the air and fire elements.

Put all of your heart into its desires and savor your creativity by exploring it in ecstasy.

Water: Joy

"Joy in looking and comprehending is nature's most beautiful gift." – Albert Einstein

Air is movement, fire is ignition and water brings balance. It deepens into the natural flow of the universe to lengthen and strengthen the abundant flow in your life.

Water is fluid but is more viscous than air and much more nurturing than the fire element. It can also be destructive, but its force is slower and more powerful. The creative and destructive effects are longer lasting.

Water represents joy in life, but the other side of the coin of joy is fear. Life moves between the two smoothly and seamlessly.

Additionally, water is all about the sacral chakra. With water, you dive deeply to know yourself fully. In this knowing of yourself, you survey your life and those who share it.

Review the people with whom you spend time. Who is serving you and lifting you up? Who is competing with you or bringing your down? Who is reflecting your truest self at this time? Perhaps, you want to winnow the people in your life based upon your growth and expansion.

By connecting to yourself and your joy, you're also given the possibility of letting go of fear.

Tapping into your inner child, realizing self-love and giving yourself permission to find joy brings renewal and regeneration.

Water is strong and deep.

Let's begin its exploration.

"It is not happiness that makes us grateful, but gratefulness that makes us happy." ~Brother David Steindl-Rast

Creating abundance with the elements of air, fire, water and earth involves your mind, heart, power and physical world.

Working with the elements eases your mind, inspires your heart, powers your joy and facilitates manifestation.

In this section, the strength of water is employed. Connecting water with your solar plexus and sacral chakras establishes a channel for joy. You can power it with your solar plexus and open it with your sacral chakra.

What is joy? According to the dictionary, joy is:

➤ *the emotion evoked by well-being, success, or good fortune or by the prospect of possessing what one desires; gaiety*

➤ *the expression or exhibition of such emotion;*

> *state of happiness or felicity;*

> *source or cause of delight.*

Joy is a few things. It's a combination of happiness and achievement.

You need to work for joy. There's an edge to it. Hence, the combination of the solar plexus and the sacral chakras. The solar plexus is activated with the passion, inspiration and creativity activities with the fire element.

Now, the focus is on the water element with its flow, flexibility and strength.

Tapping into water and the sacral chakra involves using this flow by aligning with the flow of the universe.

As you know by now, there's a natural flow to life.

Go with the Flow

There's a daily, weekly, monthly and annual cycle that happens naturally and gracefully.

Night becomes day, the moon waxes and wanes, tides rise and fall, seasons change and a new year begins.

You love this natural flow. You revel in its constancy and marvel as it unfolds.

"Come look – it's the full moon."

"Let's go to the beach and watch the sun rise. It's so beautiful."

"Autumn is at its peak. Let's go see the leaves in all of their glory."

You love this natural flow– for nature. You enjoy the rhythms and appreciate the splendor of winter becoming spring with new growth and the vibrancy of life.

Yet, you also do your best to circumvent these natural cycles in your own life.

You continually want things to expand, grow, begin, so you do everything you can to avoid when things contract, die or end. You have trouble letting go gracefully and effortlessly, so you cut off the natural cycle mid-stream and try to maintain a constant expansion.

When have you forgotten there's is a natural rhythm to the world – one of expansion and contraction? This rhythm is evidenced in the cycles of the moon, the tides of the water, and the lungs in every one of you. The moon waxes for two weeks and then wanes for two, twice a day the tides come in and go out, every few seconds, you breathe in and breathe out.

You appear so much happier when things get bigger, when there's more, when things move faster. You get a rush by a BOGO (buy one, get one) free coupon –even if you don't need or can't use the second one. You hear, 'more is better', 'faster is more efficient', and 'bigger is better.' Why?

The BIG GULP is now the regular size soda, you have so much stuff that you can't keep it in your home, so you rent storage units and have close to a million channels on TV.

When did 'more' become everything and 'less' become so scary you can't even contemplate it?

Think about less.

Take a deep breath and think about less.

You feel so great when you clear out the clutter, when you take a vacation to a remote place and unplug, and when you resist the temptation to buy more than you need. So why are you so scared when you think about less?

The cycles of the Universe are irrefutable. Contraction will always be tied to expansion. Your breath will always involve an inhale **and** an exhale.

So, what are you to do?

As the cycles of life are here to stay, it seems you have a few things to tackle if you want to minimize the potential roller coaster ride. Minimizing how you deal with the lows or contractions and shoring up your response to the ever-changing flow of life will ease the cycles for you.

There are three exercises in this section:

- Overcome your fear of contraction.
- Increase your state of gratitude.
- Use the Tarot and Goddess to gain insight into ways to deepen your connection.

Fear of Contraction

Firstly, how do you overcome your fear of contraction?

Change Your Perspective

I think the most important thing to do is to **change your perspective** of what contraction or less means in your daily life.

o If you have less, you don't have to rent a storage unit.

o If you buy less, you have more money in your bank account.

o   If you do less, you have more time for relaxation.

So, why is 'less' scary?

Take a deep breath. Note your feelings and exhale to let them go. Do this repeatedly when the fear of 'less' arises.

<u>Inevitable Change</u>

The next thing to realize is ***change in life is going to happen*** regardless of how much you may want things to remain exactly the same.

o   Summer becomes autumn. Winter bursts into spring.

o   You will age.

o   Your children will grow up.

o   People move. Bosses or teachers leave. Companies open and close.

If you can gracefully navigate all of the natural changes that happen in every life, you'll have more bandwidth to handle the unexpected ones.

So, knowing you need to accept the natural changes in life is part of the equation and an important one. However, let's look at those changes that are unexpected first.

When something changes for the better, you're happy. When something changes for the worse, you feel badly. What defines better and what defines worse?

Perhaps when you hear about a change, you can take a moment and think about what this change REALLY means for your life.

The Head of School just quit without giving notice? You ask yourself how this REALLY impacts you as the average school family.

Your favorite grocery store is selling out to the far inferior competition down the street? You know you need the prepared healthy dinner feature to get you through the week, so where else can you shop to replace this necessity?

Your gym is closing, your dishwasher is on the fritz, your very dear friends are moving, your child's teacher is leaving, your favorite products are discontinued, your partner is changing jobs, your career is no longer giving you energy...unexpected change that could feel constricting is upon you. What should you do?

1. Alter your perspective.

2. You can take a pause moment to think about how this unexpected change will REALLY affect you.

3. Allow your feelings of disappointment, frustration, sadness, angst, aggravation, or fear. Honor these feelings, thank them and then move on.

4. Take action. Action is the very best thing you can do in these moments.

Fear of Contraction Exercise

Think of an actual event or circumstance you fear losing or becoming less.

Contracting Event/Circumstance *(A close friend's moving, buying a smaller home, losing a job...)*

1. Alter Perspective *(How can this work out for you?...a new place to visit & more quality time, lower expenses & less time spent cleaning, a chance to learn something new & do something different...)*

2. The REAL effect *(Change the rhythm of the friendship, give away a lot of things & pare down, tighten budget & retool skills…)*

3. Feelings *(What feelings do these changes bring up for you? Allow them and process them.)*

4. Take Action *(Make travel arrangements, go through items and give away to charity, do resume, take classes, reach out to recruiters…)*

I chose real and scary circumstances to contemplate in this exercise. Contracting events can be actually nerve-racking and life changing. However, there is a silver lining in most circumstances. In loss of life experiences, these circumstances call for grief counselling and processing.

Take a few breaths and contemplate altering your perspective. Imagine being more buoyant to the fluctuations of life.

Increase your State of Gratitude

Having an attitude of gratitude brings much happiness into your daily life. Truly being grateful and giving thanks shifts something inside of you, so that things flow more effortlessly. You also gain more grace when things don't go smoothly.

Story: Finding Gratitude in Adversity

"There was construction on my street, that's why I can't make it to our meeting this morning. I had to move my car earlier…" I hear when I answer my phone as I am sitting down at the local café to begin said meeting the other morning.

"Well, I emailed you this morning and it's a busy time of year with the holidays," the voice continues.

The excuses escalate with my lack of effusive response and the tone starts to get defensive. "It is such a busy time of year and we never confirmed the meeting and I called you this morning and you didn't answer. Well, we'll just have to reschedule for January."

I'm grateful for my ability to immediately separate myself from growingly dramatic situations.

I ignore the fact that there's no apology for such a late cancellation. I ignore the fact that the tone has changed from defensive to offensive. I ignore the fact that this has somehow become my fault when I'm the one sitting at the meeting place at the designated time. I ignore all of this and respond with the truth that any rescheduling can't occur until the next season, which is when I'm currently booking meetings.

Yes, it's busy time of year and I'm also grateful for the busyness, as I love the holiday season and the energy of the hustle and bustle that leads to the reward of relaxation and reflection during the actual holidays.

I hang up and sit down to take a moment and mentally rearrange my day. I'm grateful for this newfound time. I originally didn't have time to do a few personal errands that absolutely needed to be done today – tailors, dry cleaners, bank and post office. How lucky am I to have gained this time to do these mundane, yet important things?

As I'm driving away, I also take a few deep breaths, as admittedly, I'm also aggravated. I'm aggravated that I've scrabbled to make the meeting, as getting two children, one who was sick with a cold, off to school that morning, was unusually hectic.

I'm aggravated that I stayed up past midnight to finish getting the proof changes for the new book to the production person as I had meetings scheduled throughout the day.

I'm aggravated that I've made time in my busy schedule to, in addition to making a business connection, give business advice. This business owner specifically pulled me aside during a recent networking meeting and asked if I could help with her business. I often do this. It's pro bono work and one I committed to when my husband and I started our first business strategy company, many, many years ago.

Knowing that I'm aggravated, I ask myself, "What's the lesson here? What message am I being given right now?"

Firstly, I go through the events of the entire exchange to look for clues as to the deeper meaning:

- The original networking event was lovely and my first foray back into the networking world as my new business persona. *Okay, nothing there.*

- A quick review of the email message trail verifies that we did indeed commit to the meeting, so it's not my needing to pay more attention to details. *Nope, that's not it.*

- A review of my feelings before the meeting reveals absolutely nothing. I have no feelings whatsoever. *Okay, no emotional work is required about this. That's good.*

- A look at my calendar tells me that I'm no more or no less scheduled than usual. *Okay, my schedule is always ridiculous, but I'm happy with my commitments.*

What can it be?

Then, I realize one of the things I'm aggravated about is that I immediately responded to a request for a meeting that I had to follow up to schedule, when I didn't need to conduct this meeting for any reason at all. There's very little to gain for me.

277

I quickly and frequently respond to requests for help without any thought as to what I gain from the encounter. Why do I extend effort to give free advice and to make connections for other people? Hmmm...how one sided is that?

Oh, thank you. It's epiphany time. YES. How grateful am I that I've gained incredible insight with very little effort and no negative results? How truly lucky am I?

The deeper meaning is the pro bono work I committed to for my original business is proportionate. My paid work is so healthy that the pro bono/paid work ratio is miniscule.

For my new venture quite frankly, this isn't the case. My paid work is minimal at this point and my unpaid is phenomenal. Adding pro bono work on the business side is ludicrous. Oh, sweet epiphany. Thank you. I feel wonderful about this encounter now, as I've gotten a clear and important message with relatively little effort. Yay.

Why do I go into such excruciating detail about all of this and can I please get to the point?

When things are going well, it's incredibly easy to feel grateful. Giving thanks on a daily basis is an easy habit to form when you're taking your first moments of the day before any of it has unfolded before you.

Yet, the day unfolds and often, it's fraught with disappointments, irritations and frustrations. So, having a strategy of four easy steps is handy to change an aggravating situation into something positive.

Now, I'm no Pollyanna. I can get just as pissed off as the next person, maybe even more so, because I have a temper.

However, going through these four steps during irritating times has helped me enormously.

They may help you too.

Four Steps for Increase Gratefulness

When a situation arises that's off-putting or aggravating:

1. Tangible and Personal

Immediately think of something tangible and personal for which to be grateful. This will give you a moment of pause to reset yourself from reacting to responding to the situation. Responding puts you in the driver's seat, reacting puts you on the defensive.

Think of a few things for which to be grateful during and right after any encounter, such as; the ability to separate myself, the holidays, and my newfound time.

2. Objective and Efficient

Handle the situation with as much objectivity and efficiency as possible.

Being silent allows the conversation to be mostly one-sided and ends the call as succinctly as possible with the comment about booking meetings in the next season. Don't fully engage. It's completely unnecessary and just prolongs the encounter.

3. Feelings

Allow your feelings. Welcome them and process each one as it comes.

After separating from the encounter, recognize and allow your feelings, such as mine of aggravation.

279

4. Deeper Meaning

Look for the deeper meaning behind the situation.

Look beyond your natural trigger points and explore the situation from the beginning. Processing your feelings helps see the deeper meaning.

This takes practice, but it gets easier over time. You'll notice patterns and be able to quickly review your natural trigger points.

At first, these trigger points will provide your answer. Over time, you'll be handling these trigger points, so they'll not provide the answer. By removing them while continuing to review the situation, your answer will emerge. Then you can work on the answer that presents itself.

Gratitude Exercise

Think of a circumstance that triggers you. It can be personal, family or business.

Situation/Circumstance *(Parents calling, friends cancelling, boss delegating, children fighting...)*

1. Tangible and Personal Gratitude *(Think of something to be grateful for...parents caring, more time, better responsibility, healthy children...)*

2. Objective/Efficient *(How can you be objective during a call, date, work or fight...)*

3. Feelings *(What feelings do these encounters bring up for you? Allow them and process them.)*

4. Deeper Meaning *(Is there a deeper meaning behind the triggers of these encounters? Acting mature, using your voice, standing up for yourself, listening and spending quality time…)*

Improving your ability to can be helped by increasing your feelings of gratitude.

Deepening your Connection to the Flow

Use the Tarot major arcana cards to get answers to go with the flow in your life.

Do a spread to deepen your connection to the natural flow of the universe.

You can also gather the energy of the card as it relates to the Goddess. There is aligning energy between the two.

In this exercise, you have the choice of using the message of the Tarot and the energy of the Goddess to deepen your connection.

The meanings of the major arcana cards and related Goddesses are:

Major Arcana	The Goddess
Fool Child 0 – Law of Natural Expression	**0 – Beginnings - White Tara**
Innocence, Faith, Beginnings. Innocent, spontaneous, curious and playful. Breath of fresh air. Life force of the great spirit. Brings joy and new life. Represents the child within each one of us. Place your trust in the hands of the universe. Be a beginner. There is mastery in beginning and being completely open to anything, despite everything.	*Origin:* Hindu and Buddhist goddess, who is said to have 21 manifestations – everyone a different color. White Tara is the one of compassion. She is known as a star or she who brings forth life; She is said to be a feminine Buddha. *Description:* An enlightened one, who has attained the highest wisdom, compassion and capability. She may retain human form,

Major Arcana	The Goddess
Negative side: You may never grow up.	yet remains in oneness with every living thing. *Message: "You can trust, be free from worry and remain open to the world with joy in your heart."* *Crystal:* Tibetan quartz
Magician I – Law of Talent	**I – Magic - Isis**
Creativity. Guile. Personal Power. Symbolizes creation. You are a transformer and materializer – manifest your dreams and visions. You can make miracles by taking spirit and bringing it into physical form. You learn to conduct the elements of intellect, spirit, earth and emotion – tools to bring to life whatever you desire. *Negative side: Black magic – ego from too much power.*	*Origin:* Egyptian goddess of magic and giver of life, married to Osiris, mother of Horus. *Description:* Divine goddess of magic and alchemy. She taught her people practical and reading skills. She is also known as the goddess of medicine and wisdom. *Message: "Gain knowledge of all that is by calling on me. I will help you gain insight into your soul by recalling your past lives, ancient wisdom or spiritual inspirations."* *Crystal:* Apophyllite, carnelian, lepidolite, malachite
Priestess II – Law of Inherent Wisdom	**II – Wisdom – Dana/Danu**
Embodies the intuitive. Intuition. Calm. Spiritual Assistance. Intuit the truth, be still and reflect. You are a temple – see clearly and counsel wisely. Quiet yourself to hear intuition. Be a mirror for others – a reflecting pool. Be calm, cool, stoic and withdrawn. *Negative side: You may withdraw too much from life.*	*Origin:* Ancient Celtic goddess, known as 'The Flowing One' – the Mother of the Gods *Description:* She births wisdom and inspiration into the world. Ancient wisdom, magical powers, way-shower. Spiritual teachings – written or oral. She holds both earth and water magic. *Message: "Use your ancient wisdom and divine knowledge to help others. Teach, speak, show the way."* *Crystal:* Labradorite, lapis lazuli
Empress III – Law of Preservation	**III – Fertility - Arianrhod**
Nurturing. Receptivity. Divine Mother. Honors and respects all of life for its richness and beauty. You are able to	*Origin:* Welsh goddess of stars and reincarnation

Major Arcana	The Goddess
recreate, resurrect and revive. One with all. Creative union. Mother Goddess. Protect that of value to you. See the value, know the value, stand up for the value. *Negative side: You can become too possessive and smothering.*	*Description:* Known as Silver Wheel. Primal figure of feminine power. Woman who is complete unto herself. Rules fertility and childbirth. Weaves the tapestry of life. Responsible for souls of warriors who fell in battle. *Message:* "Be wise. Be free. Be creative. Be unto your own self." *Crystal:* Aquamarine, danburite
Emperor IV – Law of Worldly Development	**IV – Power - Freya**
Leadership. Discipline. Divine Father. Be a builder who contributes to the material evolution of the world. To achieve your clearly defined goals, have the leadership, will, decisiveness, daring and organization of the great kings. Aspire to the top. *Negative side: Too much control – inflexible.*	*Origin:* Norse goddess of destiny, love and beauty *Description:* Leader of Valkyries, Freya had considerable power. She represents boldness, bravery and risk-taking. Her softer side involves love, beauty and passion. She is often depicted in a golden chariot through the skies, pulled by two large blue cats, a gift from Thor. *Message:* "Fully embrace yourself and your feminine power. Be bold, take action and reach for the stars." *Crystal:* Amber, aquamarine, cat's eye
Hierophant V – Law of Life Mastery	**V – Tradition - Ariadne**
Knowledge. Tradition. Guidance. Life is your teacher. Be like a child learning through the tests of life and growing through experience into Buddhahood – full enlightenment. Practice sacred rituals. *Negative side: Get too caught up in tradition and become fixed and dogmatic.*	*Origin:* Greek moon and star goddess – spiral of life – Golden Thread *Description:* Goddess of healing and emotional development. Symbolized by the labyrinth. Helps heal inner self and find your way through the creative process. It's about finding the center and the way out – at the same time. *Message:* "Call on me if you're stuck in the maze of your life. I can help you find your way." *Crystal:* Blue apatite, lapis lazuli

Major Arcana	The Goddess
Lovers VI – Law of Union	**VI – Love - Aphrodite**
Union. Choice. Relationship. Communion with others, and integration of inner self-polarities. Find your inner lover, and inner soul mate. Force of attraction. Seek out the different and you will become whole. Together but not together. Duality. Live with ambiguity, contradiction and paradox. *Negative side: May become codependent in relationship.*	*Origin:* Greek goddess of love, beauty, passion and eternal youth *Description:* Depicted by myrtle trees and doves. She knows you need to love yourself before you can fully love another. Loving others means being able to love them exactly as they are. *Message: "The love for self must come from within. The heart is the source and beginning of all beauty. Without heart, there is nothing. The love must start from within and work its way out. Not the opposite."* *Crystal:* Rose quartz, kunzite
Chariot VII – Law of Motion	**VII – Movement - Athena**
Movement. Triumph. Travel. Challenge yourself. Movement brings change and change brings new experience, learning and growth – leads to achievement of your evolutionary destiny. Maintain an inner stillness as you move about. You then become centered in the midst of changes and your movement becomes effortless. *Negative side: You may get carried away.*	*Origin:* Greek goddess of wisdom and war, daughter of Zeus, symbolized by the owl (She's synchronized with Roman goddess Minerva). *Description:* She is a warrior goddess who helps protect life. She's also know for creativity and intellectual pursuits. She strategizes and boosts ability to see both sides and big picture. *Message: "Quiet your mind and call upon me for protection, wisdom and inner guidance. I remind you who you are – you too, are a warrior goddess!"* *Crystal:* Azurite, lapis lazuli
Balance VIII – Law of Action and Reaction	**VIII – Justice - Maat**
Balance. Patience. Inaction. Eight represents balance among everlasting change. Balance is an infinite dance. Keep the mind moving, body fluid and spirit soaring.	*Origin:* Egyptian goddess of harmony, balance and truth. She's also known for justice and order. *Description:* It's said she came into existence at the moment of creation. Regulating stars, seasons, set order to the universe.

Major Arcana	The Goddess
Teach yourself through your continuously changing incoming stimuli – learn through adjusting. *Negative side: May be overly judgmental and critical.*	Adherence to divine order, tradition, bound all things together. *Message: "Surrender your ego and trust in the wisdom of the whole."* *Crystal:* Diamond, clear quartz
Hermit IX – Law of Wholeness/Perfection	**IX – Contemplation - Ceres**
Wisdom. Introspection. Spiritual Guidance. Use your inner resources fully. Meditate. Take a moment to celebrate your success so far and then get to work again. Take your time and do your work right with correct planning, proper sowing, constant nurturing and timely harvesting. Use your work in the world as a spiritual path to achieve your higher destiny. Nine – unity of mind, body, spirit. *Negative side: You may retreat too far into yourself.*	*Origin:* Roman goddess of agriculture and abundance, order and transitions *Description:* One of goddesses responsible for life itself and for the seasons. With Ceres, create, produce and then celebrate the harvest. She represents fruitfulness and fertility. She facilitated the movement of humanity from nomad to communities. Women in transition are under her protection. *Message: "Create to nourish yourself."* *Crystal:* Angelite, amethyst, bloodstone, selenite
Fortune X – Law of Prosperity	**X – Fortune - Lakshmi**
Abundance. Reward. You prosper by knowing how to receive the wealth of opportunities that come to you from the cornucopia of the universe. Manifestation of your talents so that you are rewarded in return. *Negative side: Subject to delusion of grandeur. May become exploitive and manipulative.*	*Origin:* Hindu goddess of abundance or fortune *Description:* Wealth, health, luxury, fortune, prosperity and beauty. Lakshmi bestows power, wealth, and sovereignty. She clears obstacles in your path as she works with Ganesha. She holds the promise of material fulfillment and contentment. *Message: "Call on me to bring abundance to you now."* *Crystal:* Aventurine, malachite, jade
Strength XI – Law of Self-Dominion	**XI – Strength - Brigit**
Willpower. Recovery. Success. Strength is the free and controlled total expression of your being. Total living.	*Origin:* Celtic triple goddess – maiden, mother and sage; feminine counterpart to Archangel Michael.

Major Arcana	The Goddess
Live in full accord with the undiluted multiplicity of your being. Be like the lion – live fully and completely. *Negative side: Vanity, prideful ego.*	*Description:* She's celebrated on Imbolc and symbolized by fire. She is the sun and moon, action and inspiration, achievement and creativity. She is fierce and she is known as a warrior goddess. She also represents creative expression, divinity and deep wisdom. *Message: "Don't back down. Stand up for what you believe is right."* *Crystal:* Ametrine, carnelian, red jasper
Hanged Man XII – Law of Reversal	**XII – Sacrifice - Aeracura**
Surrender. Release. Timing. Victory and success is achieved by doing the opposite of what is expected. Salvation is attained by passive surrender rather than by assertiveness and forceful resistance. Let go, surrender, give it up. Assume a holding pattern when boxed in. You're in suspense, a limbo. Accept yourself – look at your shadow side. *Negative side: Tendency to despair, feel sorry for yourself, drown your sorrows in drink or abuse yourself.*	*Origin:* Celtic and Germanic goddess – Earth Mother and Fairy Queen. *Description:* Multitasks as deity and creates a bridge between earthly life and spiritual one. She helps put goals and challenges into perspective and eliminates needless stress. Assists artists and inventors. *Message: "Be patient with yourself and your process. Get outside and enjoy nature to help you rejuvenate. You may need rest, but don't give up as you're just getting started."* *Crystal:* Blue lace agate, moss agate and fuchsite
Death XIII – Law of Impermanence	**XIII – Transformation - Ceridwen**
Rebirth. Renewal. Cycles. All things must end. Accept it. Death can occur by a natural, evolutionary shedding, letting go or release. Shed what is dead in your life. Like the Scorpion, death is a life-giving transformation. *Negative side: To fear death is not to live.*	*Origin:* Welsh goddess of magic and transformation, known as dark goddess *Description:* Keeps the triple cauldron of transformation, inspiration and rebirth. She represents the womb of the Goddess from which all life manifests. She is the Wheel of Life. *Message: "Things are changing in your life. Something needs to die so it can be reborn in another form. Do not fear the change."* *Crystal:* Charoite, sunstone, moonstone

Major Arcana	The Goddess
Art XIV – Law of Creativity	**XIV – Balance - Sarasvati**
Consider yourself an artist in all areas and phases of life. Creativity is an alchemical art of dissolving old forms and recombining them into a new synthesis. Combine, put together, integrate and synthesize. Weave together new elements – revolutionize. Create and become naturally whole and healed. *Negative side: May become unbalanced, addicted to creativity.*	*Origin:* Hindu goddess of knowledge, learning, wisdom, music, arts. She embodies the wisdom of Devi. Her name means 'The Flowing One'. *Description:* She is the river of consciousness that enlivens creation as she dispels darkness of ignorance. She embodies the pure and sublime in nature. She's considered the originator of speech and of all of the arts. Her name means 'essence of the self'. *Message: "What you speak of with intention shall manifest. You are blessed with the creative power."* *Crystal:* Ammonite – fossil, fluorite, blue calcite
Devil's Play XV –Law of Celebration	**XV – Temptation - Laetitia**
Attachment. Desire. Live fully and joyously. Sense of humor, vitality, originality. Laugh your fears and sorrows away. Lift your spirits by passion and play. Recreate yourself through recreation. *Negative side: You risk stepping off the edge into intoxicated madness.*	*Origin:* Roman Goddess Description: Joy, gaiety, celebration, linked with holidays and festivals. Often found on coins in 3rd century. Known for common joy to all. Patron of the games. Message: *"I bring you joy. Celebrate the successes of your life.* Crystal: Rhodochrosite, sunrise aura quartz
Tower XVI – Law of Purification	**XVI – Oppression - Kali**
Change. Opportunity. Awareness. Revolutionary self-cleansing of all levels of your being. Purge your impurities. Burn out what does not belong in your life. See the mental patterns and beliefs you must destroy, see negative emotions to put to flame, and physical toxins to expurgate from your body. Melt down the old inner and outer structures.	*Origin:* Hindu goddess of the cycles of life – Triple goddess – virgin, mother and crone. Dark Mother – consort of Shiva. Image of the feminine – creation and destruction *Description:* The whole universe rests upon her, rises out of her and melts into her. She liberates souls. Rebirth, cycles, joy and courage are her themes. *Message: "You are ready to embrace your wholeness. You are the divine feminine – creator*

Major Arcana	The Goddess
Negative side: May lack the will of the warrior and project your anger and frustration onto others.	*and destructor. Fear not. You are ready to be wholly and authentically you."* *Crystal:* Black obsidian, pietersite
Star XVII – Law of Luminosity	**XVII- The Star - Venus**
Peace. Compassion. Miracles. You are the light. Shine like a star. Self-esteem comes with recognizing the star you are. Self-recognition brings attainment. Recognize your star light and you will succeed and star on all levels of being. Give of yourself with compassion in service to others so they may find their starlight. *Negative side: Spaced out, too far removed from your light to help yourself and others.*	*Origin:* Roman Goddess of Love *Description:* Venus represents charisma, charm, sensuality, discernment, calm, peace, love, beauty, sex, fertility, prosperity, and victory. She knows her truth and demonstrates strength and courage in that truth. She attracts, shines and selects who to show her love. *Message: "Bestows peace, love and beauty to all who call upon her."* *Crystal:* Rose quartz, amazonite
Moon XVIII – Law of Cycles	**XVIII- Moon – Maeve**
Mystery. Imagination. The Goddess. Allow yourself to experience gentle, conservative evolutionary changes. Inner changes through contemplation will in time quietly usher in a new phase. Conservative change. Quiet, smooth, flowing and ever-changing. You are naturally psychic, particularly at night. Cultivate your dreams. *Negative side: Emotional instability.*	*Origin:* Celtic goddess of femininity. Queen of the Fay. Uses feminine powers of persuasion. *Description:* Cycles, rhythms, fertility, sexuality, phases of a woman's life, go with emotional flow. Powerful magic, very wise, warrior goddess, balances white and black magic. *Message: "Pay attention to the cycles and rhythms of your life for they hold the keys to your personal power. Call on me when you need strength to take action in a sticky situation."* *Crystal:* Black moonstone
Sun XIX – Law of Life	**XIX – The Sun - Rhiannon**
Vitality. Creativity. The God. Be alive, animate and active. You are awake. Your mind is alert, your body light and your heart sunny. Move with purpose. Be a full participant in the dance of life. You have great power and influence. You are a life force.	*Origin:* Welsh goddess of the sun and inspiration. Divine Queen of sovereignty and governance. *Description:* Pulls the Sun across the sky very day. Represents accumulated wisdom, supernatural will, ambition, power and strategy. Sorceress.

Major Arcana	The Goddess
Negative side: Burn out by ignoring your inner life.	*Message:* "*You are a magical person who can manifest your clear intentions into reality.*" *Crystal:* Amazonite, danburite, howlite
Time-Space XX – Law of Karma	**XX – Time Space – Xi Wang Mu**
Destiny. Chance. Karma. *Traditionally known as judgment card.* Direct the course of your life by examining and altering psychological and behavioral problems. Live in a world of cause and effect. Through your vision, alter the future and redirect your karma. *Negative side: Space out and ignore physical and worldly needs and responsibilities.*	*Origin:* Shamanic great goddess of China. Her peaches grow every 3,000 years on the Tree of Life *Description:* The tree is a cosmic axis between heaven and earth, a ladder traveled by spirits and shamans. She controls time and space. *Message:* "*The exquisite creations shall stand the test of time and offer a legacy of comfort, encouragement and divine grace for generations to come.*" *Crystal:* Stromatolite
Universe XXI – Law of Universality	**XXI – The World - Gaia**
Completion. Attainment. Mastery. You are the universe. You carry the universe in your genes. You possess within yourself a universe of possibilities. You are whole and perfect. Always in a state of becoming, you are simultaneously completing and beginning. *Negative side: Overloaded with possibilities, you become paralyzed.*	*Origin:* Greek goddess of the earth. *Description:* Created herself out of primordial chaos. Working to achieve harmony and balance. She heals, nurtures and supports all of life on this planet. *Message:* "*There is a type of spiritual power you can co-create which benefits and protects you while mutually empowering others to take the journey and experience divine success.*" *Crystal:* Agate (any and all), ocean jasper, smoky quartz

Tarot card spread

The card spread for deepening your connection involves the following 3 cards. You may use the Tarot cards and relate the meaning to both the Tarot and the Goddess.

What archetype is your natural expression? Who are you when things go smoothly?	*What do you need to handle the lows or the contractions in life?*	*What energy helps strengthen your connection to the flow in the cycles of life?*

You can amplify this energy with the following guided meditation.

Tarot Card and Goddess Energy Meditation
Before you begin, look at your cards and read the messages. You may use all three or choose one. Refer to the Goddess energy for each.
Now, take a deep cleansing breath and expel anything that no longer serves you. You're here for you and only you. You're centered and grounded, relaxed and open to the healing energies of the Tarot and Goddess. You're in a place of pure white crystalline light aligning your body, heart, mind and soul. You're filled with gratitude for all of the blessings in your life.
As you continue to breathe, picture the white pure loving light of universal source above your head. This white light opens the top of your head and enters your crown chakra. As you inhale and exhale, this light travels from source through your crown and into your third eye - opening it to be all seeing. You can now see the unseen and know the unknown. Third eye wide open. Third eye wide open. Third eye wide open.

Tarot Card and Goddess Energy Meditation

Breathing fully, this universal source light goes into your throat chakra, brightening it as this pure white light clears your voice to allow you to speak your authentic truth without apology. As you continue to breathe with this light, you can feel your heart chakra expand will all of the love of the universe. It swells in this glory of love and support of all that is. Next, this light enters your solar plexus – powering your will and sparking your yang energy to take action.

Now, welcome this light into your sacral chakra – the chakra that brings you joy and helps let go of your fears. Finally, your root chakra – the manifestation one creating your life in this physical realm. The light completes its journey by diving deeply into the earth.

You know what happens next. This pure crystalline light grabs all of the nutrients from Mother Earth, travels through all of your chakras and out of your crown. The light then connects to universal source and recreates its journey down your chakras into the earth. This channel clears, balances and aligns all of your chakras and blends with the healing of the earth and spiritual source of all that is.

As you breathe, you are connected to Mother Earth and all of her goodness. You are connected to the divine and all of its miracles. You are connected to you and all of your magnificence. And, you're connected to the energy of the Tarot and Goddess.

Remember the images, your messages and the Goddess.

See this images and messages from your cards.

Envision the Goddess before you.

As you breathe, you can feel the loving and supportive energy of the cards.

Feel your connection.

See the Goddess.

Revel in the feeling of being in the presence of this deep loving energy.

Make any notes in your journal.

Deepening your connection involves recognizing the natural flow of the universe and allowing these cycles. Increasing the gratitude expression in your life and using magical tools can help improve your ability to deal with your fear of contraction.

Inner Child and Self-Love

"Our first and last love is self-love." – Christian Nestell Bovee

When you imagine self-love, you feel the love, kindness and compassion of the universe. You feel nurtured, safe and secure.

When you think of joy, you think of fun, wonder and the feeling of freedom.

Combining these feelings create true joy – one where your foundation is solid and you're free to fly to the highest points.

There are ways to discover your joy and you'll explore them.

There are methods to increasing self-love and you'll delve into those as well.

Self-Love

To experience the feelings of self-love and joy, you may be reminded of the innocence of childhood.

In this next exercise, you're going to meet your inner child. *(I'll use she as the pronoun for simplicity sake).*

She's happy and healthy and welcoming your visit.

Meet your Inner Child

An inner child is in each one of you. You cannot ignore her, ask her to be quiet or make her go away. She's in every cell of your body - in every single cell. She's part of you – ingrained, intertwined and interwoven.

You need to reach out to her. Ask her to show herself.

You need to get to know her.

Who is she?

What does she want and need?

What does she have to say?

You want to welcome her into your life.

Invite her into your daily life.

Ask her to go with you on fun trips, adventures and even to work.

Ask her to get ready in the morning when you take a shower, have breakfast and start your day.

Ask her to accompany you throughout the day, then to eat dinner with you and climb into bed.

Say good night to her in the evening and then good morning upon waking.

Start a relationship. One filled with love, care and tenderness.

Get to know her and get to know yourself.

For this guided meditation, you're going to bond with the love, kindness and compassion of Kuan Yin. Connect to her image and feel her mothering influence.

Meeting Your Inner Child Meditation

Take a deep cleansing breath and expel anything that no longer serves you. You're here, present, centered and grounded. You're in a safe space, one of white light, pure intentions, clear thoughts, positive emotions and relaxed physicality. You're at peace in every part of you.

As you continue to breathe, welcome yourself into this space — you're here for you and only for you. You're going to be filled with the love and support of Kuan Yin in this moment.

As you breathe, you're going to clear yourself in the form of a bright white pure loving light and picture it entering your root chakra. This cleansing illuminates and heals your root chakra and then your sacral one. Next, your solar plexus and your heart. You can feel your heart chakra expand with all of the love of the universe. It swells in the glory of the strength and support of all that is. Your throat chakra brightens as this pure white light clears your voice to allow you to speak your authentic truth without apology. Now it goes into your third eye, opening it to be all seeing. You can now see the unseen and know the unknown. Third eye wide open. Third eye wide open. Third eye wide open. You can see Kuan Yin's image in your mind's eye. She is here in your presence at this moment. As you breathe in her energy, the white light blends with Kuan Yin's loving energy and continues its journey. It goes to your crown chakra opening it wide and connecting to the energy of all of the loving kindness and compassion available to the world.

Kuan Yin's compassion, blended with the pure white light, sends her beautiful loving kindness energy back down into your crown chakra through your third eye, throat, heart, solar plexus, sacral, root and going into the ground beneath you. The universal love and compassion travels deeply into the core of the earth. As you breathe, feel the connection between the earthly and universal realms going through your body — grounding and connecting you. You're filled with the loving kindness of the pure white light.

Meeting Your Inner Child Meditation

Knowing you're safe, supported and loved, you're now going to meet your inner child. You're safe. Any emotions that arise have no power. You're completely safe.

With your third eye wide open, your crown chakra connected to the spiritual realm and your root chakra connected to the earth's heart, you are going to see your inner child. In your mind's eye, ask your inner child to let herself be known to you. It's safe, you won't hurt her. She's totally safe. You're totally safe. Can you see her? Where is she? What is she doing? What does she look like?

Your inner child is asking you to listen to her. What does she have to say? As you breathe, listen — quietly and patiently. What does she have to say? Will she tell you? Let her know you are here for her and will listen to everything she has to say. Sit quietly in front of her, take one of her hands and gently caress it, if she'll let you. Apologize for not paying attention to her sooner. Say you're sorry for not listening before now. Let her know that you are here and you're not going anywhere. What does she have to say?

Once you hear her, thank her for her messages. Hug her. Tell her you love her. Tell her she is beautiful, strong and perfect. Tell her you love her again. Let her know she is safe, supported and loved. Let her see Kuan Yin with you. Let her feel Kuan Yin's love for both of you.

Now let her know you need to be going now, but will come back very, very soon. Let her know Kuan Yin will be staying with her. Tell her you will be listening to her more often, you will be asking her to come out and play, you will be talking with her and loving her.

Hug her again.

Let her feel your love for her. Give her a kiss and a smile.

Now that you've seen her, you know she's just a child. One who seeks comfort. One who wants support. One who needs love.

Meeting Your Inner Child Meditation

You also know she's part of you – always. Your love, support and compassion for her is love, support and compassion for you.

Drench yourself with the love, kindness and compassion of Kuan Yin. Feel it in every fiber of your being. You're bringing this level of love to yourself and your inner child from this point forward.

Take a few deep breaths in the splendor of the loving kindness.

Make a commitment to yourself – one of love. Thank your inner child and Kuan Yin.

As you take your next breath, bring your awareness back to the room.

When you're ready, open your eyes and gaze softly in front you – seeing nothing, yet aware of everything. If you'd like, wiggle your fingers and toes and do any gentle stretching your body requires. Breathe in again and open your eyes fully.

Make any notes in your journal.

Loving your inner child helps you love yourself. Embrace her and embrace yourself. You can also enhance your feelings of self-love by choosing it. You can choose to love yourself. Let's look at ways to do this.

Choose Self-Love

o   State positive affirmations every morning in the mirror.

"I am a gift."

"I love myself deeply and fully."

"I am lovable."

"The universe loves me."

298

"I am worthy of love."

"Love is my birthright. I am loved."

"I am enough."

"I am loving and loved by many."

○ Set an intention for self-love.

Write down your intention to love yourself.

Perform a ritual during a new moon.

Celebrate yourself during this ritual by creating a sacred space and luxuriating in it.

Meditate on your self-love intention.

○ Embrace a Goddess of Love.

Aphrodite is the Greek Goddess of love and passion. She epitomizes beauty, joy, passion and pleasure. She is associated with Venus and wants you to bask in your inner Goddess.

Freya is the Norse Goddess of beauty, love and destiny. She fully embraces her inner power. She is known for her boldness and bravery.

Inanna is the Babylon Goddess of war and sexual love and is the personification of Venus. She is the feminine in its fullness – the entire creation cycle of creativity and destruction.

Oonagh is the ancient Celtic Goddess of love, nature and relationships. She loves to dance and move her body. She represents transitions, creativity and magical guidance.

o Stop comparing yourself to others.

Seriously, get off of those social media sites. Close your laptop, turn off your iPad or phone and remove yourself from the input of others' movie lives. They're presenting their very best selves online and you're living your b-reel. Life is real and the reality is not being represented on social media. Remind yourself of this fact when you feel yourself being knocked down as you're comparing the traction of your life with others.

o Celebrate your successes.

Get a piece of paper or a notebook and make a listing of things you've done that you're proud of. Write down more than accomplishments. Write down those times you feel good about yourself. Write down your choices that've been right for you. Write down those times you chose yourself. These are your successes.

Look at your list. Look at all of the things you have accomplished and those times you've chosen yourself.

Think of a way to celebrate YOU.

Do a bigger celebration now and then each time you choose yourself – do a small one that's meaningful to you. It could be something simple like taking a walk, looking at the moon, smelling the flowers or having a cup of tea. It could be connecting with friends, having a beautiful dinner or buying yourself a treat.

o Lean into the energies of crystals and stones for love and support.

Rose quartz - calms, soothes and fosters love of self and others. It also encourages compassion. This stone eases emotions and releases tension.

Rhodochrosite - is a stone of selfless love and compassion. Helps you to feel loved, removes denial and allows for emotional release. Confronts issues, reveals emotions and soothes emotional stress.

Rhodonite - is a stone of grace and elegance. It opens the heart chakra and promotes self-love. It assists in personal growth, creates calms and brings confidence.

Infuse a crystal with your loving energy.

Meditate with it and feel its loving energy.

Carry it with you in your purse or backpack.

○ Ask Kuan Yin or Mother Mary for their loving kindness and compassion.

Kuan Yin is an Ascended Master who chose to stay on Earth to help healing. She is a divine and loving mother of mercy and compassion. She offers healing, guidance and forgiveness. She has gentle and nourishing energy. Relate to Kuan Yin through the energies of either amethyst, jade or rose quartz.

Mother Mary is Mother of the World and Queen of the Angels. She helps with enlightenment, evolvement and growth. She also opens the feminine principle and is involved in spiritual healings. She is the

301

connector of miracles. You can bond with her through the energy of blue lace agate.

o   Buy yourself flowers regularly. Peonies and roses are good choices as they promote self-love.

Delve into Water to Explore Joy

Water is nourishing, relaxing and refreshing. It's also strengthening, psychically empowering and invigorating.

These are the same elements of joy. Relating to water helps you find joy in your life.

With the various bodies of water on Earth, you can envision water's influence.

Oceans are strengthening.

Rivers are empowering.

Streams are invigorating.

Lakes are nourishing.

Ponds are relaxing.

Rain is refreshing.

Lean into water's influence through the following exercises.

Water Exercises

- Go swimming.
- Take a bath.
- Drink lots of water.
- Meditate with either ocean jasper or selenite.
- Walk in the rain and jump in puddles.
- Plunge your feet into a foot bath.
- Relate to a water deity such as; Goddess Coventina, a Celtic water goddess or Goddess Sedna, an Alaskan goddess of the sea.
- Envision water relating to joy in your life.

Do the following visualization with the element of water.

Water Visualization

Get into a comfortable position and turn off your phone. You don't need to sit in lotus position on the floor — a comfortable cushion, couch or chair will do just fine. Settle yourself into your seated position.

Close your eyes and take a nice refreshing breath by inhaling deeply and exhaling gently. Take another deep breath in and gently breathe out, slowly expelling all of the air out of your lungs. Surround yourself with protective white light directly from the source energy of the Universe. You are protected at all times.

Imagine the ocean as you walk onto a beach. You're safely on the sand with the Sun shining and a gentle breeze blowing as it ruffles your hair. You see the waves crashing on shore and notice the waves retreat as the ocean pulls itself back. You see only suds remain on the water's edge as the waves move forward and back, forward and back.

You align your breathing with the movement of the waves. You feel the power, strength and movement — of the water and of life. There's a natural flow of the Universe — there's a rhythm, a cycle and its flow.

Water Visualization

You feel the power of breath — it's life-giving, refreshing and invigorating. You know this is the same as the ocean. Water and air — both nourishing, sustaining and ever-lasting.

As you breathe in and out, you focus your attention on the ocean. You notice the sunshine glistening off of its surface. As the water moves, you notice ripples of color.

They look like a rainbow. There's a rainbow of color.

See the color red on the water's surface and understand this color supports your physical needs. Red means passion, power and strength. Let red wash over you completely. Know all of your physical needs are met and exceeded. You feel passionate, powerful and strong. Feel your passion. Feel your power. Feel your strength. Integrate these feelings throughout your being.

See the color orange in front of you and understand this color supports your emotional desires. Orange means joy. Let the color orange spread throughout you completely. Know all of your emotional desires are supported. You feel joyful. Integrate this feeling throughout your being.

See the color yellow in front of you and understand this color supports your will. Yellow represents energy and happiness. Let the color stretch around and within you. Know your will power expands and deepens to fuel your passion. Feel your energy. Feel your happiness. Integrate these feelings throughout your being.

See the color green in front of you and understand this color supports your heart as it fills with love. Green means healing and growth. Let the color green spread throughout you completely. Know your love fills your entire being — mind, body and soul. Allow the feelings of health and vitality flow throughout your being.

See the color blue in front of you and understand this color supports your voice. Blue means trust and wisdom. Know the truth you speak. Let the color blue spread from your throat to every cell in your body. Know each cell hears your voice and follows its vibration and sound. Allow your truth to flow throughout your being.

See the color purple in front of you and understand this color supports your intuition. Purple represents nobility and spirituality. Let the color purple fill every area of your being. Know your intuition is strong, clear and powerful.

See the color white in front of you and understand this color connects you to the universal energy. Let the color white spread from the top of your head to the sky above you. Know you are connected to the universe.

You sense your body filling with white light. You feel nourished, rejuvenated and connected. You see a rainbow of colors – red, orange, yellow, green, blue and purple swim around you and the ocean.

Take a deep rejuvenating breath.

When you're ready, return your attention to your body and notice the chair beneath you.

You continue to breathe gently allowing yourself to quietly come back to the room. Open your eyes and softly gaze in front of you.

You feel alive, yet at peace. You are ready to reenter your day.

Journal any thoughts about the feeling of joy.

Quiet Joy, Loud Joy

As with the other elements, water has a flow. It's both active and passive. Joy is part of water, so has the same flow. It requires both action and allowance.

It's the passionate component to joy that's often overlooked. It has a forward motion. It's dependent upon feeling good about yourself or the attainment of a desire. It's exuberant. It's edgy. It requires a jolt of thrill to experience.

This is what I call loud joy.

On the other hand, joy also means *a state of happiness or a source of delight.*

There's a more passive and quieter component to joy. This is the one most commonly known. It's soft, content and calm. This is quiet joy.

So, joy is both quiet and loud. Let's explore both.

Quiet Joy

Think of something that gives you great pleasure and doesn't take any effort or material expense to incorporate into your life. This thing or activity should make you smile, should lift your heart a little bit and NOT give you any feelings of guilt over incorporating it into your life.

So, I don't want you to go out and buy that brand-new Kate Spade bag you've had your heart set on for the last few months. This step in finding your joy isn't about an excuse for a shopping spree or spending any money.

This step is about giving yourself joy on a daily or weekly basis. For me, I absolutely love flowers and buy a bouquet when I do the weekly marketing. Every time I look at the flowers, it gives my heart a little lift and I feel a tad indulgent.

For you, perhaps, you love candles, music, chai tea or ice cream cones.

Think of something small and really easy to obtain or do, but near and dear to your heart.

Here are some ideas:

Quiet Joy Ideas
Use fun pens
Chew refreshing mints
Go out for coffee with a friend
Eat chocolates
Ride your bike
Take foot baths
Write notes with elegant stationary
Drink smoothies
Chomp bubblegum
See movies
Take long walks
Tend to plants
Savor luscious fruits & berries
Bake a yummy dessert
Read a really good magazine
Buy funny magnets
Take bubble baths
Use fresh herbs
Indulge in gourmet cheeses
Do your own nails
Read books
Take a nap

Pick a few ideas and make sure you incorporate them into your life on a daily or weekly basis.

You want to experience pleasure regularly and effortlessly. Write your ideas for quiet joy and then note how often you will indulge yourself.

Loud Joy

Now think of something that makes you feel TRIUMPHANT. Yes, triumphant.

For this exercise, you don't need to achieve a single thing. In fact, I don't want you to put any effort into an end result. This should be effortless and produce nothing but fun.

For me, I turn on the music full blast in my car and then sing as loudly and robustly as I can along with the music. This blows out any cobwebs in my head and lifts my spirits no matter what the circumstances. So, how can you sound your barbaric yawp?

Here are some ideas:

Loud Joy Ideas
Roll down a grassy hill
Sing in the shower
Laugh out loud
Swing
Run while waving your arms in the air
Skip
Hula hoop
Twirl
Play hopscotch
Dance
Ride your bike
Honk your car horn
Climb a tree
Go to an outdoor concert
Gallop
Go to an amusement park
Roller blade
Play kickball
Jump rope

Pick something from this list or another idea and do it today – right now. Experience your feeling of triumph.

Hello joy – you quiet and loud friend. Welcome.

People Weaving

"Have you been best friends for 20 years or were you best friends 20 years ago?"

When deepening your connection toward joy, the people in your life come up for review. You may hear advice about the people in your life.

- "Just spend time with people who make you happy."

- "Get rid of all of the people who bring you down and your life will be better."

- "Smile all of the time and you will have a happier life."

These lines are sprinkled throughout books about being happier and living your very best life and they're good advice for people who live in a world filled with rainbows and moonbeams.

For the rest of you, however, there's reality and that reality includes all types of people in all kinds of moods. In this reality, people come in all shapes and sizes and bring all of their own stuff into your life on a daily basis.

310

These people are your family members, spouses, partners, bosses, clients, coworkers, friends, employees, neighbors, relatives, acquaintances, parents of your child's friends, store clerks, drivers, customer services representatives, hair stylists, waiters, coaches, …you get the idea – LOTS of people, LOTS and LOTS of people.

Now getting rid of the people who aggravate you or bring you down may not be practical.

Only spending time with people who make you happy may carve the list of people you deal with down to so few that you create an incredibly solitary life.

Smiling all of the time? Well, that may make you look like the village idiot in the face of that teenage clerk who snidely shoves all of your groceries into the bag on top of your eggs.

So, how can you move toward joy in the face of all of these daily interactions with people, who quite frankly, create aggravation, bring chaos or just annoy the crap out of you?

Well, thankfully, there is a way and the first step is to figure out how the people in your life affect you.

For this step, you need to create a list that separates the people in your life by layer and then by category. The layers are basically the relationship that these people have to you. The categories are how they affect you. Classifying people by both criteria is useful, as your responses should change dramatically depending upon where that person fits into your life.

People in Your Life

There are people in your life on a daily basis. Those who have impact on your life and those who don't. Typically, you interact most with people who actually don't have any real impact on your life. So, let's look at who has real impact and who doesn't.

Impact
Intimates, best friends, good friends, close relatives, close acquaintances, bosses, clients, co-workers.

No Impact
Facebook friends and other social media connections, former friends, acquaintances, neighbors, parents of your children's friends, people at your yoga or fitness studio, clerks, teachers or administration at your children's school and general public.

Qualities of People Affecting Your Life
What qualities do you want the impactful people in your life to have? What characteristics are important to you at this stage?

Layers of People

The layers involve:

Layer	Type of People
Intimate	Spouses, romantic partners, children, relatives living with you, best friends, soul mates
Hold Over You	Immediate family members who are older than you, bosses, long-term clients
Bonding	Good friends, coworkers, teachers, classmates, intimate healing practitioners
You Control	Extended family, neighbors, employees or vendors
Not Lasting	Acquaintances, clerks, waiters, instructors, other parents, drivers on the road, Facebook only friends, Linked In contacts, basically the general public

Categories of People

It's not surprising that the categories are:

Positive	Neutral	Negative

More specifically, for each category, ask yourself some of the following questions:

- Positive
    - Do these people make you feel happy, safe, supported, loved, interesting, curious, energized, youthful, vibrant, joyful, or light-hearted?
    - Do they make you laugh?
    - Do you WANT to see them and wish you could see them more often?
    - Do you have fun with them?
    - Do they make you feel better for having seen them?
    - Do they listen to you and I mean really listen?
    - Are they willing to help you if you were to ask them?
    - Do you feel that the time has flown when you're with them and you find yourself wishing you could extend your time with them?

- Neutral
    - Do these people have absolutely no impact on you whether you see them or not?

313

- o If you see them, do you put them out of your mind immediately once they're gone from your physical presence?
- o If you don't see them, do you think about seeing them at all?

This is neither good or bad, it just is. There are some people who don't impact you either way and noting it is important as you may be giving these people more time than they deserve. Alternatively, some of these people in this category may be in your second category of family members, bosses or clients. If this is the case, good for you. They don't press any hot buttons – yay you!

- ▪ Negative
  - o Do these people aggravate, annoy, irritate, or anger you?
  - o Do they sap your energy and strength?
  - o Do they make you feel sad, uncomfortable or out of sorts?
  - o Do they make you feel emotionally unsafe?
  - o Do you find yourself NOT being yourself when you're with them?
  - o Do you put off seeing them?
  - o Do you talk about them in negative terms when they're not around?

Think about **how** the people in the first three layers affect you and make a quick note next to their name.

Seriously, spend some time categorizing the people who are in your first three layers of relationship: intimate, hold over and bond. These are the relationships that have the greatest ACTUAL impact on your life. The other relationship layers may be the ones that you spend a lot of time and energy on and they should have little *actual* impact on your life.

By combining the layers and categories, you can start to formulate a pattern of who's in which category and how you can either celebrate the relationship or change it to fit into your life more effectively.

So, let's make a table of these layers and categories I think you'll be surprised by how many people you allow to affect your life who should, in fact, have no lasting effect on it.

Once you realize this, you can adjust your reactions and responses according to how much effort you want to put into these relationships.

Conversely, I think you may also be surprised by how much time you're giving to people who really do not positively impact you and how little you give to those who do.

People Table Exercise

Here's a blank table for you to fill out the names of people who fit into each category. Spend the majority of your time on the first 3 layers: intimate, hold and bond.

Layer	Categories: Positive	Neutral	Negative
Intimate: *Who lives w/ you? Spouse, partner(s), children, parents, relatives, siblings, roommates* *Best friends &/or soul mates*			
Hold Over You: *Immediate family (not living w/you and older*			

Layer	Categories: Positive	Neutral	Negative
than you) & people who pay you: bosses, long-term clients			
Bond: *Good friends, coworkers, teachers, classmates, intimate healing practitioners*			
You Hold/Control: *Relatives, not living with you, neighbors, employees, vendors*			
Not Lasting: *Acquaintances, coaches, instructors, other parents, clerks, waiters, Facebook only friends, social media contacts, basically general public*			

Next, you're going to explore the different ways to handle how people affect you in each layer and category combination. You'll be spending the most time dissecting the first three layers and making suggestions on how to handle those who negatively impact you in these relationships.

In the meantime, after you make your list, call up one of your friends you haven't seen in a while who you miss and makes you feel great. Have so much fun!

Your Response to Your People

In the previous step, you talked about the people in your life and you had an opportunity to identify who they are, their relationship to you and your reaction to them.

In this exercise, you're going to go through each layer and category combination to employ strategies to deal with those individuals who drive you crazy, to appreciate those people who have very little influence on your life and to value those who have a positive impact.

Your overall goal is to spend time with people who lift you up and if you need to spend time with those who have a negative effect on you, then to turn adverse **reactions** into positive **responses**.

As an overview, there are 5 layers and 3 categories, so there are 15 combinations. The first 3 layers are connected to you in some lasting way and the last 2 are not. Basically, if there is negativity in your inner layers (1st 3), you need to deal with your reactions and it could be a big deal. If there is negativity in your outer layers, this should be easier to deal with, so my advice is to do it quickly and easily or let it go. You have many more valuable things to do with your time and energy.

Conversely, if there is great positive influence in your outer layers, there may be people you want to spend more time with, so identifying those people and reaching out could create more joy in your life.

NOTE: This is a long and in some cases, arduous process. My advice is to take it in stages. If you have someone in your 'outer' world who's annoying you, take care of it right away or let it go. However, if it's someone in your 'inner world', take your time. Do this in bite size pieces.

Let's get right to it.

Layer/Category Combination Detail:
(There is an exercise at the end.)

Intimate People

Who lives with you? This layer involves everyone who lives in your home. It could be your partner, your spouse, your friend(s), your children, your parents, your parent(s)-in-law, other relatives, and/or your pets.

This layer is near and dear. It's as intimate as it gets. Your home is sacred and you should feel safe, supported, loved, respected, and cherished when at home.

Yet, every one of the people who live with you could be going through something; toddlerhood, teenage years, menopause, illness, job stress, an emotional crisis, etc.

So, when thinking of these people and their impact on you, think over the long term and look for any trends.

If they're typically positive, but have few moments of negative, put them into the positive category. Yet, if they are typically negative with few positive, then put them into the negative category.

Positive

This is great. If your intimates are positive, then sing from the rooftops and enjoy, enjoy, enjoy! You have nothing to do unless you want to let them know how much you love them and how thankful you are they are in your life.

Neutral

For this layer, we need sub-layers because if your live-in in-laws have neutral impact – hooray, but if your partner or spouse does, then that's not good.

Spouse/partner

The first questions you need to ask yourself are, "How long has my spouse/partner been in the neutral category?" and "Do I want him or her to be there or do I want more out of my relationship?"

If you're satisfied with a neutral relationship, then that works for you and you can look at the other relationships in your life.

Yet if you want more from your partner relationship, then you need to explore this for yourself. In this case, I suggest taking some time to figure when and how the relationship has become stale, determine what you want from a partnership relationship and lay out a description of your needs as best you can. I also suggest coming up with proposed solutions.

Remember, all of this is from your perspective, so be ready to hear things from your partner that you may need to do as well.

Now you know I'm not a therapist, so seeking someone to talk to may be the best in this situation. What I am suggesting here is that finding your joy is much more difficult with an unsatisfactory partner relationship, so you either want to isolate it or make some changes.

Children

If you're neutral about your children, I want to ask, 'How did you accomplish that?' I'm anything but neutral. Seriously, if your children are in the throes of toddlerhood or the teenage years, then neutrality is your friend. Embrace it.

However, if they're not and you're chronically neutral about them, then you may want to delve into how you're feeling about your life in general. You may be experiencing a situation where you may need to talk to someone professional about what is going on with you right now.

If you have a neutral response to anyone else who is living with you – YAY you. You've achieved a Zen-like state to which all of us can aspire. Stay the course.

If it's a pet, then perhaps those family members who begged you to get said pet should help you take care of it. Pets are loveable to everyone who doesn't hold all of the responsibilities of caring for them. Sometimes they are lovable to those people too. If you're not one of those people, get your family members to help!

Negative

In this intimate layer, anyone who you have a negative response to needs to be dealt with and it may be a delicate and complex process. Take this seriously and take it slowly. And always seek support when you need it. Remember, I'm not a therapist, I just want to help you find your joy.

My advice is to make it about you and your feelings without being judgmental or accusatory.

You need to ask yourself three (3) questions:

1. Can I walk away from the issues and let them go, but keep the relationship intact?

2. If I can't let the issues go, can I change my negative reactions into positive responses when issues arise and do this on my own without confrontation?

3. If I need to confront the issues with my partner/spouse/live-in parent, how can I do this and get the best result for me?

Try the first two options before going to the third one. The third option is never fun or easy.

1) If you need help letting the issues go, then you have a few choices such as; writing down your issues and feelings in a journal to gain clarity and objectivity, talking out your feelings and issues with a close friend for same, and/or seeking support from a therapist for same.

#2) This also holds true for the first step in changing your negative reactions into positive responses. However, there's more to it than just gaining clarity and objectivity.

Here are a few tips:

- Determine what's making you crazy. Exactly what are the specifics that are annoying you to the point of negatively affecting your life?

- Figure out the origin. Figure out the history. When did this situation begin? What underlies the issue? What hot buttons does it push for you? Are these hot buttons directly or indirectly related to the other person or situation?

- Does it even have anything to do with the person pushing your hot buttons?

- What can you do to defuse these hot buttons?

- Do you need help with the underlying issue from an outsider or a professional?

This is for you alone.

You're reacting to things that may not have anything to do with the person who's pushing your buttons. Disentangling it from the other person is actually very helpful in changing your negative reactions. It makes in much simpler to work on your responses, then embroiling another person in something that they do not need to be embroiled.

#3) So it is really the other person. If you can't walk away and need to confront the situation, here are a few guidelines:

- When confronting the situation, be mindful that you're confronting the situation, not the person.

- Make it about your needs, your feelings, your perceptions and your interpretations of their words and actions.

- Know what your objective is and specifically what your needs are.

- Be calm and as objective as possible.

- Write it all down first so it's as clear and straightforward as possible.

- Get a reaction of your draft from a friend or relative. You want to make sure that you're not being accusatory or lashing out in anger. You want to defuse the issue not fire it up. You want to be heard. You want to achieve your objective of peace and harmony in your home.

- Invoke some positive into the dialogue. Remember this is your spouse, partner, child or live-in parent. This person is in an intimate relationship with you and he/she deserves respect and dignity even if he/she is driving you crazy.

- Be calm. Be calm. Be calm.

- Try to insulate yourself from a completely immature response. You're taking the high road in this situation by being calm, objective and stating everything in a manner that reflects you, not them. However, not everyone has this ability. This is a talent that needs to be learned and you're the instructor right now. The person you're confronting may become angry, defensive, or belligerent. Walk away if you need to and come back to it when they have calmed down. Conversely, this person may be calm, but pick apart your points or even worse be deliberately obtuse. Depending upon the situation, you need to decide what to do with the relationship at this point. Get help. Get support. Get relief.

- Have an outlet for your feelings.

- Depend upon friends to be supportive to help you through this. This isn't easy.

- Respect yourself and your needs. That's of utmost importance.

Children

The above still holds true, however, remember you're the adult in the relationship and it's ALWAYS your responsibility to take the higher road, to be compassionate, and to demonstrate unconditional love. You're still entitled to your feelings and issues, but you're the parent. Period. End.

Hold Over You

Immediate family (not living w/ you) & people who pay you: bosses, clients

Positive

Yippee. How lucky are you? Enjoy.

Neutral

Good for you. You have relationships with people that could be fraught with anxiety and angst and are not. I recommend keep doing what you're doing. So, you think you want to be closer to your boss, clients or immediate family? Think again. You have the right response to people who could be pushing your hot buttons. Relax into your neutrality and focus on other relationships that may deserve more attention, time and care.

Negative

Sub-layers are necessary for this category as well.

Immediate Family

Ugh. This is messy and complex. Refer to the negative partner/spouse combination above.

Bosses

Okay, so your boss is awful to you. Is he/she really or are your hot buttons being pushed, so it's really about you and not him/her? Refer to the section above for ways to gain clarity and to change your negative reactions into positive responses.

If, however, your boss is just really awful, you may need to try to change the situation. If you have an HR department, you could talk to them about your issues. Be calm, be professional, be objective. If you don't have an HR department, is there a mentor type person, either in the company or outside, you can talk to who can help you with your situation? If so, reach out to them in a professional and objective manner. Be fair. Be concise. Be ready to know what kind of help you're asking them for – is it advice? Is it to stand up for you? Is it to help you find something else?

If you can't get relief and your situation with your boss taking over your life, you need to look at your situation and determine if you can make some changes. Do you need to find another job? If so, update your resume and hit the pavement. Take your time. Be smart. You deserve better.

Clients

Get a new one. I know this sounds easier said than done, but seriously get a new client. Life is way too short and work is way too hard to be dealing with a client who's just awful to deal with. Work with them for as long as you have to, but work harder on getting a new client. Sometimes money is just too expensive.

Bonding

Friends & coworkers

Positive

I just love having positive friends and co-workers. Really the only question is: do you spend enough time with these friends? If not, figure out how you can spend more time together.

Neutral

A neutral co-worker is perfect. A neutral friend, however, may not be. It depends. If the friend is a casual one, great, neutral isn't bad. Also, if the friend is part of the family-pack, then neutral is also not bad. (Family-pack: Your partner has a friend and this is his/her partner, or if your children have close friends and the families all get together – that is part of the family pack.)

If, however, you have a neutral relationship with a close friend, I would say start spending less time with this person. A close friend shouldn't be neutral in your life.

Negative

Friends

Okay, you need to ask yourself why you're actively engaged with the person. Is it because you have been friends for x years? Think about it. Have you been friends for x years or were you friends x years ago? This is a real question. Sometimes we lose sight that people come into our lives for a period of time, but they don't need to stay in our lives forever. This is hard, especially if one person has more of an attachment than the other. How often do you see this friend? Can you disentangle from this relationship delicately and without confrontation? Can you just be too busy with your life to see him or her? Can you just let it fall by the wayside? If so, this may be the way to go. If your friend has become a non-friend and it doesn't tie you up in knots, then I say let it go as gracefully as possible.

If, however, this person does tie you up in knots and you can't let it go without expressing your feelings, then go for it. Try to keep it objective. Try to keep it about you and your feelings and your responses.

Co-workers

You know what? You can just be busy if you don't want to deal with an irritating co-worker. You can make sure that you're not open or available for them to invite themselves into your life. If, however, they just drive you bat-shit crazy and you can't avoid them, you may want to say something.

Here are a few options:

- If you have an HR department, you can go to them. This is right up their alley and they should be able to handle it in the right way.

- You could go to your boss and delicately explain the situation. This obviously depends upon your relationship to your boss and his/her ability to handle personnel issues adequately.

- If neither of these are options, you probably and unfortunately need to say something to your co-worker. You need to be delicate, calm and objective. You need to be professional. You need to be above the fray. This isn't fun, nor is it easy. Practice what you want to say and then say it to a friend. Yes, you need to practice. You need to role play a little bit. You need to do this because you want to make this situation better, not worse. Chances are this co-worker drives everyone nuts, but talking behind his/her back, gossiping, or venting just gives this situation more energy. You want to defuse it, not wind it up. So, take a few deep breaths, go forth with a calm demeanor and start with your planned comment. Keep your fingers crossed and hope for the best. Seriously, good luck.

You Hold/Control

Relatives, neighbors, employees

Positive

It's always good when you have positive relationships with relatives, neighbors and employees. Fingers crossed they remain positive! Keep the relationship in integrity and don't cross any lines that you shouldn't cross with employees.

Neutral

No worries. This is great. Neutral relationships at this level are considered a positive thing.

Negative

Relatives

The only question is: how often do you see them? It's probably only for holidays and you're most likely with a number of other people. Avoid them. Seriously, don't let them get to you. It's not worth it. If you must say something, do so, move on and let it go.

Neighbors

Again, how often do you see them? Don't. You can easily avoid neighbors. Drive by and wave from your car. Done. If they insist on trying to get in touch with you to see you socially, tell them you're busy. You don't owe them anything more. You owe them to be neighborly, but not friendly. There's a difference. Respect and civility are easy commodities to dispense. Friendship is precious.

If your neighbor contacts you to complain about things, listen, and respond appropriately. Don't take unnecessary grief. If you or your children did something wrong, own up to it, fix it and move on. If you didn't, tell them and still move on.

Really the only thing to do here is let it go.

Employees

Okay, this is an area you need to handle delicately and professionally. Don't you wish you would have only positive relationships with your employees? But, alas, that's not the case. There are always people who push your buttons. If they're good employees and get the job done, suck it up. It's your issue, not theirs. Seriously, unless they're doing something out of line and you need to dispel discipline, suck it up and let it go.

If the employee is out of line or if they're not doing their job, you need to handle this. You need to follow the HR guidelines that your company has issued. Most times, the process involves an initial conversation, a verbal warning and then a written warning. Each step needs to outline the issue, your expectations, your deadline for change and the consequence if acceptable improvement isn't made in the allotted time. This is difficult to handle if you're not experienced in these types of situations. Seek help and support from your HR department or your boss. You need to handle this appropriately and professionally.

Not Lasting

Acquaintances, coaches, instructors, other parents, clerks, waiters, Facebook only friends, social media contacts, basically general public

Positive
Yay.

Neutral
Yay.

Negative
What's the issue here? These people don't have lasting impact on your life. Cranky clerk? Say something and move on. Other parents at your child's school? Avoid them. Waiter? Say something, tip appropriately, talk to a manager if necessary and move on. Social media contacts? Really? It's so easy to unfriend, unfollow, don't read or disengage.

The only issue here is how you react to people who affect you negatively in this category. In most cases, if there's a lasting negative impact, it's due to your response or lack thereof.

Response to Your People Exercise

Look at the table in the proceeding section for the names of your people in each category. Compare their names with the suggestions in the following table.

Highlight the names of the people you need to deal with and prioritize the list.

Take it slowly. You don't need to blow up all of your relationships at once (unless you actually really do).

Layer	Categories: Positive	Neutral	Negative
Intimate: *Who lives with you?*	Nice job. Stay in the flow. Tell them how great they make you feel.	Phew. Just go with it. If it's children, you may want to look into it a bit more deeply.	Ugh. This is messy and complex. Ask yourself 3 questions: * Walk away & let it go? * Change my negative reactions into positive responses without confrontation? * How can I confront and get the best result for me? Get outside help if needed.
Hold Over You: *Immediate family (not living with you) & people who pay you: bosses, clients*	Lucky you. Be so grateful.	Not bad. Take it in stride. It could be worse.	Ugh. This is messy and complex. Ask yourself 3 questions: * Walk away & let it go? * Change my negative reactions into positive responses without confrontation? * How can I confront and get

Layer	Categories: Positive	Neutral	Negative
			the best result for me? *Boss:* Do you need to change jobs? *Client:* Get a new one.
Bond: *Friends & coworkers*	Reach out and keep in touch with these people. Make sure you spend quality time with them.	Are you spending time with people who do not fill you with joy? Are there others you would rather spend time with instead?	Life is too short to spend time and energy on people who bring you down when you don't have to be with them. Coworker? Stay too busy to get involved. Friend? Avoid – tactfully if possible.
You Hold/Control: *Relatives, neighbors, employees*	Yay you. Is there anyone you want to see more regularly? Anyone you want to turn into a friend?	No worries. Stay steady. There is no need to change a thing.	Say something if it bothers you and you can do it without any adverse impact to you. If not, let it go. It's not worth getting into a huge ordeal.
Not Lasting: *Acquaintances, coaches, instructors, other parents, clerks, waiters, Facebook only friends, social media contacts,*	Smile. This is a great way to cruise through life. Ask yourself if there is anyone you want to reach	Since there is no impact, do not spend any time on this layer/category combination.	Who cares? Seriously, there is no lasting impact. If you want to say something, do. If not, walk away. In either case, let it go.

Layer	Categories: Positive	Neutral	Negative
basically general public	out to get to know better?		

The goal of this step is to create more joy in your life by changing your negative relationships into positive ones whenever possible.

Sometimes, you need to say good-bye to relationships that are no longer serving your best interests.

If you have a particularly difficult issue, get professional help if you need it.

Always rely on friends and positive family members to help you out.

Take this slowly and in bite size pieces.

This is a process.

Letting Go

If you need help letting go, lean into the energy of water. Water washes away and cleanses. It purifies and forgives. It refreshes and nourishes. All of these things are helpful as you're letting go. Recognize the letting go process is difficult.

Everyone has a tendency to hold on, but it's helpful to remember a quote from Lao Tzu, "When I let go of what I am, I become what I might be."

Let's say this again, "When I let go of what I am, I become what I might be."

You're letting go to make space for yourself.

You're letting go to become more of yourself.

You're letting go to bring more joy into your life.

Allow yourself to let go.

Let Go of Other's Input

Most of your thoughts and beliefs aren't your own. You've been conditioned to believe certain things that may not be true. When you feel yourself being brought down, remind yourself that these thoughts, beliefs or feelings aren't yours.

Say, "These are not my thoughts, beliefs or feelings, return to sender."

Say it as many times as it takes for you to believe it.

Let go of other's input.

Let Go of Other's Conditioning Beliefs

Same.

Let Go Exercises

Loving yourself means letting go.

Here are a few exercises to help you:

o Use the energy of water. Write down anything you'd like to get rid of, put the paper in an empty glass bottle and throw it into the ocean. Watch the waves carry it away.

o Allow yourself to feel your feelings, put Epsom salts in a bath and soak in the bathtub until you're feeling refreshed.

o Walk by the ocean or lake when you're feeling out of sorts about some people or circumstances in your life. Pick up a few stones and envision each person in your mind's eye. Throw the stones into the water and watch them sink to the bottom or wash away from the shore. You're letting go of these circumstances or these people and their input.

Attract Others

Once you remove those pesky people and let them go, you have more room to invite others into your life. The following guided meditation may help you attract people who're supportive, loving and interested in you and the happenings in your life.

Attract Others into Your Life Guided Meditation
Think of the people you love to be with. Picture them in your mind. Smile at their ways. Express gratitude for having them in your life. Anchor light and love for them in your heart.
Think of the type of people you would like to attract into your life. What characteristics do they have?
Close your eyes and take a nice cleansing breath. Inhale deeply and exhale fully. As you breathe, feel yourself sink more deeply into the seat beneath you. Feel your body relax as you take a few moments to be present with yourself.
You're here right now in this moment to quiet your mind, open your heart to welcome others into your life who love and support you.

Attract Others into Your Life Guided Meditation

Take a deep cleansing breath and envision this bright white pure light of Universal source coming down into the room and filling it completely with light and love.

Now picture your crown chakra opening at the top of your head. The pure crystalline light of universal source pours into your crown chakra and travels through all of your chakras, filling them deeply and completely. Your third eye, throat, heart, solar plexus, sacral and root chakras. The pure crystalline light then flows down your legs through your feet and into Mother Earth. These roots of light burrow deeply into the earth, alighting it with Universal source energy.

You bring the light from Mother Earth up through the bottoms of your feet and into your being, filling yourself with light, and connecting you to the heavens above and the earth below. As above, so below. Heaven and earth. So above, as below.

As you continue to breathe, this light surrounds you in a gorgeous white and golden healing glow. See it swirling around you, gently, patiently, and serenely. You are glowing in and of this light.

As you breathe in this glowing light, focus on your heart. Feel it beating within your chest and in your mind's eye, see it surrounded by the glowing white light. Imagine the beating of your heart synchronizing with this glowing white light. Your breath is in sync as well. As you breathe in, this glowing light flows inside your body and filters into your heart. As you breathe out, it expands beyond you, into the room and out into the world. Continue to breathe and notice the flowing pure light.

See it safely receiving beautiful loving energy back from the world. Now imagine your heart sending this glorious loving energy out into the world. See it opening to the love from the universe. Feel this love. Feel the compassion, kindness and support.

Open your heart to the universal source energy and to the heavens and earth. Connect to the love and support. Connect to the flow of the universe. Connect to all that is.

As you revel in your heart opening, see yourself surrounded by the type of people you would like to have in your life. What characteristics do they have? What relationships _do they have with you? How do they spend time with you? How do they interact with you? What do you do with them?_

Now, picture yourself with them really seeing you, actually listening to you, knowing you, supporting you and loving you. Feel their love, support and warm embrace of compassion, curiosity, generosity and heart-felt care. Breathe this in. It's just for you — being you. They see you. They know you. They love you.

Take a few moments to revel in all of this love and support for you. Bask in this new experience of love and support.

Take a few deep breaths to integrate the energies.

As you take your next breath, bring your awareness back to the room.

Cross your arms over your heart to center your energy.

When you're ready, open your eyes and gaze softly in front you — seeing nothing, yet aware of everything. If you'd like, wiggle your fingers and toes and do any gentle stretching your body requires. Breathe in again and open your eyes fully.

Now, take a few minutes to write down any thoughts or insights in your journal.

Becoming aware of the impact others have on your well-being and making adjustments accordingly is healthy. It creates space for you to be with those who lift you up.

Renewal and Permission

"Find a place inside where there's joy, and the joy will burn out the pain."
— Joseph Campbell

Water is strength, joy and renewal. Water is associated with feelings and emotions. It's related to the sacral chakra and as you remove fear and input from others, you connect to more strength and joy in your life.

Renewal is part of water and requires allowance and acceptance. However, working with water requires choice. It also requires action and both of these activities involve the solar plexus. There is will, drive and commitment involved.

Renewal is a choice as is everything. Since everything is a choice, why not make healthy and joyful ones?

The first one is to choose to be in a good mood. It's you choosing to be positive.

The second choice is to select to start something new. Make a plan and give yourself permission.

The third choice is to give permission to be YOU.

All of these choices involve action and allowance.

1. Buoyancy of Mood

Life happens in flow – there are positive and negative events occurring in cycles. During the positive times, it's easy to stay in the flow. It's easy to accept life and its happenings.

Yet, in the times of trial, we reach into our depths to gather strength, stoicism and courage. During these times, we need renewal, and sometimes, we need to CHOOSE.

We need to choose to remain positive.

How can we remain positive? How do we you keep your mood intact as you pass from one cycle to the next?

If you have a stable foundation, it'll provide a buffer for your mood. So, establish regular habits of moving your body, eating well and getting enough sleep.

The other ways you can maintain buoyancy of mood is to:
- o   Actively focus on the positive.
- o   Seek levity and relief.
- o   Connect with friends.

Making a habit of each of these will help in the moments when life feels as it's contracting or changing in ways that you may not immediately identify as constructive.

Buoyancy Exercise

Establish Good Habits *(Is there anything you can do to improve your sleep, exercise, diet routines? If so, jot down a few notes.)*

Focus on Positive *(What can you do to stay positive? What can you be positive about? What do you have to be thankful for? What gifts do you have? Remind yourself of all of the goodness in your life.)*

Levity and Relief *(What can you do to lighten up? What makes you laugh? What gives you relief? What will help? Who can help you?)*

Connect with Friends *(Who do you wish to see now? Reach out to friends who are supportive and bring you joy. Reach out to them, they want to help.)*

2. Start Something New

Having passion for something in your life makes it easy to renew and rejuvenate.

However, how about starting something new to experience joy?

It's exciting, challenging and ever changing as all new things are at the beginning.

It's shiny and scary and fun.

Story: Be a Middle-Schooler

"Don't be afraid to start something new," our Head of School begins his address to the incoming parents of the middle school class. "We expect our kids to try new things all of the time and they're at a great age to do just that, but I challenge each of you to do the same thing. Don't be afraid to start something new."

I love this idea and roll it around in my head for a few days and realize that yes, this is exactly right. It's time to start something completely new.

This is a few years ago and the final kick in the pants I need to begin this venture into writing, illustrating and publishing. It's a new line of work, in a new industry, with new contacts and although I can reach back into my experience base, most aspects are brand new.

It's exciting, challenging and ever changing as all new things are at the beginning. It's shiny and scary and fun. Some days it just takes my breath away. Whoosh…there it goes, all of my breath is gone. Again. Apparently, this is what breathtaking means.

I want to share this feeling. I want you to experience being so full of something that it requires all of your attention and fills you to the brim. I want you to feel so incredibly ALIVE. Remember one facet of joy? It's exuberance.

This is the perfect next step in finding your joy – start something new.

So, what's whispering to you?

What yearning do you have to begin something just for you?

340

What beckons you?

Perhaps you have so many ideas you cannot choose. Perhaps you have absolutely no idea how to even begin to find something new. Perhaps you have wanted to do something for a long time and have never given yourself permission to do so.

Let's separate these things and then break them down into bite size pieces. Select the section where you need support.

Too Many Ideas – Need Help Choosing

Are there so many ideas swirling in your head that you cannot decide? If so, do NOT look at the list in the following section. You don't need any more ideas!

You need to spend a little bit of time on this, however, as you need to create a list. I talk to many CEO's who have so many ideas they're paralyzed by what to do first. I realize this is a little different as these are enjoyable things and not work-related, but the strategy of tackling the issue is exactly the same. Skip the next idea section and go directly to the idea selection section.

No Ideas?

Are you stumped by the idea of doing something new?

Here's a list:

• Cook	• Skate	• Yoga
• Bake	• Ski	• Tai-chi/Qi-gong
• Entertain	• Snowboard	• Meditate
• Garden	• Surf	• Tarot Card reading
• Farm	• Bike	• Palm reading
• Write	• Run a marathon	• Become a psychic
• Paint	• Knit	• Witchcraft

341

• Draw	• Crochet	• Juggle
• Learn a foreign language	• Sew	• Learn magic tricks
• Sing	• Quilt	• Ride a unicycle
• Learn an instrument: piano, guitar, flute, saxophone, etc.	• Scrapbook	• Learn Morse code
	• Candle-making	• Play poker, cribbage, bridge, or chess
	• Jewelry making	
• Karate	• Woodwork	• Learn about wines
• Fencing	• Printmaking	• Make beer
• Tennis	• Cartooning	• Get a(nother) degree
• Golf	• Graphic design	• Start a business
	• Interior design	

What speaks to you? If there's not anything on this list, talk to a few friends and get their ideas. Perhaps you could start something together.

Once you've selected an idea, go to the numbered list in the giving permission category and get some information you'll need to begin.

This is exciting.

It'll be fun.

Idea Selection

In this section, write down all of the things you want to do in your journal. Don't think about any one thing. Just write all of them down.

Look at the list in your journal and think about each one. Take a few minutes and ask the following few questions:

1. How long have I wanted to do this?
2. How will I feel doing this week after week?
3. How will I feel once I have accomplished it?

4. Do I still want to do this?

You'll be able to pare the list down slightly as there'll be a few things that have been in the running only because you wanted to do them at one time. They may not have staying power.

Seriously, there may be things that you feel you should still do, as you wanted to do them at one time. This isn't an exercise in completion. This is about joy. Permit yourself to cross off the ones that don't hold excitement or desire and then cross them off of your list.

Wait a bit and then return to the list. Put them into categories – life skills, art and music, physical, crafts, fun, home, metaphysical, and career. If you don't have things for every category, don't add more ideas. I merely want you to categorize your ideas, as you may be able to combine a few or decide among them to pare down your list.

Life Skills	Art & Music	Physical
Crafts	Fun	Metaphysical
Home	Career	Other

Look at your categories and rank the categories themselves. Are you more interested in learning life skills or doing something fun? Would you rather spend time doing something physical or artistic? Prioritize by category.

Based on the category with the highest ranking, select one of your ideas. Save your list to revisit once you've completed your first idea. You're not retiring your selected ideas; you're just prioritizing them. You can always pursue the others as you complete each one.

Once you've selected your idea, go to the giving permission step and answer the questions to make a plan for pursuing your idea.

Give Yourself Permission

You want to start something new and you have a prioritized list of things you want to do. Now, you need to give yourself permission to begin.

Say Yes

Firstly, breathe. It's okay. You deserve to do something just for yourself. You're not talking about getting a manicure or hiring a cleaning service, although those are good ideas. You're talking about delving into something that you want to do and perhaps have wanted to do for quite a while.

- o Something that you need to carve out time, effort and energy.
- o Something that you can go to week after week.
- o Something that will fill your heart.
- o Something that will lift your spirit.

You need to say "Yes" to do something new - just for you.

So, say, "Yes."

Say it out loud.

Say "Yes."

Make it your mantra.

"Yes, I'm going to do something just for me."

Take another breath and believe you're going to do something for yourself.

"Yes, I deserve to do something for myself."

Smile and say it again, "Yes, I'm going to start something new."

"Yes, I'm going to……"

Take one more deep breath. You're ready.

<u>Plan for something new</u>

Secondly, you need to make a plan by answering the following questions:

1. How much time will you need on a daily, weekly or monthly basis?
2. Will you need instruction? If so, where can you get it? How much will it cost?
3. Will you need support for child or elder care? Do you need support for pick-up/drop-off? Do you need coverage over dinner time? If so, do you need support for making dinner? If you need support in any or all categories, write it down and then list names of people who can help you.
4. Do you need materials? If so, list them and the source(s).
5. Review your list and realize that you're most likely not asking for a lot. Become comfortable with this.

6. Ask your partner and family for their support, explain how much it means to you to have their support, and then tell them when you're to begin.

7. If you're without a partner or any household support, reach out to friends and family.

Plan for Something New

Time Required:

Daily-
_____

Weekly-
_____

Monthly -
_____

Instruction Required:

What -
_____

Where -
_____

Cost -
_____

Support Required:

Care -
_____

Driving -
_____

Meals -
_____

Have so much fun and remember to keep breathing. Know that you deserve to do this one thing just for you.

Let's all start something new.

Permit yourself to begin and make a plan.

Outreach

Thirdly, gather your resources and get coverage. It's time to reach out to schedule your classes, buy your materials and call in favors to get the support you need to begin doing something just for you.

Ask, ask, ask.

Remember all of those times you've offered support to others so they could do something just for themselves. Recall all of the coverage you provided, willingly and lovingly. Expect the same response from those around you. They're just as willing to help you as you have been to help them.

Ask.

Begin.

Now, it's time to begin.

Nothing more – just begin.

Have fun – this is about joy.

3. Permission to be YOU

Let's deepen the permission you just gave yourself to start something new. Give yourself permission to be more of yourself.

I love Marianne Williamson's words:

"Our deepest fear is not that we are inadequate. Our deepest fear is that we are powerful beyond measure. It is our light, not our darkness that most frightens us. We ask ourselves, 'Who am I to be brilliant, gorgeous, talented, fabulous?' Actually, who are you not to be? You are a child of God. Your playing small does not serve the world. There is nothing enlightened about shrinking so that other people won't feel insecure around you. We are all meant to shine, as children do. We were born to make manifest the glory of God that is within us. It's not just in some of us; it's in everyone. And as we let our own light shine, we unconsciously give other people permission to do the same. As we are liberated from our own fear, our presence automatically liberates others."

Imagine.

Brilliant. Gorgeous. Talented. Fabulous.

Shining brightly.

Reflecting all of the glory of the world.

Envision your magnificence.

Permission to be YOU Affirmation

In your mind, I want you to say, "I permit myself to be the very best version of myself I can be. I give myself permission to achieve my very best life - to live it fully, deeply and without apology. I forgive myself for not doing it sooner. Now is the perfect time. I am ready."

Now I want you to say aloud by repeating after me; "This is my life. I will not apologize for being powerful, brilliant, beautiful, abundant and joyous. I will not shrink from my own glory. I am absolutely magnificent."

I also want you to repeat, "I am completely in love with myself. I totally love myself. I am in love with me – just me – potently, poetically and abundantly – in love with ME."

Perhaps write these words and post them on your bathroom mirror.

Read them daily.

Love yourself enough to pursue joy in your life.

Give yourself permission.

Permission to choose a good mood.

Permission to start something new.

Permission to be you.

"Joy is prayer; joy is strength; joy is love;
joy is a net of love by which you can catch souls." – Mother Teresa

Working with water means working with your deepest feelings and emotions.

It means deepening your connection to your truest self. It requires you to love, care and attend to yourself.

As you pursue self-love, you discover ways to align with a more nourishing life.

This leads to more joy in your world as you then let go of people who aren't supportive and loving towards you.

These actions require you to gather your willpower and to take action to bring joy toward you. You give yourself permission to start something new and make a plan to actually do it.

As you give yourself permission to love yourself, you permit yourself to pursue your soul's desires.

By living your soul's desires, you're living in abundance.

Living in abundance is the greatest joy.

Earth: Authenticity

"That inner voice has both gentleness and clarity. So, to get to authenticity, you really keep going down to the bone, to the honesty, and the inevitability of something."
— Meredith Monk

Using the natural rhythm of life, think back to the prior elements of ether, air, fire and water. These elements relate to the connection, clarity, passion and joy in your life to provide you with the ingredients to create more abundance.

However, the earth element involves making it real. Making these components real involves solidifying each one as you clarify air, discover fire and empower water.

In some cases, there are new exercises and in others, you revisit the former.

So far, you've connected to ether, but have you integrated it into your daily life?

352

You've cleared your mind through air, but to what end? The same can be said with fire and finding your passion and tapping into your creativity. Or for water, and releasing your fear and stepping into joy. What have you folded into your daily life at this point?

In this section as you work with the element of earth, you anchor these newfound qualities to welcome abundance into your days.

To bolster clarity, you visualize your true self. You do exercises to get to your core values and then use these values to make decisions in your life.

To discover your true self, you review your passions. You determine your likes and dislikes and wants and needs.

To empower your true self, you allow for opening, healing and forgiving. This is about joy and as always with joy, there's a reflective nature to it. Next, you fire it up with drive and energy.

To embody your true self, you become YOU. You embrace your clarity, passion and joy to create real abundance in your life.

To make it real with the element of earth, you anchor your connection and solidify the progress from the other elements. You've gained clarity, passion and joy and now you get to your core authenticity by visualizing, discovering, empowering and embodying YOU.

The bottom line is the earth element is about making it real using inputs from the other elements. Let's make your true self real in the world.

"The only thing worse than being blind is having sight but no vision." – Helen Keller

Making it real creates substance and solidifies your being in material ways. Due to this, you want to revisit your discoveries by delving deeply into the core of you.

This is all about AIR. Refer to the air section and think back to wishes and blessings, intentions and beliefs, surrendering pre-conditioning and heightening manifestation power.

- o What vision do you have for your life?

- o What is your truth?

- o Who are you at your core?

Paring down to the core of who you are and getting to your authentic roots requires honesty, courage and commitment.

o   Be totally honest.

o   Be brave.

o   Commit to yourself.

You're worth it. You're worth all of the honesty, bravery and commitment in the world.

Once you've gained clarity, you'll discover more of yourself and then you can empower and embody you into your purest form.

Aligning with your authentic self in this way creates abundance in your outer world by drawing magic into your sphere and connecting with the unlimited possibility of the universe.

In alignment, you attract all of the bounty and blessings the world has to offer.

The first step is to clarify the vision of your life and to do this, you want to winnow down your assessment from the intentions exercise from the air section.

Assessment for Awareness and Truth

You want to review the areas of your life from Kaleidoscope Wheel of Life ™

Inner Life	Outer World
Health and fitness	Environment
Intellectual life	Career
Creativity (heart)	Family
Love… (heart)	Friendships

Inner Life	Outer World
Spiritual life	Relationships
	Adventures
	Community

Greatest desires in life – carved into 3 basic areas – life mission, love & relationship, blessings.

Ranking & Priorities

- o Based on the questionnaire and referring to the Kaleidoscope Wheel of Life ™ on page 96, what areas do you want to pursue?

- o Which ones are areas of strength to leverage?

- o What are your steps to revealing yourself to yourself?

Area of Life Assessment Priorities

Recall the areas of life assessment. What are your priorities for each?

Inner Life:
- ■ Create wellness | health & fitness – *physical/earth - make it real*
- ■ Spark mind | intellectual life – *mental/air – calm*
- ■ Satisfy heart | creativity & love – *emotional/water – joy*
- ■ Fill soul | spiritual life – *spiritual/fire – passion*

Outer World:
- ■ Improve living conditions | environment – *home, office, car, furnishings, clothing, finances, administration, second home, if applicable*

- Relish life work | career – *'work' is defined as job, career, business, volunteer positions, position & role in society*

- Boost fun with friends | family, friendships, relationships – *entertain, host parties & family events, celebrate holidays, relax throughout week, do fun things on weekends, gather with friends, see them regularly, stay in contact, connect intimately with besties and partner, go on dates, laugh, be frivolous, welcome levity*

- Expand your horizons | adventures & community - *adventure, travel, new discoveries and experiences, meet new people, cultural explorations, philosophy of life, establish community, be in service, engage actively to create a better world*

Where do you want to expend your energy?

Refer to the exercise in the air section for intentions and beliefs. If you've been doing your intentions over the last few days and weeks, you may have experienced shifts in your life. If so, you may want to revisit the exercise in the intentions and beliefs section and fine tune your priorities.

If you're satisfied with your areas of focus, review those and prioritize them. Rank them from highest to lowest. Make a list.

Clarify You Meditation

Another way to gain clarity is to perform the following meditation and journal your findings.

Clarify You Meditation
Close your eyes and breathe deeply by taking a long inhale and exhaling fully. Take a moment to gather yourself. You have spent these last few moments thinking about what you value and who you are at your core. It's not as easy as it first appears. *Take a moment to center yourself and quiet your mind. All is as it should be. Do not force the answers. Be open and allow them to come to you. Now, let's go deeper to gather wisdom and clarity to see what shows up. We welcome all that will come to us today.*

Take another deep breath. Inhale and exhale. Envision three basic areas of your life in a circle as pieces of pie ringing around a centerpiece titled harmony. This harmonious center brings you peace and joy. It powers you at your core to tackle every aspect of your life brilliantly and with ease. Take a moment to bask in its essence. Breathing in this beautiful, bountiful essence, see the other areas of your life circling the center. You will visit each one, imagining its fulfillment and welcoming any information about the value or values associated with each.

The first area of your life is your life mission. Here it is filled with wisdom, learning, creativity, abundance, fame and recognition. Imagine you are living your life mission. Breathe it in. Smile with the fulfillment of attaining your greatest desire in this area. See yourself in your mind's eye. Feel yourself living your life mission. Wrap this feeling around you and breathe it in. Take a few moments. You are safe. What value comes to you? Envision yourself encapsulating this value – what is its essence? Tuck it away into a corner of your mind imagining it underneath the title of life mission. You will remember this.

We leave your life mission to look at the love and relationship area of your life. This area is filled with a loving partner, supportive family, wonderful friends, and helpful people. Breathe it in. Smile with the fulfillment of attaining your greatest desire in this area. See yourself in your mind's eye. Feel yourself filled with love & supportive relationships. Wrap this wonderful feeling around you and breathe it in. Take a few moments. You are safe. What value comes to you? Envision yourself encapsulating this value – what is its essence? Tuck it away into a corner of your mind imagining it underneath the title of love and relationship. You will also remember this.

Lastly, let's look at the blessings area of your life. It is filled with health, wealth, prosperity, travel, and fun events. Breathe them in. Smile with the fulfillment of having all of your heart and soul desires in this area. See yourself in your mind's eye. You are vital and in perfect health. Your body moves with ease and grace. You have balance, flexibility, coordination, endurance and strength. You are youthful in feeling and appearance. Breathe in perfect health. What does it feel like? You also have the comfort of wealth and prosperity. What does it look like? You have the fun of experiencing travel and going to see places and people who interest you. What does that sound like? You are living your blessings every day. Feel yourself enmeshed in these blessings. They are swirling around you and within you. Breathe them all into your being. Take a few moments. You are safe. What value comes to you? Envision yourself encapsulating this value – what is its essence? Tuck it away into a corner of your mind imagining it underneath the title of blessings. You will remember this.

You are ready to see all three areas of your life:

Your life mission…

Your love and relationships…

Your blessings…

Now picture the values that came to you under each heading. Envision them.

Now come back into the room, open your eyes.

Write your responses in your journal.

- o My value of my life mission is…

- o My love and relationships feel like…

- o My blessings are…

Core Values

At the center of your harmony and power of who you are, you're going to look at the values you want to use to guide your life.

Values are pillars to coalesce your priorities, make your decisions and filter your choices.

Selecting values is a process. Don't think about it. You're going with your gut instinct for the first pass.

Look at the images on the next pages and see if any words jump out at you.

If so, either circle them or write them down in your journal.

Creativity WISDOM Joy

LOVE *beauty* Grace *imagination*

curiosity *radiance* Faith

peace strength **passion** FUN

discovery trust *sexuality*

abundance commitment

BALANCE *freedom*

honesty kindness *FRIENDSHIP*

wonder family justice integrity

vitality compassion HEALTH

elegance adventure

vital   harmony   CONNECTION

enchantment

leader

Unique   stable   Energy   influence

reputation

sensual

solid

authentic

respect   generosity   open   ACHIEVER

growth   popular   mysterious   fair

gravitas   serenity   intuitive

CONTRIBUTOR   DELIGHTFUL   BOLD

evolving   famous

Next, refer to the following table for the definitions of words. See if any resonate with you. This process is a bit more thoughtful, but don't belabor it. Think and ponder, but don't agonize. There are no wrong answers.

Core Value	Merriam-Webster Definition
Abundance	Relative degree of plenty, affluence, wealth
Achiever	A person who brings to a successful end; attains with great effort
Adventure	Exciting or unusual
Advocacy	Support a cause
Attractive	Pleasing appearance, charming, alluring; providing pleasure or delight
Authentic	Genuine, real; representing one's true beliefs and nature
Authority	Power to determine, control, command
Balance	Mental and emotional steadiness
Beauty	Qualities in a person or a thing that give pleasure to the senses or the mind
Bliss	Complete happiness
Bold	Break the rules without hesitation, courage, daring
Brave	Having or showing courage
Calm	A peaceful mental or emotional state
Charisma	Special charm or appeal that causes people to feel attracted and excited by someone: Special magnetism
Charm(ing)	Extremely pleasing or delightful
Commitment	Attitude of someone who works very hard to do or support something
Community	Group of people who have the same interests
Compassion	Feeling of wanting to help someone
Competent	Having skill, knowledge, experience; properly qualified
Connection	To become joined, to establish a relationship, rapport or communication
Contribute	Give time, money, knowledge, assistance for charitable purposes
Courageous	Being brave, showing strength to face danger, fear or difficulty
Creativity	Having or showing an ability to make new things or think of new ideas
Curiosity	Desire to learn or know more about something or someone

Core Value	Merriam-Webster Definition
Delightful	Highly pleasing
Desirable	Having good or pleasing qualities; worth having or getting
Determined	Resolute, staunch, decided, resolved
Discovery	Act of finding or learning something for the first time
Duty	Something that you must do because it is morally right
Elegant	Refined grace or dignified propriety
Enchant(ing)	To attract and move deeply
Energy	Natural enthusiasm and effort
Equilibrium	A state of emotional balance or calmness, intellectual balance
Evolving	Developing gradually, become into being
Expert	Special skill or knowledge, authority in field
Fair	Free from bias
Faith	Strong belief or trust in someone or something
Family	Group of people who are related to each other
Famous	Having widespread reputation, renowned, celebrated
Fitness	Quality or state of being in good physical shape
Freedom	Quality or state of being unrestrained or free
Friendship	State of being friends - people who you like and enjoy being with
Frivolity	Lack of seriousness: the quality or state of being silly or frivolous
Fun	Someone or something that is amusing or enjoyable
Grace	Charming or attractive trait or characteristic & ease and suppleness of movement or bearing
Gravitas	A very serious quality or manner, commanding respect
Growth	Increase by natural development
Generosity	Freely giving; showing kindness and concern for others
Happy	Feeling pleasure and enjoyment
Harmony	Internal calm, a pleasing arrangement of parts
Health	Condition of being sound in body, mind, or spirit
Honesty	Quality of being fair and truthful
Honor	High respect, esteem.
Humor(ous)	A funny or amusing quality
Imagination	Ability to form a picture in your mind of something that you have not seen or experienced

364

Core Value	Merriam-Webster Definition
Influence	Capacity or power of persons to be a compelling force to produce effects or actions
Integrity	Quality of being honest and fair: the state of being complete or whole
Intuitive	Having the ability to know or understand things without any proof or evidence
Joy	A source or cause of delight: the emotion evoked by well-being, success, or good fortune or by the prospect of possessing what one desires
Justice	The process or result of using laws to fairly judge and punish crimes and criminals
Kind(ness)	Having or showing a gentle nature and a desire to help others
Knowledge	Information, understanding, or skill that you get from experience or education
Leader	A guide, conductor, director who shows the way
Learning	The activity or process of gaining knowledge or skill by studying, practicing, being taught, or experiencing something
Liberty	The power to do or choose what you want to
Light-hearted	Having or showing a cheerful and happy nature, not serious
Love	Strong affection, attraction, desire, admiration, attachment, enthusiasm, devotion
Loyalty	Having or showing complete and constant support for someone or something
Magic	Extraordinary power or influence from supernatural source
Magnanimous	Generous in forgiving, free from pettiness; high-minded, noble
Magnetism	Person who attracts, lodestone
Master	Person with ability or power of expertise
Movement	The act of moving from one place to another, or moving your body
Mysterious	Beyond understanding, secret, profound or inexplicable
Open	Not closed or barred; relatively free
Optimistic	Disposed to take a favorable view of events or conditions and to expect a favorable outcome
Passion	A strong feeling of enthusiasm or excitement for something or about doing something

Core Value	Merriam-Webster Definition
Peace	A state of tranquility or quiet
Pleasure	Frivolous enjoyment, sensual gratification, recreation, amusement, delight
Poise	To hold or carry in equilibrium
Popular	Regarded with favor, approval or affection by people in general
Powerful	Exerting force; potent
Prosperity	The state of being successful usually by making a lot of money
Radiant	Having or showing an attractive quality of happiness, love, health: bright & shiny
Recognition	Realize, identity from knowledge of appearance or characteristics
Reputation	Favorable repute, good name, estimation in which a person is held
Respect	A feeling of admiring someone or something that is good, valuable, or important
Responsibility	The state of being the person who caused something to happen; or a duty or task that you are required or expected to do
Safe	Free from hurt, danger or risk
Secure	Dependable, certain, sure, firmly established, affording safety
Sensual	Relating to, devoted to, or producing physical or sexual pleasure
Sensitive	Aware of and understanding the feelings of other people
Serene	Calm and peaceful
Service	Act of being of use, to gratify others
Sexuality	The quality or state of being sexual or desirous
Skilled	Ability from knowledge, practice and aptitude, trained, craftful
Solid	Firm, hard, compact in substance
Spiritual	Things of a spiritual, ecclesiastical, or religious nature
Stable	Lasting, unwavering, steadfast
Status	Position of standing
Strength	The quality or state of being strong; the quality that allows someone to deal with problems in a determined and effective way
Success(ful)	The fact of getting or achieving wealth, respect, or fame

Core Value	Merriam-Webster Definition
Tenacity	Very determined, persistent. Never give up.
Trust	Belief that someone or something is reliable, good, honest, and effective
Unique	Very special or unusual
Vitality	A lively or energetic quality
Wealth	A large amount of money and possessions
Wisdom	Knowledge that is gained by having many experiences in life; the natural ability to understand things that most other people cannot understand
Wonder	The quality of exciting amazed admiration
Worthy	Good and deserving respect, praise, or attention

Choose those values that speak to you. Record them in your journal.

Categories of Values

Now, you're going to look at the categories of similar values and choose the one in that category that speaks to you the most. Circle or make notes in your journal.

Creativity Curiosity Discovery Evolving Growth Imaginative Knowledge Learning Wisdom Wonder	Achiever Adventurous Bold Brave Courageous	Abundance Generosity Magnanimous Prosperity Success(ful) Wealth	Authentic Authority Competence Expert Influence Leader Master Powerful Skilled Strength Unique Worthy
Balance Bliss Calm	Charisma Charm(ing) Enchant(ing)	Advocacy Commitment Contribute	Compassion Kind(ness) Love

Equilibrium Faith Harmony Peace Serene Intuitive Magic Mysterious Sensitive Spiritual	Gravitas Magnetism Popular Recognition Reputation Status Vitality	Determined Duty Fair Honesty Integrity Justice Liberty Loyalty Respect Responsibility Safe Secure Solid Stable Trust	Open
Delightful Frivolity Freedom Fun Happy Humor(ous) Joy Light-hearted Optimistic Pleasure	Community Connection Family Friendship Service	Energy Fitness Health Movement	Attractive Beauty Desirable Elegant Grace Passion Poise Radiant Sensuous Sexual

Value Section

Refer to your priorities in area of life assessment.

Look over your values. Compare your priorities with the values you've selected. Pare down the values.

Prioritize them in alignment with the areas of your life assessment. Make a list in your journal.

Story: Values

"Values are a wonderful way to target exactly who you are and they're helpful in your business as well. Your personal values can be used in your I AM statements in mirror work or as part of your affirmation rituals," I explain to a group of business leaders who're interested in the intuitive side of life.

We continue doing the core values exercises and everyone's excited. As people are reviewing the values, I realize that I'm shifting mine in my head at this very moment.

I've been using the same personal values for a handful of years and I'm quite attached. Full disclosure, they've become a bit rote.

"I am intuition, wonder and joy," I say every morning in the shower.

At this moment, though, I realize I want to shift the intuition to magic. I want to keep my mind WIDE open to all of the mystical and intuitive possibilities in the universe. So, I make a mental note to change this value in my morning ritual.

My new personal mantra will be, "I am magic, wonder and joy."

After the class, I realize this will open the intuitive aspect of life even more.

I can't wait!

Boost the power of your values through the following guided meditation.

Values Meditation
Close your eyes and take a nice refreshing breath by inhaling deeply and exhaling gently. Take another deep breath in and gently breathe out, slowly expelling all of the air out of your lungs. Take one more and feel grounded and centered in this place.

Values Meditation

Now, you're going to create space by releasing that which no longer serves you. It does not need to be identified or named. It simply needs to be released. Ask the Universe to release that which no longer serves you as you inhale gently and exhale deeply and completely until all of the breath is expelled from your lungs. And as you do, release all the old, useless energy into a long black string that extends as long as your breath. As you stop your exhale, the black string separates from you and lies gently in the air in front of your mouth – separate and still. Now, ask the Universe to cleanse this old and useless energy into brilliant white light filled with gold and silver swirls. Each brilliant white beautiful string is now filled with the glorious energy of the Universe. These strings move toward each other and gather together to lift swiftly into the air above your head, through the roof of your house, and into the sky – lighting the way with the glory of this shifted energy. You completely let go of this energy by giving thanks for the lessons, and centering yourself back into the room.

By taking another deep breath, you settle into yourself and ground your energy into your core. Now, focus on your core values.

What are they? What are the values you feel and envision about your life mission? Breathe these in. What are the values you dream of in love and relationships? Wrap these around you. What are the values you imagine in the blessings area of your life? Soak these up into your breath and then into your body.

Take a moment and ponder these values.

Gently breathe in and out. Breathe more deeply this time as you breathe in your core values. You reach out to take them right from the Universe as it presents these to you as a gift. You fold them into yourself and embrace them into the core of your being. They are now part of you –fully and easily integrated.

Now imagine your core values starting at your root chakra and planting a new seed of physical manifestation. See the red glowing roots of your core values and power as they plant themselves into the world and light up with energy.

Values Meditation

Notice that red energy moving up your body into your sacral chakra and gathering emotion to generate even more feeling and desire. Notice as the orange desire swirls and moves into your solar plexus where it builds power and conviction. See the yellow power of your conviction blending into green as it touches your heart. Smile as your power and essence fill your heart with joy.

Your joyous heart is singing with love as it spreads this love and support into your throat chakra to give it voice. The blue of your throat moves your vibrational sounds into your third eye, opening it to peer out at the indigo creation of your magnificent insight. Your crown chakra is waiting with bated breath to receive your insight and sing it into the spirit world and the Universe.

With your core values achieving grounding, gathering desire, harnessing power and conviction, receiving love and support, giving voice, gaining clarity and insight and connecting with the Universal power of all that is, you are ready to live at your highest potential.

You are ready to create your vision and achieve success. You're ready to live your very best life. Breathe this in with all of its magnificence. Breathe in all of your magnificence. You are utterly magnificent. You are absolutely powerful. You are loved beyond measure.

Take a few moments to bask in all of this magnificence.

Now, be thankful. Be grateful to the Universe for making your dreams and desires come true. Thank you, universe. Breathe in deeply. You're completely abundant in all things. Your life is fulfilled, ric, and full of joy.

Now as you breathe in this goodness and joy, feel the bliss of being alive. Take another deep breath and fill yourself with the bounty of life. Allow this state of bliss to accompany you on your return to your room.

Your values are…

Writing your values and posting them where you can see them will help you incorporate these into your life.

Including your values in your intentions adds power to them.

Saying your values as mantras or affirmations also helps.

"Find out who you are and do it on purpose." - Dolly Parton

Use the power of earth to make your recent self-discovery of who are you a reality. From fire, you remembered, then used the creation cycle to tap into divine creativity. There's passion with fire that you'll use here to make your creations real.

Use logic and reason to bring forward fire and to lean into the energy of earth by connecting to yourself. The following meditation allows you to do just that.

It's time to imagine your best self.

Imagine Your Best Self Meditation
Get into a comfortable position and turn off your phone. You don't need to sit in lotus position on the floor – a comfortable cushion, couch or chair will do just fine. Settle yourself into your seated position.
Close your eyes and take a nice refreshing breath by inhaling deeply and exhaling gently. Take another deep breath in and gently breathe out, slowly expelling all of the air out

of your lungs. Surround yourself with protective white light directly from the source energy of the Universe. You are protected at all times.

Now one more deep cleansing breath in, exhaling gently and fully.

This is your time. Time - just for you. Things have been a bit frenetic lately leaving you feeling disconnected and potentially disengaged.

So, you're investing in yourself by taking a few precious moments to reconnect and imagine your best self.

Inhale deeply and exhale fully.

Continue your breathing – in and out, in and out, you feel centered, grounded and relaxed. As you continue breathing, imagine your very best self.

Picture yourself completely. Imagine you are living your life as you always have wanted to. You are happy, healthy, joyful, passionate and filled with love.

Breathe in and out, in and out. Imagine yourself. This is your very best day. You have everything you have ever hoped for. You are all that you can be.

Picture yourself. Feel yourself. Know yourself.

What are you doing?

What are you wearing?

Who are you with?

How do you feel?

What have you done this day?

Imagine Your Best Self Meditation
Why are you so happy and alive?
Take a few moments.
When you're ready, open your eyes and make a few notes.

Jot down any notes of your experience.

Wants and Needs

You've just imagined your very best self. You pictured yourself – happy, healthy, and fully alive. You're completely in love with yourself.

In this state of mind, do the following exercises.

Wants

So, when you imagined yourself in our guided meditation exercise, who are you? You imagined your very best self. What is it you want? What do you wish? What do you desire? You don't have to pick and choose. This is a list of wants, desires and wishes. There are no limits.

It's good to want, desire and wish...

Write three wants, three wishes and three desires.

Wants	Wishes	Desires

Now, what do you **need** to attain your wants, wishes and desires?

Time? Money? Resources? Skills? Support? Expertise?

What do you need? Write down your needs.

Now, explore a few steps to get your needs met.

Needs:

Step
1:_____

Step
2:_____

Step
3:_____

What do you want and need to create your very best life?

After, you've listed what you want and need, turn these into HAVE statements. You've asked yourself the questions as want and need ones to get to the particulars of how to create your very best life.

In the practical sense, develop your plans, reach out to others and ask for support and resources to attain your desires.

In the magical one, change these to "I have" statements to call in these energies into your life.

In your journal, write each one as "I have…".

Likes and Dislikes

In the passion section, you discovered your talents – what you're really good at and what makes you unique. This is insightful as leveraging your strengths builds confidence and creates ease in forming structure to live your very best life.

However, what you're good at may not be what you like to do and how you like to spend your time. For example, I'm very good at handling details, yet I loathe spending lots of time muddling around in them. I'm also good at the administrative side of things and also hate dealing with these seemingly mundane items.

Likes and Dislikes *(+ for like/ - for dislike)*

What do you like to do? What gives you energy? At the end of the day as you review it in your mind, what do you feel good about accomplishing?

Entertaining	Baking
Hosting	Catering
Planning parties and events	Cooking
Tending bar	Crafting
Making music playlists	Creating
	Sewing
Field trip traveling	Taking classes
Long journeys	Doing online courses
Short weekends	Reading
Beach vacations	Attending workshops
Mountain vacations	Purchasing learning materials
Camping	Working with mentors
Quick trips	Being a mentor
Traveling for business	
Working out	Yoga
Exercising	Breath work
Strength training	Meditation

Biking Running Stretching Walking	Going to the spa Doctor appointments
Phone calls Meetings Conversations with others Handling conflict and negotiations Helping people with their issues Managing difficult situations Connecting with people	Beautifying Designing and harmony in spaces Shopping Buying and selling Hunting for things Tracking things Adopting new technology Working online
Teaching Coaching Mentoring others Giving advice Listening to others Talking with others Answering questions	Networking Writing copy and content Creating marketing materials Communicating with prospects Designing sales proposals Making deals Expanding current client work Social media – word and video Using social media sites
Administrative details Cleaning and organizing Checking things off a list Finishing projects Organizing Juggling multiple tasks Keeping a planner or agenda Scheduling appointments	Creating products and solutions Innovating service lines Producing client content Client delivery Communicating with clients Follow-up with clients Invoicing and collecting
Number crunching Inventory Financial numeracy: P&L, B/Sheet, C/Flow Key metrics Budgets and forecasts Projections and targets	Investigating and researching Brainstorming Looking at the long-term Solving puzzles Seeing the big picture Formulating patterns Making connections Strategic lens Goals and objectives

Doing errands Paying bills Keeping the family schedule Running the household Fixing things around the house Maintaining household systems Contacting workers Conducting work on your house	Taking pictures Creating photo albums Scrapbooking Journaling family history Organizing memorabilia Ancestry or genealogy
Charitable work Being of service Giving to charity Care giving Nurturing Helping others	Dieting and nutrition Sleeping Napping Using a Fitbit or keeping track Vitamins and minerals Herbs
Spiritual work Going to church Magic and mystery Dream work	Manicures, pedicures, facials Hair appointments Make-up and jewelry Dressing up Latest trends

Conversely, what do you dread? What do you put off doing? How do you procrastinate?

Review the list above and select those things you do NOT like doing or what you feel is a complete waste of time.

Take some time over the next few days and notice what gives you energy and what depletes it. Become aware of what you're eager to do and how you procrastinate.

Make a list.

Knowing your likes and dislikes is helpful to being true to yourself.

Discover Yourself through the Goddess

Use this method to shore up those areas of your life you need support and to amplify your strengths.

There are Goddesses who can help you in every area of your life. These follow your inner life areas of wellness, emotional life, intellectual prowess and soul desires. Your outer world is represented by living conditions, relationships, life mission and adventure and fun.

Refer to the Goddess listing below if you want information about the Goddess before doing the meditation.

Brigid – Physical body/Create wellness
Origin: Celtic triple goddess – maiden, mother and sage; feminine counterpart to Archangel Michael.
Description: Celebrated on Imbolc. Get in touch with your feminine power; speak your truth and be unwavering in your convictions.
Crystal: Angelite, sodalite

Hathor – Emotional life/Satisfy heart
Origin: Egyptian goddess of mother; sun and sky goddess
Description: Feminine energy of receptivity. Helps with receiving from the physical as well as spiritual worlds. Brings abundance once blockages are removed. Be thankful for all of the gifts you receive.
Crystal: Malachite, turquoise

Athena – Intellectual prowess/Spark mind
Origin: Greek warrior goddess, daughter of Zeus
Description: Goddess of wisdom and war, helps protect, creativity and intellectual pursuits. She strategizes and boosts ability to see both sides and big picture.
Crystal: Azurite, lapis lazuli

Kali – Spiritual life/Fill soul
Origin: Hindu goddess of the cycles of life: Mother earth
Description: She liberates souls. Rebirth, cycles, joy and courage are her themes.
Crystal: Black obsidian, pietersite

Diana – Living conditions/environment
Origin: Roman moon goddess, daughter of Jupiter
Description: Helps with childbirth, animals and connecting with nature, particularly the elementals. Aligned with oak tree for strength and focused intention.
Crystal: Amethyst, moonstone

Freya - Love and relationships
Origin: Norse goddess of beauty, love and destiny.
Description: Friday is named after her representing time to celebrate. She had many lovers, unbridled sexuality and unyielding passion. Boldness. Bravery. Risk-taking.
Crystal: Amber, aquamarine, cat's eye

White Tara - Life Mission/Career
Origin: Buddhist mother of liberation through success in work and achievements.
Description: Enlightened activity, compassion, power and prosperity.
Crystal: Tibetan quartz

Sekhmet – Growth/expand horizons/adventures
Origin: Egyptian warrior goddess and is depicted as a lioness.
Description: She is the powerful one who protected and led pharaohs into war. She also can bring disease and heal it.
Crystal: Fire agate, sunstone, pyrite

Discover You Goddess Meditation

Close your eyes and reenter your connected space. You're already connected to the earthly and spiritual realms. You can feel your chakras spinning clearly and actively in the appropriate directions. You know you're an open channel of light traveling from the earth up through your chakras and connecting to the pure universal light of all that is.

Your heart, third eye and crown chakras are wide open to receive the powerful energy of the Goddess. Your solar plexus, sacral and root chakras are rooted to the earth – centering and grounding you.

Now, you're going to tap into your inner goddess to gather your willpower for pursuing your authentic self. We're calling in the Goddess for each area of your life – physical, emotional, mental and spiritual inner life and living conditions, love, life mission and growth in your outer world.

Your physical self – your health, fitness and wellbeing. You embrace and worship your body with your choices about food, water, exercise and sleep. You relish the opportunity to show your body how much you love it. If you need motivation to take care of your body, call on Brigid, the Celtic Triple Goddess. She is the counterpart to Archangel Michael. She protects you and gives you the motivation and drive you seek as well as the support you need. She understands the knowing that's required to be merged physically and spiritually. She's compassionate about the emotional twinges as well. She helps you with your integrity with your body. Call on her to make healthy choices.

Your emotional body yearns for all of the receptivity available in the Universe. You want emotional safety, you desire to be listened to and heard. You want to be known. Hathor is the essence of divine feminine energy. She is the Egyptian Sun and Sky Goddess. She represents the Universe itself. She helps you feel safe enough to be open to all of the gifts of the universe. Embody her to help you receive in the natural flow of the Universe.

Now, for your mental body. That beautiful brain. The power of your thoughts. You move your attention to Athena – the intellectual. The strategist. The wisdom. Call on Athena when you're feeling confused or fuzzy and you are suddenly filled with all of the wisdom of the universe. The ideas flow – freely and frequently. Your insights – astound. You are intellectual. Potentially, intellectually superior to all. You're able to tap into your mental body at will shifting from your thoughts to those of the universe –easily, seamlessly. Your mind is a wonder – filled with genius. It's greatly entwined with your intuition. Your mental facilities make you fierce, strong, and capable. You are strategic. A warrior. Breathe in your mental prowess.

Your spiritual life represents wholeness – there is light and dark. As you need courage to explore the depths, call on Kali. She is the Hindu Goddess symbolizing Mother Earth. She is the wise woman – she represents the cycles of life. She helps you go deep. She liberates the soul as you embrace your wholeness. Make the connection and see your spiritual life strengthen.

Discover You Goddess Meditation

Your living conditions need improvement – you want to make more money, create sanctuary or give yourself permission to have abundance. You need someone on your side – you need an advocate. Call on Diana the huntress as she is aligned with the strength of the oak tree. A tree that grows to tremendous height and strength from a tiny acorn. Diana can help you plant acorns to grow into giant, lasting trees. She is focused intention and can help you manifest in ways that matter to you. Be strong. Breathe in Diana's strength and know it's yours. You are strong. Advocate for yourself to improve your environment.

Your love life needs sparkle and passion. You want romance, sensuality and deep abiding love. You yearn for your soul mate or want to strengthen and intensify the love already in your life. Call on Freya – the Norse Goddess. She is bold and brave and true. She knows herself fully and loves herself completely. Freya will help you attract and celebrate your loving partner into your life. Be bold and call on her.

You desire a more potent, powerful and prosperous career. You want to align with your life mission. You need to overcome obstacles and blocks in your authentic life mission expression. White Tara is here to help. This Buddhist Mother can liberate you in work through success and achievements. Ask White Tara for help.

Call on Sekhmet when you're in a rut. If you're stuck or lack drive, ambition or passion to learn new things, expand your horizons or go on adventures. You may feel timid or lackluster. Sekhmet will help you find your discipline or courage. You may feel afraid to do what your instincts are guiding you to do. Sekhment is pure power. She's a warrior. She tells you, "You can recover from any pain through the courage, commitment and bold loving devotion in what matters most to you." You can do anything you desire. Believe in yourself.

Take a few moments to breathe in all of the energies of the goddess. Call on Brigid, Hathor, Athena, Kali, Diana, Freya, White Tara and Sekhmet. Embrace the Goddesses and call on them as needed. They are here for you.

Discover You Goddess Meditation

Thank them for their energies, guidance, insight, power and support. Fill yourself with the cleansing and pure white light of the universe. You are connected to the divinity in you.

Take a final deep breath – breathing in all of the aspects of yourself. You're centered, grounded and present. Close the energy by crossing your arms over your chest.

As you take your next breath, bring your awareness back to the room.

When you're ready, open your eyes and gaze softly in front you – seeing nothing, yet aware of everything. If you'd like, wiggle your fingers and toes and do any gentle stretching your body requires. Breathe in again and open your eyes fully.

Make any notes of your experience.

Remember pertinent messages.

Post them in visible places.

"The ultimate value of life depends upon awareness and the power of contemplation rather than upon mere survival." - Aristotle

Empowerment involves allowance through forgiveness and willpower through action. From water, you have deepened your connection with joy, experienced your inner child, let go of people no longer uplifting to you and given yourself permission to choose yourself.

Now it's time to allow, forgive and take action.

Allowance

Opening

Opening your mind and heart in alignment helps open the channel of giving and receiving.

Assess how open your mind and your heart are in particular ways.

<u>Open Mind</u>

Circle what's true for you.

Wonder	Interest	Contentment
▪ Plethora of reading: up-to-date on periodicals, current events & best seller list ▪ Explore new information continuously ▪ Currently, learning new skills ▪ Seeking cultural exploits ▪ Visionary mental abilities ▪ Constantly able to think critically ▪ Solve problems regularly ▪ Impeccable memory ▪ Decisive ▪ Insatiable curiosity ▪ Constantly aware of surroundings ▪ Connected intuitively ▪ Flexible thinking	▪ Try to keep up-to-date on periodicals, current events & best seller list ▪ Like to pursue new information regularly ▪ Want to learn new skills ▪ Enjoy cultural exploits ▪ Sometimes think in visionary ways ▪ Occasionally able to think critically ▪ Solve problems occasionally ▪ Good memory ▪ Somewhat decisive ▪ Like to be curious ▪ Observe surroundings ▪ Can connect intuitively	▪ Only a little bit interested in reading – fiction or non-fiction ▪ Welcome new information if it's presented to you ▪ Satisfied with your current skills ▪ Would rather not go to the theater, opera or ballet ▪ Like details and information in bite-size pieces ▪ Forget things easily *(it's a running joke!)* ▪ Would rather have someone else make decisions ▪ Usually don't notice things around you *(probably another running joke!)*

Wonder	Interest	Contentment
<ul><li>Integrative philosophies/big picture life</li><li>Facile with paradoxes</li><li>Actively solve mysteries</li></ul>	<ul><li>Able to think flexibly</li><li>Able to accept alternative philosophies</li><li>Able to accept paradoxes</li><li>Able to solve mysteries</li></ul>	<ul><li>Have trouble connecting to your intuition</li><li>Have strong opinions and stick with them</li><li>Really don't enjoy puzzles or mysteries</li></ul>

Where are most of your circles? Are in you a state of wonder, showing interest and curiosity or contented with your current level of knowledge?

There are no wrong answers. You're just looking for alignment. Be honest. Be brave and committed to your authenticity. The truth is what it is.

Open Heart

Circle the true statements.

Open	Welcoming	Satisfied
<ul><li>Live with open heart</li><li>Trust self and others</li><li>Surf emotional cycles smoothly and harmoniously</li><li>Healthy connections with friends and family</li><li>Welcome and provide intimate relationships</li><li>Satisfy perceptions and senses</li></ul>	<ul><li>Desire to live with open heart</li><li>Somewhat trusting of self and others</li><li>Surf emotional cycles with flexibility</li><li>Basically, have healthy connections with friends and family</li><li>Ability to welcome and provide intimate relationships</li></ul>	<ul><li>Are afraid to open your heart – you don't want to get hurt</li><li>Have trouble trusting yourself (*afraid to let yourself or others down*)</li><li>Others haven't earned your trust (*you've been hurt too many times*)</li><li>Have intense emotions/really like drama</li></ul>

Open	Welcoming	Satisfied
▪ Seek joy regularly ▪ Feel happy and content on a daily basis ▪ Nurturing and full of caring for self and others ▪ Nourishing and active self-love ▪ Balance between giving and receiving ▪ Engaged in harmonious intimate relationship ▪ Connected to soul mate ▪ Always allow heart to rule	▪ Want to satisfy perceptions and senses ▪ Desire to seek joy ▪ Feel happy and content on a regular basis ▪ Able to nurture and care for self and others ▪ Occasionally active in self-love ▪ Striving for balance between giving and receiving ▪ Engaged in intimate relationship – working towards healthy ▪ Desirous of soul mate ▪ Sometimes allow heart to rule	▪ Have broken connections with friends and family ▪ Are afraid of intimacy – either timid or fearful ▪ Don't understand how to satisfy your senses ▪ Would rather be content than joyful ▪ Happiness is oftentimes an illusion ▪ Care too much about others to care for yourself – you put yourself last ▪ Haven't figured out how to engage in acts of self-love ▪ Either give too much or expect others to give to you too much ▪ Not engaged in intimate relationship & don't want one ▪ Think soul mates are a myth

Where are your circles? Compare these with your mind. Are they similar? If so, then your mind and heart are aligned.

If your mind is more open than your heart, look for ways to open your heart. If your heart is more open than your mind, look for ways to open your mind.

Oracle cards can help you find answers, solve problems and assess situations. These can help you open your mind to rely on your intuition and open your heart to trust your instinct.

Oracle Cards

If there are oracle cards that speak to you, use them to help you assess situations, open to solutions and forgive in relationships, if necessary.

Relationship Readings

There are two separate relationship reading spreads – one for self-love and the other for relationship with a partner or close friend. They are both powerful spreads.

Self-Love

	I.	Something to love about myself		
II. Where can I be more patient with myself?		♥	III.	Where can I be kinder to myself?
	IV.	Energies to draw upon & strategies to incorporate		

1 *You & what you are relating to the here and now in the relationship*	*2* *The other person / the other person's input*
3 *The combined energies*	*4* *The insight of guidance in this situation*

Situations: *The Cross*

	5 *Resolution*	
2 *Subconscious influence which you are unaware*	1 *The issue*	3 *External influence of which you are aware*
	4 *What is required for resolution*	

Energizing the Answers

- o Leave the cards out for as long as you desire.
- o Take pictures of the layout answers if you feel they require more attention, focus, energy, time for you to gain their full meaning.
- o Spend some time in meditation with the cards you have chosen or have chosen you.
- o Journal about the answers you have received.
- o Carry the card(s) with you throughout the day.
- o Charge the card(s) further with crystals or stones.

Forgiveness

Striving for forgiveness can help you open your heart.

Definition of forgiveness:

➢ *Process of forgiving or being forgiven.*

Definition of forgive:

> *To stop feeling angry or resentful toward someone for an offense, flaw or mistake.*
> *To cancel a debt.*

Imagine cancelling karmic debt – removing it from your physical life, mental activity, emotional power, energy field, aura and entire being. Imagine removing it from your karmic expanse. Your soul will no longer have to carry it from one lifetime to another.

Forgiving is actively reaching for abundance, magic and freedom.

It's saying *'yes'* to change.

It's taking a step toward a better life.

It's about you becoming free. Free to pursue your own life.

Forgiveness is all about you – not the other person. It doesn't matter what they think, feel or desire regarding this situation. It doesn't matter what their story is or who they tell. It doesn't matter how many people they get into their 'corner'.

Forgiveness is only about you – your response, your feelings, your freedom.

Complete forgiveness is the Holy Grail.

However, it's a process.

Here are ways to make it more palatable as you begin:

1. Journal to free your thoughts and feelings

2. Work out, dance, shout, scream or sing loudly to express excess energy from this person or situation

3. Write a letter to the person stating your feelings and don't give it to them

4. Define boundaries to have moments that free you of the person or circumstance you are in the process of forgiving

5. Let go of the story – seriously, release it to the Universe

6. Create laughter and frivolity moments in your life

7. Lean into your joy

8. Remember it's a process – be patient and kind to yourself

Forgiveness Visualization

Close your eyes or gaze softly in front of you. Start your regular breathing pattern.

Envision yourself sitting comfortably in the middle of a grassy meadow surrounded by gorgeous trees, bushes and flowers. The grass is soft under your feet and the sun is shining brightly in the clear blue sky. There are birds singing beautifully in distance and butterflies and bumblebees are flying gently around the flowers.

As you're sitting comfortably, you recall a situation that is still bugging you today. You bring it into your mind's eye and then call the person responsible into your comfortable sitting area in the meadow.

Breathe in patience and loving kindness. You are safe, loved and supported by the universe.

Feel the love the universe has for you.

Return your attention back to the person sitting in front of you.

> ### *Forgiveness Visualization*
>
> *Tell the person what he/she did and how it made you feel. He or she sits quietly without any comment as you tell your side of the story. It feels so good to have him or her listen without responding. You let this person know all of the thoughts and emotions you've experienced.*
>
> *Take a deep breath and ask for a response. The only thing he or she says is: "Thank you for telling me. I'm sorry."*
>
> *You then say, "I forgive you. I also forgive me. I forgive you. I forgive me. I forgive you. I forgive me."*
>
> *Repeat until the forgiveness feels complete.*
>
> *Continue to breathe. Welcome love, compassion and kindness into your sphere.*
>
> *Sit for a few moments in complete bliss. You feel free and happy to be alive.*
>
> *Cross your arms over your heart to ground yourself.*
>
> *Express gratitude and return to the room.*

Action

Thomas Edison has said, "Genius is 1% inspiration and 99% perspiration". He's right. When you're inspired, you're swept up with your inspiration. It makes you think everything's going to be easy. It makes you think there's nothing you cannot do. It makes you filled with energy, ambition, and verve. You're on fire!

It's great that you're on fire. You can use it. You can use it to push through the initial stages of planning and research. You can use it to figure things out and to push through obstacles. You can use it to do quite a lot.

However, you can't use it to do everything as inspiration alone isn't going to get the job done. Perspiration is critical. You're going to have to work - very hard. You're going to have to work - long hours. You're going to have to work and learn many new things. You're going to have to work and admit you don't know everything.

So, for that 99% perspiration, it pays to get help.

Asking for support helps you open your heart. It allows you to receive and making plans activates your mind as it gives you clarity.

For more heart opening and mind expansion, ask for support.

Support

"Friends…they cherish one another's hopes. They are kind to one another's dreams." – Henry David Thoreau

Who do you know?

You're going to review the prior step of likes and dislikes to identify things that you may need help.

Do you like to handle details or stay in the big picture?

Do you like to spend time with people or alone?

Do you know how to make a plan to achieve your passion?

Do you know how to get the funds you may need to make your passion a reality?

Do you need schooling to gain a degree or information?

Make a list of the activities you need to complete to be successful. Put your name next to the ones you can do – easily and well. Put a dash next to the ones you can do, but not very well. Put a star next to the items you cannot do.

Look at the list of starred items.

Who do you know that can do these things? Put their names down next to the star(s).

Collate the items by name. Look at the names, determine the best way to handle your request and gather the contact information.

Reach out.

Reach out to the people on your list.

Hire or engage them immediately.

Do it today – that 99% perspiration is much better handled together than alone.

Develop a Plan

"Failing to plan is planning to fail." – Alan Lakein

It's time to develop a plan.

Nothing happens without a plan.

You've spent time in mediation and reflection, so what's your passion?

Say it to yourself and then write it down. When will you achieve it?

Write a date next to it.

Now, list a few high-level goals. Be specific, but think longer term. Here are a few areas as examples:

1. Gather information.
2. Learn something new.
3. Gain experience.
4. Save money to achieve your passion.

5. Allow time, resource and focus to shift in order to transition from one thing to another.

6. Launch your passion.

Next, include a few key steps for each high-level goal.

To expand on the example, here are a few steps for each goal;

1. Gather information.
   - Research new area of focus.
   - Talk to people in this new area.
   - Reach out to experts for advice or support.

2. Learn something new.
   - Order and read books or periodicals on this subject.
   - Take an online class or workshop.
   - Enroll in a program.

3. Gain experience.
   - Perform practice protocols, services or build prototypes.
   - Volunteer.
   - Apprentice with someone more experienced than you.

4. Save money to achieve your passion.
   - Make a list of expenditures.
   - Develop a budget.
   - Stick to it.

5. Allow time, resource and focus to shift in order to transition from one thing to another.
   - Make a transition plan.

      o   Communicate it with those impacted.

      o   Shift time and resource from one to the other.

6. Launch your passion.

      o   Let the world know.

      o   Complete transition.

      o   Begin.

Where do you need help?

Write down the names you thought of in the 'Who do you know' exercise.

Now's the time to reach out to these people if you have not already. Include these names into your plan in the appropriate areas.

Finally, include dates on your plan. Work back from your launch date. Review the dates to ensure you're being reasonable and ambitious.

Empowerment Meditation

Look over your support requests and your plan. Instill power to your allowance and actions.

Empower YOU

Close your eyes and take a nice refreshing breath by inhaling deeply and exhaling gently. Take another deep breath in and gently breathe out, slowly expelling all of the air out of your lungs. Take one more breath and feel grounded and centered in this place.

As you continue to breathe, envision a rainbow of color above your head. It's the most magnificent rainbow you have ever seen. It's bright – the brightest colors you have ever seen. The reds, oranges, yellows, greens, blues and purples are gorgeous- simply and utterly gorgeous. Each color sparkles. It's as if the colors are filled with jewels.

You imagine these colors flowing above your head and know they are connected to all of the abundance of the universe.

As you breathe, you welcome these colors into your being. You see them swirling all around you and entering your head at your crown chakra. You are filled with all of the abundance, bounty and beauty of the universe. This is the pure crystalline light of the universe. The light of the universe is shining through you.

As you breathe, lean into the powers of the colors. You breathe in connection to the divine and the spirit of all that is. You feel the magical elements of the world run through you.

Inhale and exhale. Focus on your insight and intuition and know you can see your gifts reflected in the universe. Breathe in your knowing.

Move your focus to your throat and allow the flow of the rainbow to enter into your throat. You find your voice and can hear yourself shouting your truth from the rooftops.

Now your heart- it's open and filled with all of the love Mother Earth and her inhabitants have to offer. You are loved beyond measure. Fill yourself with this love.

Breathe into your power center and feel your strength, bravery and boldness. You are strong. You are brave. You are bold. You reach for your potential —without restraint. You take action to live your life to its fullest.

You feel all of the joy and pleasure you can imagine entering into your body. It swirls as it delights and enchants. You fill yourself with faith, optimism and the intense happy light of the Sun. You are glowing.

Now ground all of this energy into the Earth to make it real in your life. Ground the intuition, the insight, the truth, the love, the power and the joy for you to tap into whenever you desire.

Surround yourself with all of these energies. Immerse in them. Relish in the forces of universal love, support and abundance.

Fill yourself with the universal light of all that is.

Your light begins to glow brighter and brighter. Your colors - even more brilliant. Your insight, power and joy are limitless. You become the light. You embody the energies. You immerse yourself in the powers.

Immersed in the glow, you realize this light has always been inside of you – always. You are the insight, love, power and joy. Feel it growing brighter and bigger until it spans the entire world. The power of the entire universe lives inside of you, always.

Gently breathe in and out. Breathe more deeply this time as you breathe in your power.

Take a few moments.

As you take your next breath, become aware of the seat beneath you and the presence of the room. When you are ready, open your eyes and gaze softly in front you – seeing nothing, yet aware of everything. If you would like, wiggle your fingers and toes and do any gentle stretching your body requires. Breathe in again and open your eyes fully.

Welcome back – your life is bountiful and joyous.

You're to open to the abundance of the universe and are ready to take action in the world.

Write your experience in your journal.

Post empowering messages in visible places – perhaps on your bathroom mirror.

"You have no need to travel anywhere. Journey within yourself, enter a mine of rubies and bathe in the splendor of your own light." - Rumi

Embodiment is the culmination of all – an open mind, a grateful heart and an authentic will.

To embody yourself, you need an open mind filled with wonder, a grateful heart to allow for the truth and the will to pursue your authentic self without end.

Let's begin with the mind by opening it and embracing wonder. There are practical and magical ways to do each.

Open Mind

- o Change your thoughts
- o Revisit your beliefs
- o Assess the areas of your life
- o Determine your intentions

- Use the element of air
- Say 'yes' to your intuition
- Question, question, question
- Envision the fairies

To embrace wonder, here are a few practical ways:

Practical Exercises to Embrace Wonder
- Read children's books.
- Walk in nature.
- Swing on a swing set.
- Say "yes" and be curious about life.

There are magical ways to embrace wonder as well. Here's an astrological one.

Astrology's Expression of Wonder

Gemini's quest in life is wonder. Gemini has the ability to hold paradox and believe in both sides with curiosity and joy.

Gemini ♊
Ruled by Mercury | 3rd House
Gemini likes communicating.
Archetypes: Witness, Teacher, Storyteller, Journalist
Description: Versatile, communicative, problem solver, multi-dimensional, quick-witted, lively, inquisitive, explore everything, gathering knowledge, messenger, inquiry, curious, adaptable, interpret lots of data quickly, wander and explore and hold two-sides of an issue and believe both to be true. State of wonder.

Where is Gemini ♊ in your chart?

The following example shows Gemini in the 3rd house with Jupiter in Gemini in the 2nd house. So, there's Gemini energy in both the 2nd and 3rd houses with the energy of Jupiter.

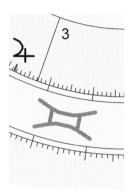

For this person, the learning, teaching, speaking, writing and communicating house is in its own sign. The 3rd house is affiliated with Gemini. The sense of wonder is desired in the early educational years and in the character of siblings and neighbors. So, it's an extra boost to have the same sign and house combination. This person has the ability to access wonder more easily. However, there's only one expression of wonder in this person's chart, so he or she is missing another expression of it.

The 2nd house energy is enlivened by Jupiter whose energy is big, bold and expansive. It's a good luck charm in the 2nd house – the house of resource, connection, competence and self-worth, but doesn't energize the 3rd house. It's only noted as it's included in the image.

Now, where does wonder lie in your chart?

   o   In which house does Gemini lie?

   o   What does it mean? *(Refer to the house table).*

- Do you have a planet here? What's its energy? *(Refer to the planet table)*.

- Do you any other planets here? What's the energy? *(Refer to the planet table)*.

- Can you put the information together?

If you have more than one planet here in different signs, it gets really confusing very quickly. You may want to refer to an astrologer or a reputable online interpretation.

After you've expanded your mind, it's time to fill your heart with gratitude.

Again, there are practical and magical ways to do this.

Grateful Heart

Practical ways to fill your heart:
- Count your blessings
- Practice gratitude
- Listen to your instincts
- Strengthen spiritual connection
- Love yourself
- Forgive – yourself and others

There are also magical ways to open your heart.

Flower Power

Flowers have meaning. Use the power of flowers to open your heart. Flowers are happy and bring joy to those who grow or buy them for their enjoyment.

Flower	Meaning
Daffodil	Inner beauty and connection
Lavender	Healing and protection
Rose	Love
Rosemary	Memory and protection
Violet	Simplicity and modesty; discern relationship within groups

Buy roses for love, lavender for healing and daffodils for beauty.

Essential Oils

Essential oils are medicinal, but also affect emotions. Either diffuse or use in the bath as appropriate.

Bergamot – uplifting and soothing. It builds confidence and stabilizes moods. It's phototoxic, so be careful with sunlight.

Geranium – good substitute for rose oil. Provides a sense of happiness and wellbeing.

Jasmine – symbol of hope, happiness and love. It's known as the Queen of the Night. It's uplifting and joyous, opening the heart to more love and compassion.

Lavender – Calms strong emotions and allow life force to flow through your body. It helps you relax and release fear.

Neroli – harmonizes mind and emotions. It uplifts the spirit.

Palo Santo – banishes negative energy. It helps you reconnect with your loved ones and yourself.

Rose – heart healing and soothing. It helps with grief, bereavement and comfort in dark times.

<u>Angels</u>

Connect to the angels to open your heart, feel more compassion and act in loving kindness.

> *Archangel Chamuel* - guides you to find whatever you're seeking, including love and romance. He manifests self-love.

> *Archangel Jophiel* – a feminine energy who brings beauty to everything – including you, inside and out.

> *Archangel Raguel* - instills harmony within relationships, ensuring peaceful communication. He brings forgiveness, peace and calm.

> *Archangel Raphael* - helps hearts heal from the past. Allows you to stay open to present and future love.

These are the practical and magical ways to maintain an open heart.

Listening to your heart and following it shows your gratitude. Your heart knows how wonderful you are, don't let yourself forget it.

Now, for your will. You need to take action to realize your dreams.

Authentic Will

The mind, heart and will need to align in order to embody yourself fully and completely.

For authentic will:

- o Go inward to explore your wholeness
- o Receive healing support
- o Accept your perfection

- Find your bravery
- Speak your truth
- Take action
- Commit to yourself

Exercises to Speak your Truth

Do things to use your voice. Speak up. Stand up for yourself or others. Advocate for a cause you support.

Use the following crystals to help you find and use your voice.

Crystals

Blue Calcite – quiets the mind, opens communication and helps purify energy. Creates emotional intelligence, calms the mind and boosts memory. Eases anxiety and releases negativity.

Blue Topaz - helps you see where you strayed from your truth and brings you back to your core. It ensures you to live up to your own aspirations. It assists you to write your own script.

Lapis Lazuli – leads the soul to immortality and opens the heart to love. It's considered a royal stone that's the key to spiritual enlightenment. It's peaceful, while highlighting the power of the spoken word. It stimulates higher thinking, clarifies mental facilities and brings objective awareness. It helps with problems of the nervous system.

Sodalite – unites logic with intuition, harmonizes the third eye and deepens meditation. It stimulates trust, brings emotional balance and encourages interdependence. It helps with panic attacks.

Turquoise – dispels any negative energy and electromagnetic smog from your surrounding environment, allows clear thinking and calms your nerves when speaking in public. It releases old vows, inhibitions and helps your soul express itself.

Crystal Grid

Use a grid to power your voice. Use the four points of three stars to utilize the power of 12 and 3 in numerology. It's about mastery. Gain mastery in claiming your power and using your voice.

Ways to Commit to Yourself

Committing to yourself takes courage and practice. The universe will test you by putting things in your path detracting from your commitment. Don't back down.

- o Be brave.
- o Embrace yourself in your entirety.
- o Recognize wholeness.
- o Be authentic. Be unapologetic. Be unstoppable.

Embodiment through Colors

Use the meaning of colors to help you embody certain traits. Choose the traits you wish to embody, then do the color meditation.

Color	Color Meanings
Red	Energy, passion, love, strength
Orange	Joy, enthusiasm, attraction, encouragement, success
Yellow	Happiness, cheerfulness, warmth
Green	Growth, harmony, healing, freshness, luck
Blue	Communication, loyalty, wisdom, confidence, faith
Indigo	Intuition, intelligence, contemplation, solitude
Purple	Royalty, luxury, wealth, magic
White	Innocence, purity, safety, cleanliness
Brown	Earthy, home, nature, comfort
Grey	Modesty, maturity, reliability, old age
Black	Power, protection, elegance, formality, mystery

Color Meditation

Get into a comfortable position and remove any distractions from your space.

Think of the color you want to invoke depending upon its meaning:
Red - Energy, passion, love, strength
Orange - Joy, enthusiasm, attraction, encouragement, success
Yellow - Happiness, cheerfulness, warmth
Green - Growth, harmony, healing, freshness, luck
Blue- Communication, Loyalty, wisdom, confidence, faith
Indigo- Intuition, intelligence, contemplation, solitude
Purple - Royalty, luxury, wealth, magic
White - Innocence, purity, safety, cleanliness
Brown - Earthy, home, nature, comfort
Grey- Modesty, maturity, reliability, old age
Black- Power, elegance, formality, mystery

> ## Color Meditation
>
> *Silver – Feminine and lunar energy*
> *Gold – Masculine and solar energy*
>
> *Close your eyes and begin to breathe. You can feel your body relaxing as you are comfortable, content, grounded and centered in this moment.*
>
> *As you breathe, think of the color you selected. Imagine it as a ball in front of you and see it expanding as you continue to breathe.*
>
> *Watch it as it envelopes you completely. You can breathe normally and are relaxed and safe. Picture your color completely surrounding you and then gently entering your body. You become your color. You're wearing it so beautifully.*
>
> *Now think of the meaning of your color. Imagine its meaning totally enveloping you. Breathe it in. In your mind, say 'I am (and your color meaning)." Say it to yourself a couple more times. Take a few moments and continue to breathe. Bask in your color and its meaning.*
>
> *As you breathe, know you are grounded, centered and completely alive with the meaning of your color.*
>
> *Thank the colors of the rainbow and express gratitude for your general well-being.*
>
> *When you're ready, take a final deep breath and return your focus back into your room. Return to your day feeling calm, yet refreshed.*

Embody YOU

Think of your I AM statements. Write a few from the previous exercises. Do you have core values, powers or traits you wish to embody. Write them down and then perform the following meditation.

Close your eyes and take a nice refreshing breath by inhaling deeply and exhaling gently. Take another deep breath in and gently breathe out, slowly expelling all of the air out of your lungs. Take one more and feel grounded and centered in this place.

Now, we are going to create space by releasing that which no longer serves us. It does not need to be identified or named. It simply needs to be released. We ask the Universe to release that which no longer serves us as we inhale gently and exhale deeply and completely until all of the breath is expelled from our lungs. And as we do, we release all the old, useless energy into a long black string that extends as long as our breath. As we stop our exhale, the black string separates from us and lies gently in the air in front of our mouths – separate and still. We ask the Universe to cleanse this old and useless energy into brilliant white light filled with gold and silver swirls. Each brilliant white beautiful string is now filled with the glorious energy of the Universe. These strings move toward each other and gather together to lift swiftly into the air above our heads, through the roof of the house, and into the night sky – lighting the way with the glory of this shifted energy. We completely let go of this energy by giving thanks for the lessons, and centering ourselves back into the room.

By taking another deep breath, we settle into ourselves and ground our energy into our core. Now let's focus on ourselves once again. Let's think back to the earlier exercises and the questions; Who are you? What do you want and desire? What are your 'I AM' statements?

So, who are you? Feel the whispers circling around you, "Remember who you are. Know who you are. Love who you are." Feel the energy building as you envision the very best version of yourself in all of your glory. You are magnificent. You are powerful. You are unapologetically YOU.

Fill your entire being with the essence of your most magnificent you. Then wrap the essence of it all around you. It is strong. You are strong. It is deeply rooted. You are deeply rooted. It connects to the universal source. You are connected to the universal source. Take a few more moments – breathing in and out.

Now, what do you want and desire? Remember your wishes. Envision yourself asking those around you and the universal source to gift you your wants, desires and wishes. Imagine everyone around you supporting you. Feel the universe saying, "Yes. Yes. Yes." Breathe in

413

this support.   Soak it up with your breath and then feel it integrate into your body. Wrap it around you with gratitude and extend it out into the universe. You are surrounded by love and support for your wants, desires and wishes.

Let's recall your 'I AM' statements. I AM…. I AM…. I AM….. State these loudly and clearly in your mind. Watch the universe catch them with a smile and joyously lift them to all that is. Your 'I AM' statements are part of the grid and universal light. You feel their power in the universe.

Gently breathe in and out.   Breathe more deeply this time as you breathe in your I AM statements.   You reach out to take them right from the Universe as it presents these to you as a gift. You fold them into yourself and embrace them into the core of your being. They are now part of you —fully and easily integrated.

Now imagine who you are, your wants, desires and wishes and your 'I AM' statements weaving together to form a beautiful rope and then circle around itself to form a tightly woven colorful circle.

You feel this circle starting at your root chakra and planting a new seed of physical manifestation. See the red glowing roots of your woven circle and power as it plants itself into the world and lights up with energy.

Notice that red energy moving up your body into your sacral chakra and gathering emotion to generate even more feeling and desire. Notice as the orange desire swirls and moves into your solar plexus where it builds power and conviction. See the yellow power of your conviction blending into green as it touches your heart. Smile as your power and essence fill your heart with joy.

Your joyous heart is singing with love as it spreads this love and support into your throat chakra to give it voice. The blue of your throat moves your vibrational sounds into your third eye, opening it to peer out at the indigo creation of your magnificent insight. Your crown chakra is waiting with bated breath to receive your insight and sing it into the spirit world and the Universe.

Embody Your Highest Potential

With your woven circle achieving grounding, gathering desire, harnessing power and conviction, receiving love and support, giving voice, gaining clarity and insight and connecting with the Universal power of all that is, you are ready to live at your highest potential. You are ready to create your vision and achieve success. You are ready to live your very best life. Breathe this in with all of its magnificence. Breathe in all of your magnificence. You are utterly magnificent. You are absolutely powerful. You are loved beyond measure.

Take a few moments to bask in all of your glory and the glory of the universe.

Now let us be thankful. Let us be grateful to the Universe for making your dreams and desires come true. Thank you, Universe. Breathe in deeply. You are completely abundant in all things. Your life is fulfilled, rich, and full of joy.

Now as you breathe in this goodness and joy, feel the bliss of being alive. Take another deep breath and fill yourself with the bounty of life. Allow this state of bliss to accompany you on your return to this room.

When you're ready, open your eyes and gaze softly in front you — seeing nothing, yet aware of everything. If you'd like, wiggle your fingers and toes and do any gentle stretching your body requires. Breathe in again and open your eyes fully.

Welcome back – your life is bountiful and joyous.

You are embodied. Make any notes about your experience.

"Authenticity is everything! You have to wake up every day and look in the mirror, and you want to be proud of the person who's looking back at you. And you can only do that if you're being honest with yourself and being a person of high character. You have an opportunity every single day to write that story of your life."
— Aaron Rodgers

To make abundance real in your life involves clarifying, discovering, empowering and embodying your most authentic self.

Revisiting your intentions for the vision of your life helps you discover exactly who you are. This discovery is the key to living authentically and being in the pure abundant flow of the universe.

This is about earth and relying on its logic and reason. It's about using its stability and reliability. Its firmness and balance.

Earth makes manifest.

It's how you create tangible, physical representation of dreams, intentions and desires.

It's how you fuel those dreams and desires with intent, power and purpose.

It's how you gather support and develop plans to make your desires real.

Now you see your dreams as they unfold in your world.

You know your true self as you embody all of your dreams, intentions and desires.

Imagine living the life of your dreams.

Be authentic as you live and breathe in the world.

Your mind is open, your heart is filled with love and your soul and your will is activated to make your dreams manifest in this world. You are fulfilled with all of the bounty and grace of the universe.

You are ready for your abundant life.

Abundance in Evidence

LIVE ABUNDANTLY IN YOUR OUTER WORLD

Live Abundantly

"To enjoy good health, to bring true happiness to one's family, to bring peace to all, one must first discipline and control one's own mind. If a man can control his mind he can find the way to Enlightenment, and all wisdom and virtue will naturally come to him." – Buddha

Just like a glacier, 90% of life is lived below the water line. Only the tip of the glacier is seen on the water's edge and only the tip of your life is evident to the outside world. Therefore, you've spent 90% of this book focused inwardly.

The inner life is expressed in the outer world and by now you fully explored your inner life. You've connected to spirit through ether, you've gained clarity through air, inspired passion and creativity through fire, deepened joy through water. You've made it all real with the element of earth.

Now it's time to pay attention to your outer world. You have the opportunity to delve into its aspects of living conditions, life mission, relationships and expansion of your horizons.

Referring once again to the Kaleidoscope Wheel of Life™, you review an exercise from the AIR section.

When you completed the assessment in the intentions and beliefs section, what did you discover? These discoveries make have changed now that you've gone through the exercises in the book. Perhaps you would like to do the assessment again.

This isn't to ding you for not doing something. It's to recognize where you want to expend effort in perhaps different ways than before you begin creating abundance in your life.

Living Conditions

For this life area, you determine whether you're a ninja, diligent or have a casual attitude toward your living conditions and environment.

There are a few categories; car, home, style and financial administration. It may help you to recognize these as such to determine your level of focus for each.

Also, if any particular area is not a high priority for you, recognize it and move on. This is about you, not what other's think about you or believe you should do. YOU.

Be honest. This is for your eyes only.

Ninja	Diligent	Casual
▪ Love your car ▪ Car runs smoothly ▪ Love your home ▪ It's decorated beautifully ▪ All furnishings are to your taste ▪ Everything is maintained and kept up-to-date ▪ House is cleaned regularly ▪ Spring cleaning is done seasonally ▪ Landscape design is to your liking and done regularly ▪ Space is clear and uncluttered	▪ Your car is acceptable and typically runs smoothly ▪ Like your home ▪ It's decorated okay ▪ All furnishings are almost to your taste ▪ Most things are maintained ▪ House is cleaned sporadically ▪ Spring cleaning is done sometimes ▪ Landscape design is almost to your liking and done somewhat regularly	▪ Your car works, so it's perfect ▪ Your home is your home – it's useful ▪ Decorations are not a priority ▪ You have furniture – it works ▪ Maintenance is not something you think about ▪ Your house is clean enough ▪ Spring cleaning isn't done ▪ What landscape design? ▪ You don't even see the clutter

Ninja	Diligent	Casual
▪ Everything is in its place	▪ Space is not clear and is kind of cluttered	▪ Nothing has its own place
▪ Organized and practical	▪ Everything has a place and is sometimes there	▪ Disorganization doesn't register
▪ Have plenty of luxurious clothing and accessories	▪ Kind of organized and mostly practical	▪ Clothing is not a focus
▪ Haircut, make-up and clothing maintained	▪ Desire more luxurious clothing and accessories	▪ Your hair gets cut and you don't wear make-up
▪ Have appropriate outer wear and footwear for every season	▪ Try to keep up with haircuts, make-up and clothing needs	▪ Your outer wear is multi-purpose
▪ Do laundry on regular basis	▪ Have mostly appropriate outer wear and footwear for every season	▪ Laundry gets done when you run out of clothing
▪ Finances are in order	▪ Do laundry sporadically	▪ You pay your bills
▪ Taxes are done regularly	▪ Finances are kind of in order	▪ Your taxes get processed - eventually
▪ Have will, healthcare proxy, etc.	▪ Taxes are done adequately	▪ Don't have will, healthcare proxy, etc.
	▪ Want to have will, healthcare proxy, etc.	

Again, what categories are of no interest to you? This is an important question as you may want to disregard if you make the choice to let go of the category and it *doesn't* affect you to do so.

What categories are you proud of?

On what areas would you like to expend more effort?

Make a note here of those things you would like to investment time, energy and resources on to improve your living conditions.

You're worth the investment.

Remember your worth. You're worth more than all of the money in the world.

Don't forget it.

Life Mission

Are you passionate about life mission? Is it an integral part of your life? Are you a zealot, industrious or part time worker? There are no wrong answers. This is up to you. Just make sure you're not assessing with your head. Use your heart instead.

Zealot	Industrious	Part-timer
■ Have level of education necessary to work in your selected industry ■ Have necessary certifications for same ■ Passionate about your work ■ Seek to discover or learn more about your work	■ Striving for level of education necessary to work in your selected industry ■ Getting necessary certifications for same ■ So-so passionate about your work	■ Your educational level is perfect for your position ■ You don't need to spend time or money to get certified. ■ Not passionate about your work

Zealot	Industrious	Part-timer
▪ Actively strive to achieve more in your work	▪ Are fine with what you know for your work	▪ Unenthused about what you know for your work
▪ Your work supports your livelihood	▪ Try your best at work and do a good job	▪ Get by at work and do a fine job
▪ Gain energy by doing your work	▪ You leave your work at work	▪ You count the hours until the end of your workday
▪ Your work stimulates your mind	▪ Your work almost supports your livelihood	▪ Your work doesn't support your livelihood
▪ Your work feeds your heart and soul	▪ Don't leak energy by doing your work	▪ You leak energy by doing your work
▪ Your work is aligned with soul purpose	▪ Your work sometimes stimulates your mind	▪ Your work doesn't stimulate your mind
▪ At the end of the day, your work makes you feel lucky and blessed	▪ Your work sometimes feeds your heart and soul	▪ Your work doesn't feed your heart and soul
	▪ Your work isn't aligned with your soul purpose	▪ What soul purpose?
	▪ At the end of the day, your work doesn't leave you drained and exhausted	▪ At the end of the day, your work leaves you drained and exhausted

Do you have a career or a job? Do you want a career? If so, do you want it to align with life mission?

What are you willing to invest in your life mission with relation to time, effort and resource?

Are you looking to change your work? Do you need guidance on your life mission?

One of the most laser-focused ways to gain insightful and powerful information on life mission is to see an astrologer and look at your chart. All of the answers are there – waiting for you.

Relationships

Now, for relationships. How important are intimate connections, family and friends to you? Circle the areas you would like to welcome into your life.

Clan-like	Friendly	Loner
<ul><li>Live with open heart</li><li>Trust self and others</li><li>Healthy connections with friends and family</li><li>Welcome and provide intimate relationships</li><li>Engaged in harmonious intimate relationship</li><li>Connected to soul mate</li><li>Love to entertain and do it regularly</li><li>Host dinner parties – formally or informally</li><li>Host or gather with family and friends on holidays</li></ul>	<ul><li>Desire to live with open heart</li><li>Somewhat trusting of self and others</li><li>Basically, have healthy connections with friends and family</li><li>Ability to welcome and provide intimate relationships</li><li>Engaged in intimate relationship – working towards healthy</li><li>Desirous of soul mate</li><li>Like to entertain and do it occasionally</li></ul>	<ul><li>Are introverted</li><li>Don't want to trust others</li><li>Have limited interactions with friends and family</li><li>Aren't seeking any intimate relationships</li><li>Think soul mates are a myth</li><li>Don't like to entertain and therefore never do it</li><li>Don't want to host dinner parties – formally or informally</li><li>Would rather not host or gather with</li></ul>

Clan-like	Friendly	Loner
▪ Welcome open door policy for friends to drop by	▪ Sporadically host dinner parties – formally or informally	family and friends on holidays
▪ Really enjoy spending time with friends	▪ At times, host or gather with family and friends on holidays	▪ Would love to have a closed-door policy at work!
▪ Have intimate friends	▪ Would like an open-door policy for friends to drop by	▪ Love spending time alone
▪ Trust friends to lean on for support	▪ Sometimes enjoy spending time with friends	▪ Don't seek intimate friends
▪ Share secrets, solve problems and rely on each other	▪ Have intimate friends, but don't stay connected	▪ Don't want to trust friends to lean on for support
▪ Relax during the week and play during the weekends	▪ At times, trust friends to lean on for support	▪ Don't have any secrets to share
▪ Take vacations regularly	▪ Occasionally share secrets, and rely on each other	▪ Relax, play and vacation alone
▪ Relish time off	▪ Sometimes relax during the week and play during the weekends	▪ Spend time alone, but would rather spend time with others
▪ Sink into own life, love the solitude of spending time alone	▪ Take vacations occasionally	▪ Don't really know what to do with time off
▪ Enjoy frivolity	▪ Handle time off	▪ Don't like being alone – feels too lonely, you feel bereft and lost
▪ Laugh - often	▪ Like the solitude of spending time alone, but not for very long	▪ Don't laugh often
	▪ Laugh - occasionally	

Human beings need connection with others. Saying you don't want to have any relationships is not an option in this part.

So, if that's the case, you want to open your heart to allow others into your world. You may need less connection than others, but you still need connection.

Heart Opening Exercise

Simply enter a meditative state.

Once there, breathe deeply and fully. Focus your attention on your heart chakra and start breathing into it. As you inhale, expand your heart center and feel it opening. Feel it filling with love. As you exhale, feel your heart extend its love into the space in front of you and behind you. Continue to breathe, opening and extending your love. Conjure your loved ones or those types you would like to welcome into your life. Breathe in connection, breathe out love.

Take a few moments. Thank your heart for its wisdom, guidance and love. Thank you loved ones, now and future, for their kindness, support and participation in your life.

When you're ready, take a nice full breath and bring your awareness back into the room. Exit your meditative state and close your energy.

If you need more healing in regard to relationship, reach out. Get the support of others who work in this space. It could be traditional therapy or it could be energy work. Either is fine – whatever resonates for you.

If you're ready to connect with others, who do you want to contact?

Reach out.

Call a good friend and spend time talking. Chat, catch up, share secrets, laugh out loud.

When is your next party or dinner? Make a plan.

Have fun!

Expand Horizons

How much exploration do you want to have in your life? Do you want to be an adventurer, participator or spectator?

Adventurer	Participator	Spectator
▪ Invent ways to seek new adventures	▪ Welcome new adventures	▪ So-so about new adventures
▪ Find ways to travel and explore	▪ Welcome travel and exploration	▪ Don't desire to travel or explore
▪ Seek out new material – books, classes, mentors, ideas, concepts	▪ Entertain new material – books, classes, mentors, ideas, concepts	▪ Like familiar materials – books, classes, mentors, ideas, concepts
▪ Love to meet new people in either large groups or intimate settings	▪ Willing to meet new people in either large groups or intimate settings	▪ Would rather not meet new people in either large groups or intimate settings
▪ Regularly go to different events – art exhibits, sports games, soup nights, musical concerts, barbeques, plays, kid shows	▪ Sometimes go to different events – art exhibits, sports games, musical concerts, barbeques, plays, kid shows	▪ Like routine, so avoid – art exhibits, sports games, musical concerts, barbeques, plays, kid shows
▪ Volunteer for local charity – soup	▪ Thinking to volunteer for local charity – soup	▪ Give money, so don't need to volunteer for local

Adventurer	Participator	Spectator
kitchen, animal shelter, library, children's school, board room	kitchen, animal shelter, library, children's school, board room	charity – soup kitchen, animal shelter, library, children's school, board room
■ Embrace new technologies	■ Will adopt new technologies when necessary	■ Like the old ways of doing things – new technology is daunting
■ Actively and frequently try new things – learn a new sport, craft or game	■ Occasionally try new things – learn a new sport, craft or game	■ Don't want to try new things – learn a new sport, craft or game
■ Solve puzzles	■ Willing to solve puzzles	■ Satisfied with your current philosophy and approach to life
■ Expansive and inclusive life philosophy	■ Open to expansive and inclusive life philosophy	

Do you have travel plans? Do you want them? If you don't want to travel physically, do you want to explore other places through movies, videos or books?

Do you actively engage in experiencing new things? Make a plan to do one new thing this week.

When's the last time you had a philosophical discussion? Call a friend who likes discourse and begin a conversation.

Go out and meet new groups of people. Visit a game café and play a board game with others.

Reviewing each area of your life to determine where to spend time and resource is important when creating abundance.

You're increasing your blessings and targeting where these blessings go helps you decide exactly how to improve your life.

Look at the four areas of your outer world: living conditions, life mission, relationships and horizons.

Prioritize where to put your time and resource.

Look at your plans for starting something new and incorporate these findings into them. You may find these plans overlap or they may be completely different.

Either way, develop plans to improve your life. Start something new. Invest in yourself. Give yourself permission to disregard those areas that are not of high priority to you. Remember, this is about you and no one else.

The Universe rewards you for supporting, loving and empowering yourself.

Say 'Yes' to yourself and allow the Universe to support you fully and completely.

Stay connected.

Get clear.

Be passionate.

Live in joy.

Be authentic.

Get into the abundant flow by aligning your mind, heart and will.

Live Abundantly

Living abundantly is about so much more than having more money. Notice, I didn't even mention money, prosperity or wealth in this section.

The money is the easy part.

Aligning with your true self is the golden nugget.

It's pure treasure.

REMEMBER:

YOU ARE WORTH MORE THAN ALL OF THE MONEY IN THE WORLD.

Write it down.

Post it visibly.

Say it as a mantra.

YOU ARE WORTH MORE THAN ALL OF THE MONEY IN THE WORLD.

Welcome to your abundant life.

You are ready.

Begin. ☺

Wrap-Up: all about abundance

"Not what we have but what we enjoy constitutes our abundance." – Epicurus

Abundance is nuanced in your inner life and explodes in your outer world. The inner life nuances aren't subtle, they're the keys to the kingdom. To unlock your abundance, you weave between the foundational tenets and pillars of abundant flow using both practical and magical tools.

The unlocking begins with connection. When you're connected to the source of the universe, your mind, body and soul line up with abundance. This connection helps you gain awareness, appreciate wholeness and recognize the infinite nature of the universe.

The layering of the components in your inner life – connection, clarity, passion and joy – lead to authenticity. Being your true self aligns with the glory, grace and power of the universe.

Leaning into the rhythm of universal flow helps you in the elegant dance of life – the giving and receiving, the movement and stillness and the action and the allowance.

The pillars mechanize these layers by giving substance and form to your abundance. The natural elements align with your bodies:

ether - all bodies

air – mental body

fire – spiritual body

water – emotional body

earth – physical body

Each of these elements energize you in unique ways. Ether invites connection for all of your bodies. Air brings insight to your mind and clarity to your voice. Fire generates passion and creativity and links to your heart's desires. Water allows the release of fear and the power of joy. Earth induces your intentions, dreams and desires into reality.

Becoming your authentic self is a process. One involving all of the layers of abundance and the practical magic available to you.

Using the magical tools of divination, vibration, cycles and seasons and inner guides is fun and powerful. The practical means of focus, determination, vitality and action actuates the abundant flow.

Realize your abundance by living your life authentically, with connection, clarity, passion and joy.

"I can't change the direction of the wind, but I can adjust my sails to always reach my destination." – Jimmy Dean

When you write a book on abundance, the Universe, with its infinite sense of humor, is going to whack you.

I know this.

Why am I surprised?

I absolutely know this, so why am I surprised when my husband gets laid off as I approve the first proof of this book or my company is audited by the IRS or when my son totals his car after having it for 3 months? *(He's fine – walked away completely unscathed.)*

All of these things happen within a week of my receiving the first print copy of the book – on abundance.

Why am I surprised?

I know how the universe works.

As I finish the book, I imagine telling stories of how the money flows, the happiness abounds and basically, the birds sing as I'm surrounded by the earth's bounty.

Can you see the final screen cut of dancing and bursting into song?

Instead, my breath catches when I hear my husband's voice on the phone telling me he's been 're-orged', my stomach pitches when I read the audit request from the IRS and my heart lurches when I hear my son's voice on the line telling me he's been in an accident.

Oh, the Universe's sense of timing.

After my initial reaction, I take stock.

The silver lining is completely clear with my son as he's not hurt. That's all that matters and if the 17-year old new driver can learn a valuable lesson about driving in the snow and taking more care – absolute blessings and abundance abound.

It actually doesn't take long with my husband's situation. It's three-fold. 1) He can certainly use some time off and truth be told, he hasn't been happy with his position for the last handful of months. Change is inevitable. 2) As he usually travels, having him home to help and support is something I've been wanting to acclimate to as I'm learning to receive in this way. 3) It's great for him to take a step back, know how valuable he is and see what he really wants to do next. He's a wonderful provider. I have no issue in his ability to find his next step on his life mission. So, taking a breath, recognizing value and trying new things is always an abundant circumstance.

As for the IRS - well, it's the IRS, so hearts and flowers are harder to envision.

Truth be told, this one throws me.

After the initial shock, I shrug it off and begin to compile all of the records I'll need to back up the claims. It's about this business, so no worries – I have all of the receipts and I'm meticulous about declaring all revenues and recording the expenses.

Now I have reams of paper copies and am ready to respond to the audit request.

Then I look at the filing and begin to do a little research. My tax accountant has inexplicably categorized the business expenses in a casual way and I didn't catch it.

This is another thing entirely and I may need help going through this process.

I hire a tax attorney and he walks me through how the audit will happen. It looks like it will expand to three years and we may be doing a refiling.

Okay.

Also, I need to validate my very existence. I'll need proof of my marketing materials, calendars, schedules and logs. I'll need copies of my strategies and plans. I'll need back-up for all expenses, certainly, but will also need to justify the reason behind each expense.

Questions abound. What have I been doing? Why have I gone from a lucrative business consulting role to write children's books to then pursue the magic of spirituality?

Why have I allowed my revenues to dip and my expenses soar?

What are these trips I've been taking to study astrology? Am I an astrologer now? If so, what does that mean for consulting revenue?

What is my path back to high profitability? In other words, when will I return to paying lots of taxes again?

What have I been doing?

Yes, this one knocks me down. It brings me to my knees. Not the tax paying – I've got lots of tax payments under my belt and will surely have them again.

It's the questioning and validating my choice to go from the safety of business to the fringe of astrology and to my love – magic in life.

It's the fact that my path has been meandering as I've unfolded the true essence of my work over years instead of months.

It's the not knowing yet having faith.

How long can I continue in this way?

As I comb through records, every choice takes on new meaning.

- Getting the trademark registered is expensive and yet, it appears I've veered away from the children and family aspect of my business.
- Self-publishing allows freedom, but certainly requires considerable time and resource for selling and marketing.
- Learning new skills and wanting to master them also takes substantial time and resource.

The choices seem so right as I journey through them over the years, but when taken as a snapshot, what have I been doing?

I fumble and stumble for a few days. Okay truth? I completely lose my footing.

I withdraw into myself and question everything.

I've been working 60-70 hours a week for a handful of years and quite frankly, have taken a huge hit in profits. Looking at it through the financial lens, the whispers and doubts creep in.

What am I doing? I could be relaxing and enjoying my family and friends and instead, I'm working more than ever.

Am I building anything or just marking time going from thing to thing? The path is still unclear at this point and the journey looks like a mishmash. So, what am I doing? Has everything I've done been a waste of time? Is it a case of the proverbial bored housewife indulging in her creative fantasy while the doting husband funds the endeavor to keep her occupied?

And finally - *Is it worth it?*

This is the kicker.

Is it worth it?

This journey to the core of my being to allow creative expression out into the universe hasn't been easy.

Well, that's an understatement.

I've been questioned, challenged and brought to my knees more times than I can count.

The question, is it worth it, swirls in my head until I can't separate it from other questions. Do I want it? If so, how badly? What am I willing to do for it? What am I willing to risk? What aren't I willing to risk? Why do I want to risk at all?

Oh, and then, the penultimate questions surfaces, *am I worth it?*

That's the question. That's the bottom line. Finally, the essence of this situation.

Am I worth it?

Yes. I am.

Every minute, every hour, every day.

Every choice, every expenditure, every class or magical tool.

Yes, I am worth it and then the question, *is it worth it* answers itself.

Yes.

Absolutely. Without a doubt in the world.

This is my calling – the writing, teaching and allowing clients to become themselves – completely. The bridging between the practical and the magical. The wonder of getting to the core of you and the very core of existence. The demonstrating the equanimity that comes with living the spiritual way.

Yes, yes and yes again.

So, surprise from the Universe? Initially.

But, then – not at all.

When leaning into your abundant being, the Universe will lean in as well.

When it does, the Universe will ask; "How abundant are you?"

For me, the answer is - infinitely.

I am infinitely abundant.

I wish the same for you.

As always,

Kim

Snapshot: all about abundance

Ether: Connection	Water: Joy
o Create Space	o Deepen Connection
o Find Calm	o People Weaving
o Summon Spirit	o Inner Child and Self-Love
o Maintain Connection	o Renewal and Permission
Air: Clarity	**Earth: Authenticity**
o Wishes and Blessings	o Clarify You
o Intentions and Beliefs	o Discover You
o Surrender Scarcity	o Empower You
o Manifestation Power	o Embody You
Fire: Passion	**Live Abundantly**
o Remember Who You Are	o Living Conditions
o Welcome Future Self	o Life Mission
o Creation Cycle	o Relationships
o Tap into Divine Creativity	o Horizons

Acknowledgments

I would like to thank my soul sisters for travelling through the worlds with me and reflecting various aspects of my soul in this one:

Ivana - for reflecting my spiritual ninja,

Nicole – for demonstrating big buckets of love,

Therese – for activating community and engagement,

Tricia – for personifying loyalty, laughter and friendship.

I love this life and am thankful to have each of you as part of my world.

Many thanks go out my resident editor, Greg, without whom this book would have many errors and typos. ☺

I've grown to so appreciate the collective that has formed around my weekly play-and-learn series. These women are supportive, compassionate and powerful bad asses! Cheers to Annie, Christine, Jackie, Karen, Katie, Katy, Kimberly, Maureen, Nicole and Tricia.

And to those who join us along the way – Amanda, Caterina, Jennifer, Sally, Sue and Suzanne.

And always, to my family, Greg, Nick and Katy – for their love & support, making dinner, doing errands and basically supporting the house while I spend the hours immersed in being written.

Good Resources

all about calm, Kim E. Woods, CreateSpace Independent Publishing Platform, North Charleston, SC, 2016.

all about magic- beginnings, Kim E. Woods, CreateSpace Independent Publishing Platform, North Charleston, SC, 2017.

Crystal Goddesses, Alana Fairchild and Jane Marin, Blue Angel Publishing, Victoria, Australia, 2015.

Goddess Guidance Oracle Cards, Doreen Virtue, Hay House, Carlsbad, CA, 2004.

Inner Sky, Steven Forrest, Seven Paws Press, Borrego Springs, CA, 1984.

Moon Power, Simone Butler, Quarto Publishing, Beverly, MA, 2017.

The Secret, Rhonda Byrne, Atria Books/Beyond Words, Hillsboro, OR, 2006.

Voyager Tarot Deck, James Wanless, Fair Winds Press, British Columbia, Canada, 1987.

About the Author

Kim E. Woods is a revealer as she connects to the cosmos and her inner knowing to reveal your truth, potential and magic™. She combines her business, family and intuitive expertise in unique ways to weave the magical with the practical.

She's helped hundreds of clients live better lives through her one-on-one sessions, play & learn series, Facebook groups, online programs and collective gatherings. She also performs online weekly celestial rituals, writes a regular blog and puts her offerings into book format to reach those who cannot connect with her individually.

Working with Kim involves gaining insights, tools and solutions to live an intuitive, abundant and magical life.

Kim has authored six other books – the *Men in the Head*® series to help family and children and the *all about* series involving *all about magic – beginnings* and *all about calm* book and audio files to help you create calm and magic in your life.

You can purchase her books on Amazon. To schedule a reading, check out her solutions or register for an event, go to on her website at *kecfreedom.com*.

Kaleidoscope Books

all about magic – *beginnings*

Magic is everywhere and tapping into it is easy – if you know how.

Creating space in your life, learning about energy and connecting to your intuition are the first steps to living a magical life.

Next, blending practical, accessible and extensive solutions helps you access and use your magical side.

Then, learning of divination and vibrational tools, discovering the potential of cycles and seasons and realizing the quality of connecting to your inner guides amplifies your magical powers in practical ways.

This book is a survey of lots of different magical methods for you to explore. As you uncover those that speak to you, this format allows you to access them in relation to others of their kind.

Energy is magic.   Intuition is magic.   You are magic.

all about calm

Everyone should be living with calm, joy and bliss. Yet, this isn't the case. Why not?

The American Institute of Stress and the American Psychological Association find:

- 44% of Americans feel more stressed now than they did 5 years ago

- 70% of workers report that workplace stress affects their personal relationships, mainly with their spouses

- 38% of kids (ages 8 – 17) surveyed have trouble falling asleep

Everyone needs quick tips and simple solutions, easily remembered, to employ throughout the day to bring calm and relief from stress.

This book on calm has quick tips and easy solutions that fit into your back pocket. There are tips for every aspect of your life: singlehood, work, home, and family. There are even tips for your teens and children. These tips are featured in tables, highlights, stories, visualizations and guided meditations.

Are you ready to create calm and live a more peaceful life?

If so, this book is for you.

Men in the Head ® Books

Men in the Head ® books describe the brain-body connection in a fun and simple way for adults and children.

There are four books – one adult and three children's.

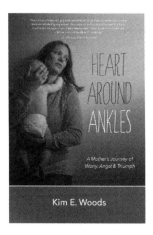

Do you know someone who has developmental issues?

If so, this story is for you.

This is a story of one mother's quest to realize her son's highest potential. She wanted him to be happy. She wanted him to appreciate humor. She wanted him to understand the nuances of social interactions.

It's one mother's story of her journey through the confusing labyrinth of child development. It's a story of frustration and worry.

Most especially, though, it's a story of triumph.

It could be your story.

Men in the Head ® Children's Books

<u>Alex & Chloe Meet the Men in the Head</u> ® is a chapter book for children ages 6 -10 years old.

Alex, Chloe and Shadow go on an adventure and meet the Men in the Head ®. The little creatures are lost and can't find their way back home!

Can Alex, Chloe and Shadow save the day with a pair of sunglasses, a pack of gum, crumbled tissues, a tiny toy parachute and a few other treasures?

Surprise! is a picture book for children ages 4 – 8 years old.

The Men in the Head® friends have lots of fun during the day. Henry, Samantha and George play on the beach, while Amanda, Gerald & Thomas work at their jobs.

In the afternoon, George plays baseball while Larry & Gary watch – well, maybe they play instead!

Meanwhile…

Shhh…the friends are planning a birthday party for Sally. Can everyone keep it a secret long enough for Sally to be surprised?

<u>So Big!</u> is a baby book for children ages 2 – 3 years old.

You met the Men in the Head® friends in our *Alex & Chloe* and *Surprise!* books and now you can see them as babies!

In this fun and entertaining tale, the babies show all of their talents. See Baby Henry splash in water and play at the beach. Follow Baby George as he learns how to walk and watch Larry and Gary play on riding toys and swings!

Kaleidoscope

Revealing your truth, potential, & magic™